JF2112 . A4   ID ε

The Idea
of Political Marketing

Recent Titles in the Praeger Series in Political Communication
Robert E. Denton, Jr., *General Editor*

The Idea
of Political Marketing

Nicholas J. O'Shaughnessy, Editor
Stephan C. M. Henneberg, Associate Editor

Praeger Series in Political Communication

Westport, Connecticut
London

Library of Congress Cataloging-in-Publication Data

The idea of political marketing / Nicholas J. O'Shaughnessy, editor ; Stephan C. M. Henneberg, associate editor.

    p. cm. — (Praeger series in political communication, ISSN 1062-5623)

  Papers originally presented at conferences held at the Judge Institute of Management Studies, Cambridge.

  Includes bibliographical references and index.

  ISBN 0-275-97595-9 (alk. paper)

  1. Campaign management. 2. Marketing—Political aspects. I. O'Shaughnessy, Nicholas J., 1954– II. Henneberg, Stephan C. M. III. Series.

JF2112.C3 I34   2002

324.7--dc21   2001054594

British Library Cataloguing in Publication Data is available.

Library of Congress Catalog Card Number: 2001054594

ISBN: 0-275-97595-9

ISSN: 1062-5623

First published in 2002

Praeger Publishers, 88 Post Road West, Westport, CT 06881

An imprint of Greenwood Publishing Group, Inc.

www.praeger.com

Printed in the United States of America

Contents

Series Foreword

Robert E. Denton, Jr.

Those of us from the discipline of communication studies have long believed that communication is prior to all other fields of inquiry. In several other forums I have argued that the essence of politics is "talk" or human interaction.[1] Such interaction may be formal or informal, verbal or nonverbal, public or private, but it is always persuasive, forcing us consciously or subconsciously to interpret, to evaluate, and to act. Communication is the vehicle for human action.

From this perspective, it is not surprising that Aristotle recognized the natural kinship of politics and communication in his writings on *Politics* and *Rhetoric*. In the former, he established that humans are "political beings [who] alone of the animals [are] furnished with the faculty of language."[2] In the latter, he began his systematic analysis of discourse by proclaiming that "rhetorical study, in its strict sense, is concerned with the modes of persuasion."[3] Thus, it was recognized over twenty-three hundred years ago that politics and communication go hand in hand because they are essential parts of human nature.

In 1981, Dan Nimmo and Keith Sanders proclaimed that political communication was an emerging field.[4] Although its origin, as noted, dates back centuries, a "self-consciously cross-disciplinary" focus began in the late 1950s. Thousands of books and articles later, colleges and universities offer a variety of graduate and undergraduate coursework in the area in such diverse departments as communication, mass communication, journalism, political science, and sociology.[5] In Nimmo and Sanders's early assessment, the "key areas of inquiry" included rhetorical analysis, propaganda analysis, attitude change studies, voting studies, government and the news media, functional and systems analyses, technological changes, media technologies, campaign techniques, and research techniques.[6] In a survey of the state of the field in 1983, the same authors and Lynda Kaid found additional, more specific areas of concerns such as the presidency, political polls, public opinion, debates, and advertising.[7] Since the first study, they have also noted a shift away from the rather strict behavioral approach.

A decade later, Dan Nimmo and David Swanson argued that "political communication has developed some identity as a more or less distinct domain of scholarly work."[8] The scope and concerns of the area have further expanded to include critical theories and cultural studies. Although there is no precise definition, method, or disciplinary home of the area of inquiry, its primary domain comprises the role, processes, and effects of communication within the context of politics broadly defined.

In 1985, the editors of *Political Communication Yearbook: 1984* noted that more things are happening in the study, teaching, and practice of political communication than can be captured within the space limitations of the relatively few publications available."[9] In addition, they argued that the backgrounds of "those involved in the field [are] so varied and pluralist in outlook and approach, . . . it [is] a mistake to adhere slavishly to any set format in shaping the content."[10] More recently, Swanson and Nimmo have called for "ways of overcoming the unhappy consequences of fragmentation within a framework that respects, encourages, and benefits from diverse scholarly commitments, agendas, and approaches."[11]

In agreement with these assessments of the area and with gentle encouragement, in 1988 Praeger established the series entitled "Praeger Series in Political Communication." The series is open to all qualitative and quantitative methodologies as well as contemporary and historical studies. The key to characterizing the studies in the series is the focus on communication variables or activities within a political context or dimension. As of this writing, over seventy volumes have been published, and numerous impressive works are forthcoming. Scholars from the disciplines of communication, history, journalism, political science, and sociology have participated in the series.

I am, without shame or modesty, a fan of the series. The joy of serving as its editor is in participating in the dialogue of the field of political communication and in reading the contributors' works. I invite you to join me.

NOTES

1. See Robert E. Denton, Jr., *The Symbolic Dimensions of the American Presidency* (Prospect Heights, IL: Waveland Press, 1982); Robert E. Denton, Jr., and Gary Woodward, *Political Communication in America* (New York: Praeger, 1985, 2d

edition, 1990); Robert E. Denton, Jr., and Dan Hahn, *Presidential Communication* (New York: Praeger, 1986); and Robert E. Denton, Jr., *The Primetime Presidency of Ronald Reagan* (New York: Praeger, 1988).

2. Aristotle, *The Politics of Aristotle*, trans. Ernest Barker (New York: Oxford University Press, 1970), p. 5.

3. Aristotle, *Rhetoric*, trans. W. Rhys Roberts (New York: The Modern Library, 1954), p. 22.

4. Dan Nimmo and Keith Sanders, "Introduction: The Emergence of Political Communication as a Field," in *Handbook of Political Communication*, eds. Dan Nimmo and Keith Sanders (Beverly Hills, CA: Sage, 1981), pp. 11–36.

5. Ibid., p. 15.

6. Ibid., pp. 17–27.

7. Keith Sanders, Lynda Kaid, and Dan Nimmo, eds., *Political Communication Yearbook: 1984* (Carbondale, IL: Southern Illinois University, 1985), pp. 283–308.

8. Dan Nimmo and David Swanson, "The Field of Political Communication: Beyond the Voter Persuasion Paradigm," in *New Directions in Political Communication*, eds. David Swanson and Dan Nimmo (Beverly Hills, CA: Sage, 1990), p. 8.

9. Sanders, Kaid, and Nimmo, *Political Communication Yearbook: 1984*, p. xiv.

10. Ibid.

11. Nimmo and Swanson, "The Field of Political Communication," p. 11.

Introduction

POLITICS AND THE MARKETING CONCEPT

There are, of course, many clear parallels between the selling of politicians and the selling of certain products. Most obviously, politics sell an abstract and intangible product; it is value-laden; it embodies a certain level of promise about the future, some kind of attractive life vision, or anything the satisfactions of which are not immediate but long-term, vague, and uncertain. Vendors of products that share the above characteristics will have legitimate things to say to politicians: the analogies are with promise-based offers. Those of us who write on political marketing have tended to see an election as, in all its essentials, a condensed consumer-product-marketing campaign. We have argued, following from Kirchheimer (see chapter 4), that the growth of a more homogeneous society creates promiscuous political allegiances: voters are no longer pre-committed, so political merchandising assumes greater significance.

Many of the methods employed correlate with those used to sell products where information is complex or contradictory and not easily retained by the audience, as in insurance or finance. Marketing is a derivative of what people seek, insofar as this can be determined. It is not simply the attempt to persuade them to a point of view.

The essence of marketing is reciprocity: "consumers" themselves bring something to bear on the selling; they are not passive objects, and the process is an interactive one. Thus, the marketing concept is distinguished above all by the emphasis that is placed on customer focus. Identifying the needs and wants of customers and fashioning products and communications shaped by that understanding is the core of the marketing task. Such understanding is garnered through marketing intelligence, and thus value is not defined in any absolute or objective sense, but subjectively from the market's viewpoint: it has been claimed that customer satisfaction is best attained by focusing on customer desires at the beginning, as well as at the conclusion, of the production process. And the marketing approach is sensitive to the fact that any customer base is not an amorphous, undifferentiated mass.

Marketing is—or should be—also very much concerned with interpreting the customer. This is something more than merely mapping out what customers say about themselves and acting accordingly: rather, it is the activity of surfacing their latent wants—the underlying desires that they cannot articulate fully. An example of this view would be that of Harrop (1990), who sees political marketing as essentially a form of services marketing: marketing a party consists in projecting belief in its ability to govern (and political parties are service organisations). But there is scepticism about services, and therefore parties need to reassure: they must eliminate all perception of risk. The ideal party, he claims, would be a political version of a Holiday Inn.

THE PRACTICE OF POLITICAL MARKETING

Practice would appear to accord with theory. Thus, much American political communication could be legitimately diagnosed by the term "political marketing." The ideological turnaround of the Clinton administration in his first term was a good example of this: "Clinton gave people what they wanted to hear, with just the right language, words and phrases that would resonate with the American public" (Johnson 1997). So far had parties internalised the marketing concept that it had apparently become the organising principle behind not only communication, but policy as well. And a popular view in Britain after the 1987 Labour defeat was that the policy review was driven not by the policy but by the communications executive: image sought substance. New policies were an important part of Labour's offer, but they were policies selected against the template not of ideology but of market appeal: populist ones ("cut NHS bureaucracy," welfare to workfare, etc.); liberal ones with an "international conscience" and a (highly selective) ban on weapon sales, reduction in taxes on the low-paid, and so forth; radical ones (abolishing the hereditaries in the House of Lords); and authoritarian ones, with the sacking of incompetent teachers, imprisonment for corrupt officials, curfews for under-tens. There were ten points and five pledges—vague, uncosted promises all. Apparently, then, political marketing would appear to have come of age, the core dynamo of political practice today and a theoretic framework accepted on occasion even by an initially hostile political-science profession. More extreme, of course, was the Berlusconi experiment in Italy: "slickly presented, adopting American political techniques in a context devoid of American restraints, Berlusconi used television with a skill that made the enigmatic arts of the Christian Democrat Giulio Andreotti as redundant a political weapon as the letters of Cicero . . ." (Sheridan 1995). Berlusconi built a movement "which was both apolitical and non-ideological. . . . Its structure is not that of a political party but of a network of football supporters' clubs" (Sheridan 1995).

Key differences between marketing and propaganda may be summarised as follows: marketing—at least if its exponents are fully educated in the market concept—is what the audience wants. The message can be framed accordingly. In contrast, propaganda is didactic. Marketing rests on the notion of exchange. The political market, as the commercial market, contains sellers and customers who exchange "something of value": the parties/candidates offer representation to customers who in turn offer support (votes). Nor is marketing just advertising, even though less sophisticated organisations see it as this, and in politics it has often been regarded merely as a synonym for political advertising. Marketing fundamentally involves the integration of some total "offer" into an overall strategy, and political marketing has advanced beyond issue and image advertising and into strategy itself (although strategy also has evolved independently from other, historical sources); beyond this, it has become a total way of conceptualising government, a core organising force.

However, prior to writing about political marketing, it is necessary to define the term, because political marketing is a new subfield of marketing and political science, and most studies do not explicitly discuss the explanandum in question. Political marketing, using a definition of commercial marketing by Grönroos (1990), can be defined as:

[seeking] to establish, maintain and enhance long-term voter relationships at a profit for society and political parties, so that the objectives of the individual political actors and organisations involved are met. This is done by mutual exchange and fulfilment of promises. (Henneberg 1996)

This definition emphasises the following aspects: a focus on exchange relationships (the crucial explanandum of marketing—Bagozzi 1974, 1978); a long-term perspective, voter-oriented (but restricted by societal considerations); and mutual benefits for all parties involved. For other definitions of political marketing, compare Harrop (1990), Newman (1994, 1999), O'Shaughnessy (1990), and Reid (1988). Nevertheless, political marketing is still a research field with only a provisional theoretical framework.

The chapters in this volume were originally papers given at several annual conferences held at the Judge Institute of Management Studies, Cambridge, which retained a research group specialising in the theory of political marketing. The aim of these conferences, which now continue at other venues, was to introduce the marketing and political science professions to each other, with the aspiration that there would be mutual learning, and not a little respect. And it was also, of course, to add to the extant theory in this specialised field of non-profit marketing, as well as to enhance research networks between the two "mother-disciplines" in order to foster theoretical developments towards more analytical depth in this research area. Political marketing has now reached a "critical mass": definitions, terminology and explanandum have been discussed (although there is still some flux), and some dedicated researchers have put much effort into the development of the research area, which has manifested itself in lively publications activities in political marketing over recent years (such as Newman 1999).

Because political marketing is an interdisciplinary research area, the organisers at the Judge Institute regarded maintaining a balanced mix of participants' backgrounds to be important. Researchers from the main disciplines of marketing and political sciences as well as from communication studies and political philosophy took part.

POLITICAL MARKETING AS ACADEMIC PARVENU

Such research is much needed. The theoretical contribution that marketing may make is, for whatever reason, doubted by some political scientists. The aim of this first volume, whose focus is on the theory of political marketing with the more abstract questions such as conceptual definitions, is to set right that imbalance in the literature. It will, it is hoped, be followed by a further volume looking at political marketing in an applied sense, particularly "political marketing management", the tactical and applied aspects of political marketing, the evolution and impact of the genre, its ethical and social consequences, and the techniques and technologies of political market research.

Political marketing is about the making and unmaking of governments in a democracy, but for some the intellectual content of this process is less appealing than are such themes as the marketing of soap powder or the planning of sales territories. But if marketers do not study this topic—and they, after all, have the relevant tools—who does? Political scientists? It is the familiar story of that interdisciplinary no-man's-land where the fields are left untended because the academic reward system does not harvest there. In spite of the attention of Philip Kotler (Kotler & Kotler, 1999), the marketing academic profession has shown very limited interest in the political ramifications of their discipline and the ethics thereof. Political marketing is "not business". Of course it is—and a vigorous cottage industry. More to the point, the comparative uninterest of the marketing profession in the external application of their techniques, technologies and concepts, especially to elections and to the permanent work of government, is perplexing, as if the only value exchanges that mattered were the monetary–material ones.

Political scientists also come to the area of political marketing with some prejudices. Marketing is seen as perhaps trivial, concerned with the cosmetics: its insights are even viewed as pedestrian, an ascription of new labels to old truths. But the real question is not what marketing has contributed, but what it could contribute—if both academic parties could accept its legitimacy. But political science, while interested in the social structure of voters, voting behaviour patterns, evolutions and so forth, is perhaps less sensitive to the fact that elections are a persuasion task writ large, most especially with the demise of inherited class loyalties, and, therefore, the study of persuasion in the analogous area of consumption—that is, marketing—may, just possibly, have something significant to say. The problem is not fundamentally with the extant content of political marketing but, rather, with the perceived image of that content.

Thus political marketing as a useful sub-discipline would appear to be winning rather limited acceptance by political scientists. Some are still suspicious, Philo (1993) dismissing what he calls a "shallow science of imagistics", while for Bowler and Farrell (1992) the marketing literature is "an exercise in rationalising success or failure in hindsight" rather than offering any theoretical insight. Perhaps this stems from political scientists' misconceptions of the nature of marketing, tending, in Scammell's (1999) words, "to view political marketing as poll-driven politics", which is "a crude follower definition that misunderstands the significance of exchange" and makes a simplistic distinction between the active citizen and passive consumer. In fact, the problem is most certainly a marketing problem insofar as marketing best describes key elements in that problem and key techniques that can help to solve it.

Several main conclusions can be drawn from this debate: first, criticism of political marketing is widespread. It comprises the instrumental as well as conceptual levels. Second, it also must be stated that most criticism is simplistic and not well founded. One does not necessarily have to embrace political marketing in every respect to notice that most criticism is grounded in normative models, in ideals of democratic behaviour (Franklin 1994; Jamieson 1992). These models sometimes seem out of touch with reality. One example is the normative model of voting decision-making based on objective information and full deliberation. Voters cannot follow this model because of the intrinsic complexity of the decision-making task; therefore, they use cognitive short-cuts and cues in order to facilitate a decision (Newman and Sheth 1987; Popkin 1994; Reid 1988; Sniderman et al. 1993). Furthermore, much criticism is based on an elitist understanding of democratic processes. Nevertheless, it seems obvious that political marketing management can cause a "new" kind of democracy, one that is more plebiscitary and populist in nature and less representative (Birch 1995). In order better to assess the ramifications of political marketing, more theoretical understanding of the phenomenon is necessary. This is, however, a difficult objective, because it is not easy to establish whether political marketing is a "prime mover" (i.e., a cause) or merely an effect of other social developments.

Others have come to recognise in political marketing a distinctiveness of contribution. For Bartle and Griffiths (chapter 2), that lies in the broader theories of demand it introduces, such as voter aspiration, and in applied tools like segmentation. Scammell (1999) echoes their further argument: "curiously, however, political science voting models seem reluctant to build in image/reputation as a major element. The standard voting model continues to rely on party identification, issue perceptions and to a lesser extent leader evaluations." She adds: "the party reputation factor, so vital to explanations of 1997, is included not as a separate and essential part of the models but as a 'political shock', an event capable of disrupting the equilibrium of the stability of the overall model." Harrop (1990) also stresses the importance of image in marketing's potential contribution to political science: most studies of voting behaviour, such as Himelweit's consumer model, stress policy and ideology. But image is also critical—such as competence or trustworthiness—and it is here that the tools of marketing analysis help. The political scientists concentrate on social division in the attempt to explain support for the different parties—a legitimate exercise, but not in isolation likely to generate richer interpretation. Scammell (1999) believes, following on from Collins and Butler (chapter 1), that an even more important contribution is the strategic focus that marketing brings: "the prime distinctive contribution of the marketing literature . . . shifts the focus from the techniques of promotion to the overall strategic objectives of the party/organisation." Thus it effectively reverses the perspective offered by campaign studies/political communications approaches.

OUR CONTRIBUTORS

Our first contributors, Neil Collins and Patrick Butler, represent both the marketing and the political science academic professions. But both recognise that it is not enough to draw, as traditional political science does, on ideology or policy alone. Strategy is also critical, and the distinctive contribution of political marketing is the stress it lays on strategy. In an essay that is replete with international examples, they argue in favour of the relevance of the marketing analogy and frameworks to political science, but with the caveat that they are in need of modification: these authors endorse the application of leader (expand, retain)–challenger–follower–nicher typologies to political market situations, a paradigm that would both clarify many a political contest and be a source of election strategy. For John Bartle and Dylan Griffiths, political scientists see marketing as encroaching on their territory and as trivial, and this is false. Marketing provides many useful tools for political scientists—market segmentation, targeting, product positioning. They criticise downplaying of party image and the impressionistic: broader theories of demand such as voter lifestyle aspirations are in their view richer than more rigidly economics-based models. Three different models of voting behaviour theory—based on social psychology, rational choice and consumer behaviour respectively—were the starting point of their analysis. It can be shown that there is considerable convergence between all three approaches. However, consumer-behaviour related models seem to grasp the complexities of voting decision-making best, although political scientists are hostile to this approach. In addition, for the purpose of political marketing management (i.e. managerial use) only consumer behaviour-oriented approaches are helpful.

John Bartle discusses the value of the insights that marketing brings to political science, a corrective to the limitations of models of voter behaviour drawn from economics and social psychology. This underpins his analysis of the British Labour Party's curious historical relationship with marketing—a flirtation in the 1960s, then blame for the party's eclipse and finally the evolution towards the apotheosis of marketing under Blair as the key organising concept of government.

Stephan Henneberg and Stefan Eghbalian undertake a reinterpretation in marketing terms of Kirchheimer's (1966) catch-all concept of party organisation and strategy (one of the most important sources on electoral strategy for political scientists). It can be shown that Kirchheimer described something like a proto-political marketing strategy which was very advanced for the time of his analysis. In general, one can argue that the development of electoral strategies from mass-integration towards catch-all parties (equivalent to a change from a selling to a marketing concept) was predominantly concerned with a shift in targeting strategies. An ever more volatile market structure of political competition necessitated a change from concentrated targeting to undifferentiated targeting (Kotler and Armstrong 1996). Henneberg also provides in a separate chapter a study on generic functions of political marketing. Besides the "traditional" elements of marketing functions like product, primary communication and cost function, four additional elements for organisational survival in the political sphere were analysed: fund raising, news management (secondary communication), internal cohesion and parallel campaign management functions.

Dominic Wring discusses the evolution of the marketing concept, its nuances, meaning and sophistication, and also its application to politics. He illuminates how the "4Ps" model of product, price, place and promotion apply to political marketing and act as a structuring device, and he reconciles this with existing political communication theory.

Two further chapters take a different track. In a discussion of political marketing and the aestheticisation of politics, Barrie Axford and Richard Huggins relate modern politics to post-modern trends. Modern politics and especially political marketing are seen by them as part of a broad post-modernist culture of signs and symbols; we should not, however, fear this, and they criticise the nostalgia of looking back to some imaginary golden age. Post-modern political marketing is really a phenomenon of dissolving class barriers, where people are bereft of traditional anchors. They take the example of *Forza Italia* as an extreme case of this, a media-created party that seemed to answer a huge appetite for change, a party people were comfortable with. Political marketing is simply part of a world of serial symbolism and media-saturated imagery, whose self-referentiality is captured in a scene from *Murphy Brown*, where she watches Dan Quayle criticising her giving birth outside wedlock.

Finally, Nicholas O'Shaughnessy poses the question of whether political marketing has itself been over-marketed, within the context of a more general discussion of political marketing as a special case of marketing with its own unique features. For example, the sequence of communication is sometime two-step, with the press as messenger and interpreter: he stresses that political advertising is in itself an autonomous political event, with unpredictable consequences, and interpretation by the mass media that can be very fickle.

CONCLUSIONS

Political marketing works because of the apoliticality of most voters, who are cognitive misers and who are thereby inadvertent consumers of political information. While different countries—largely as a result of different regulatory regimes—emphasise different media (in the US, the thirty-second ad spot; in the UK, very often, the old-fashioned street posters), it is the potential ability of political marketing to present on uncluttered image of party, candidate and issue, an image that explains its potential effectiveness. Not least, an efficient political marketing campaign can in itself be perceived by voters as a surrogate index of competence; perhaps we tend to infer from displays of competence in one area a more general characteristic of competence. Of course, the politicians themselves may come to believe this—that communication is reality, that political effectiveness and communication skill equate.

However, political marketing as a research topic is still in its infancy. Marketing theory has a lot to offer to the analysis of the political competition but political scientists too can give marketers insights into the functioning of specific non-profit markets that are highly significant in our daily life (Kotler and Andreason 1991).

REFERENCES

Bagozzi, R. P. (1974), "Marketing as an organized behavioural system of exchange", *Journal of Marketing*, vol. 38 (October), 77–81.

Bagozzi, R. P. (1978), "Marketing as an exchange: A theory of transactions in the marketplace", *American Behavioral Scientist*, vol. 21 (March/April), 535–556.

Birch, A. H. (1995), *The Concepts and Theories of Modern Democracy*, London, Routledge.

Bowler, S., and Farrell, D. (eds.) (1992), *Electoral Strategies and Political Marketing*, Basingstoke, Macmillan.

Franklin, R. (1994), *Packaging Politics*, London, Edward Arnold.

Grönroos, C. (1990), "Marketing redefined", *Management Decision*, vol. 28, no. 8.

Harrop, M. (1990), "Political marketing", *Parliamentary Affairs*, vol. 43, 277–291.

Henneberg, S. C. (1996), "Conference report: Second Conference on Political Marketing", *Journal of Marketing Management*, vol. 12, no. 8, 777–783.

Jamieson, K. H. (1992), *Dirty Politics, Deception, Distraction, and Democracy*, Oxford, Oxford University Press.

Johnson, D. (1997), *Political Communication in the Information Age*, Seminar, Wissenschaftszentrum Berlin, 5 February.

Kirchheimer, O. (1966), "The transformation of the Western European party systems", in J. LaPalombara and M. Weiner (eds.), *Political Parties and Political Development*, Princeton, Princeton University Press, pp. 177–200.

Kotler, P., and Andreason, A. R. (1991), *Strategic Marketing for Non-Profit Organizations*, Englewood Cliffs, Prentice-Hall.

Kotler, P., and Armstrong, G. (1996), *Principles of Marketing*, Englewood Cliffs, Prentice-Hall.

Kotler, P., & Kotler, N. (1999), "Political marketing: Generating effective candidates, campaigns, and causes", in B. I. Newman (ed.), *Handbook of Political Marketing*, Thousand Oaks, Sage.

Newman, B. I. (1994), *The Marketing of the President*, Thousand Oaks, Sage.

Newman, B. I. (1999), *Handbook of Political Marketing*, Thousand Oaks, Sage.

Newman, B. I., and Sheth, J. N. (1987), *A Theory of Political Choice Behaviour*, New York, Praeger.

O'Shaughnessy, N. J. (1990), *The Phenomenon of Political Marketing*, Basingstoke, Macmillan.

Philo, U. (1993), "Political advertising, popular belief and the 1992 British General Election", in *Media, Culture and Society, vol. 15*, Thousand Oaks, Sage.

Popkin, S. L. (1994), *The Reasoning Voter*, Chicago, University of Chicago Press.

Reid, D. M. (1988), "Marketing the political product", *European Journal of Marketing*, no 9, 34–47.

Scammell, M. (1999), "Political marketing: Lessons for political science", *Political Studies*, vol. 17.

Sheridan (1995), "Political theatre", *Times Literary Supplement*, 6 January.

Sniderman, P. M., Body, R. A., and Tetlock, P. E. (1993), *Reasoning and Choice: Explorations in Political Psychology*, Cambridge, Cambridge University Press.

The Idea
of Political Marketing

1

Considerations on Market Analysis for Political Parties

Neil Collins and Patrick Butler

There is growing interest in political marketing; not least because, as O'Shaughnessy (1990) warns in his examination of trends in the United States, serious questions arise about the impact of marketing on democracy itself. The triumph of Silvio Berlusconi's *Forza Italia* suggested to many that an elite-driven exercise in marketing could succeed in capturing governmental power (Donovan 1994).[1] Similarly, the gearing up of would-be candidates in New Hampshire is a reminder of the importance of the "selling of the president". Often, the tendency in much of the commentary on such events, however, is to focus on the tactical dimensions of marketing. Much coverage addresses issues at the level of political advertising, the impact of television on politicians' and parties' standing, and "spin-doctoring". Such attention can be "superficial, anecdotal, and ... focus on tactics and techniques to the exclusion of campaign strategy" (Mauser 1983, p. 30).

The concern in this chapter is to move the emphasis to the strategic level. In making this "crucial" distinction between the strategic and the tactical (Harrop 1990), it applies a broad strategic analysis to the political market. Bowler and Farrell (1992) are, among political scientists who focus on electoral strategy, exceptional by drawing attention to the elements of preparation and planning and of organisation and control. The electoral marketing starts well before the stage of campaign themes and images. A market analysis of the political/electoral competitive arena, employing a marketing technique, can prove insightful in strategic development.

The analysis here requires that the political parties in a democratic system be regarded as analogous to commercial organisations in industrial markets. Rather than analysing the parties in terms of their ideology, historical origin or policy platforms, they are considered in terms of their relative market standing or competitive position. That is, the labels used to describe the parties will be market leader, challenger, follower and nicher. These are drawn from the business strategy literature. They have been widely used for the analysis of business strategy and have been popularised by Porter (1980) and Kotler (1994). This framework offers a competitive positioning map of the market that will inform marketing and campaign decisions and guide strategic direction. It is not understood by many non-marketing analysts that tactical and operational moves, such as colour schemes for conference backdrops and the grooming of candidates and their partners, must be guided by strategy; otherwise, tactics will be the product of good luck and intuition.

The model employed in this analysis does not highlight the usual political-science questions of accountability, responsibility and electoral legitimacy; the actors are part of the strategic process. This chapter primarily adopts a marketing as opposed to a political-science perspective. It shows how marketing frameworks can be applied effectively to political campaign management.

The chapter opens with a brief overview of strategic marketing in political campaigns, considers the analogy of a company in a market and describes political parties as market players in these four positions of leader, challenger, follower and nicher, outlining appropriate strategic directions.

STRATEGY AND MARKETING

Strategy

"Strategy" has been described as "one of the most overused words in the business vocabulary" (Wensley 1987, p. 29), because management writers, practitioners and observers seek to describe business activity and prescribe management solutions using it. For the purposes of this discussion on marketing, a useful definition that makes clear the broader perspective of strategy over tactics is provided by Luck and Ferrell: "Strategy is: a scheme or principal idea through which an objective would be achieved" (Luck and Ferrell 1982, p. 2).

With such an understanding of strategy, then, a political party may decide to engage in coalition in the same way that a commercial company may decide in favour of franchising as a method of market entry. Clearly, the debate in such a political party may be couched in terms of ideology or democratic propriety, but, in the context of this analysis, the decision is taken to reflect marketing considerations.

Political scientists often find business analogies inappropriate. However, marketing principles can be successfully applied if the characteristics of the context are properly understood and addressed (Butler and Collins 1994). It would be unwise to dismiss the beneficial perspectives that marketing and strategic-management frameworks can bring to the field of political campaigning. Indeed, Dunleavy (1990), Harrop (1990) and others have welcomed the insights that marketing and other disciplines, such as economics and occupational psychology, have brought to elections.

Smith and Saunders (1990) trace the increasingly sophisticated adoption of marketing in politics. They refer to the "Strategic Marketing Era", in which marketing's influence on policy formation, as opposed to merely tactical communications and presentations, will emerge. There is evident disdain in popular political-science comment for a marketing approach. Some party activists at the local level are also reluctant to embrace marketing techniques. Their objections arise from the supposed ethical dilemma of tailoring policy to short-term electoral-campaign considerations. The strategic marketing decisions referred to here, however, are of a different order and do, by nature, involve parties taking a longer-term view. Political parties, like commercial organisations, have inherent or instinctive strategic perspectives, whatever the degree of sophistication. Mature parties in the West have strong party discipline, are established, and have clear lines of authority as do typical business organisations. They tend to have mission statements, corporate objectives and idealised aspirations. In many cases, the strategic principles do indeed flow from these.

The military roots of the idea of strategy are very clear in the marketing literature, where terms such as campaign, battle and tactics are common. Election studies are also replete with parallels between political and military contests. The rhetoric of elections suggests the constant clash of marshalled, disciplined and enthusiastic devotees. The reality of both political and commercial life is often a tedious, non-combative and thankless routine punctuated only infrequently by the excitement of competition. Generally, the political generals rely in the field on a volunteer "army", which frequently voices its own disparate ideas on strategy.

Marketing

The notion of the market here is not that of the traditional economist. Rather, the analogy employed is that the election is the market, the political party is the company and the vote is the purchase. This thinking is widely recognised, with Denton (1988), Reid (1988), O'Shaughnessy (1990) and Niffenegger (1989) all using analogous terms to deal with marketing issues in politics. Furthermore, the recent emphasis by the marketing community on long-term interactive relationships in the exchange process, with its stress on loyalties and obligations, increases the heuristic value of the framework. Such thinking goes beyond the economist's view of the perfectly competitive market as an arena for one-off transactions influenced mainly by price. For this reason, the vote, while seen as analogous to the purchase, is understood to be part of an ongoing process rather than a decision at the moment the citizen-consumer enters the polling booth.

This analysis is concerned with a particular market, namely that which Reif (1985) refers to as first-order elections—that is, elections to national parliaments. Many of the generalisations about strategy made below will apply to second-order elections, but, as Reif characterises them, they regularly have low turnout, brighter prospects for small and new parties, and national government parties' losses. For these reasons, second-order elections warrant separate treatment. Reif's principal concern was the analysis of elections to the European Parliament. Marketing complication also arise, however, in relation to federal systems. In Australia, for instance, at the 1993 national election, Labour, the market leader, retained office in Canberra despite "'thoroughly contrary' performances in South Australia and Tasmania" (Mackerras and McAllister 1994). The popularity of the parties in the state arena clearly influenced the overall national result. Nevertheless, the analysis concentrates on the national contexts.

The nature of the political market is dynamic, despite west European party systems being considered in the 1960s and 1970s to have more or less stabilised. Parties were presented as moving towards a "catch-all" strategy in response to "waning opposition" and the "end of ideology": "since the late 1970s these views were more and more contested and empirically shown to be incorrect. It appears that . . . parties have remained ideologically distinct and several countries have experienced a more volatile electoral record since the early 1970s" (Keman 1994, pp. 125–126).

In North America, electoral volatility has also been the subject of considerable attention, not least following the disastrous showing of the Canadian Progressive Conservative Party at the 1993 general election.

QUALIFICATIONS

The limitations of the "elections-as-markets" analogy and the strategic approach are noted. The primary focus of the market analysis framework is on competitive position: the final consumer in the market—that is, the electorate—and individual and community political preferences are addressed only indirectly. Further, while the strategic metaphor stresses competition and a win–lose orientation, the propensity in many industries (including politics) is to satisfice rather than maximise. Although talk is often tough, especially in more mature industries, respect for boundaries is often implicit; for the most part, political marketing is a mature, stable industry setting. The political market has other significant characteristics that should be acknowledged. Whereas most commercial markets support many firms, political "markets" generally consist of relatively few players; also, commercial markets tend to be continuous (notwithstanding seasonal variations) whereas elections are periodic (Mauser 1983).

As in the commercial sector, political market strategies are not simply the product of some universally applicable, if necessarily complex, logic. Parties in similar competitive positions in different countries may act differently. For example, in one country they may seek to adopt coalescent or cooperative strategies, while in other political cultures, competition or conflict may suggest itself more readily. Lijphart (1984) and others following his analytical framework have suggested that these strategic responses are a product of the interrelationship between social homogeneity and the extent of elite cooperation. Clearly, in citing examples of competitive strategies, national propensities towards more consensual and cooperative styles of democracy need to be acknowledged.

Finally, a great deal of the literature on marketing and politics has been generated in the United States and Britain. The contribution of this literature in broadening the scope of political science and marketing is significant, but it is important to be aware that the relatively unusual features of the electoral and party systems of those jurisdictions may have limited the insight of generalisations based solely on their experience. For example, few countries other than the United States are dominated by only two parties. To adapt this model purely to the United States, it would be necessary to allow for the impact of the federal system, the absence of a "general election", and the vagaries of presidential primaries, when intra-party competition mimics multiparty competition. Such adaptation may wish to treat the United States as a series of discrete markets: the presidential, the congressional and those within the fifty states. Nonetheless, these qualifications do not diminish the insights to be gained from the application of this strategic-analysis framework.

MARKET POSITIONS

The analysis of market positioning can be addressed from many perspectives. The top management-consulting firm of Arthur D. Little propose that a firm in a market will occupy one of six competitive positions: dominant, strong, favourable, tenable, weak, or non-viable. Kotler's (1994) broader framework of four positions—leader, challenger, fol-

Table 1.1. Market Positions, Characteristics and Strategic Directions

Position	Characteristics	Strategic Directions	Examples
Leader	highest share acknowledged orientation point subject to continuous attack	expand total market expand share defend share	HZDS (Slovakia) PSOE (Spain)
Challenger	chosen to depose leader may be several challengers	attack leader attack similar competitors attack smaller competitors	RPR (France) SPÖ (Austria)
Follower	purposeful concentration on target market imitative rather than innovative local/regional strengths broad line	clone imitate adapt	FDP (Germany) PD (Ireland)
Nicher	leader in narrowly defined market or niche specialist appeal	create niche expand niche defend niche	FPÖ (Austria) *Bloc Québecois* (Canada)

lower, nicher—is suggested here as more appropriate to politics. It is more applicable in an arena where fewer players will operate. Table 1.1 outlines these positions, their characteristics and their strategic directions.

In normal applications of the model, the four positions are defined on the basis of market share. Market research provides the necessary data, which invariably reflects units sold/volume sales. The equivalent market research in politics is the opinion poll, providing a snapshot of the electorate's views. Here, market share is taken to be votes gained at the last general election. So, for example, a party such as the UK Labour Party which was leading significantly in the opinion polls in early 1996, was nonetheless the challenger by this criterion. While this may appear somewhat perverse, elections are the only truly reliable guide; opinion polls are not definitive.

Market Leader

The market leader in any industry is the player with the highest market share. It provides the acknowledged orientation point for the others. It may not be highly regarded by competitors, nor liked nor even respected, but it is the accepted leader. Typical market leaders in a variety of product markets include Coca-Cola, British Telecom, YKK and Kodak. It is not essential for the leader to be the most innovative, most customer-friendly or most accessible, although leaders would normally score highly on such marketing dimensions. Indeed, many competitors of these organisations base their own marketing programmes on being better than the leader on one or several such factors.

A number of strategic directions are common among market leaders. For the political party, where analysis shows that the player is in the position of market leader, three appropriate types of strategy—expanding the total market, expanding market share further and defending market share—can be anticipated. By virtue of holding the leadership position, the leader is subject to continuous attack. Defensive strategies are, therefore, of particular importance. The world of commerce is full of stories of market leaders who were successfully beaten into a lesser place or who vanished in a tough competitive environment. However, it is not feasible in the long run only to defend a position. This is to assume that the market is static. Even the most narrowly defined product markets entail some competitive dynamic. So, the leader must also consider either expanding the total market, thereby gaining more sales and revenues, or increasing its already dominant share further, even where market size remains constant.

Expanding the market may be difficult for a market leader where its appeal is already to a broad section of the electorate. Very infrequently, the electorate may expand significantly as a new group of voters (e.g. eighteen-year-olds or women) are added. Even more rare is an expansion of the state itself, as in Germany in 1991. When new states are created, such as Slovakia, new parties often form from the grouping most closely associated with establishing its existence. These parties compete for market share with the initial leader using the various strategies available. Already, after only three years, the pattern of fragmentation is clear in Slovakia with the leader, *Hnutie za Demokratické Slovensko* (HZDS), losing market share to new ventures.

The problem of increasing its market share becomes a question of balancing the appearance of dominance and stability with that of being innovative and responsive to new preferences. In a political market, the leader has to appeal to a broad range of voters. It may, for example, be necessary to be seen to support farmers, whose interests are in higher food prices, and consumers who would choose a different policy. This makes it difficult for a leader to be too explicit across a wide number of issues. Nevertheless, a leader's high visibility confers upon it some advantages in credibility and recognition. New, young and inexperienced voters are likely to vote for it disproportionately (Butler and Stokes 1969). The latter authors suggest that, in Britain, people voting for the first time in 1945 were influenced by the strongly pro-Labour atmosphere. Their voting intentions continued to be biased towards Labour for a long time after they initially exercised the franchise. On the other hand, others may wish to show their independence and sophistication by not voting for the leader.

Much more straightforward for the leader is the strategy of defending market share. This involves reinforcing the party's existing image among its supporters and reminding them of the reasons for their underlying loyalty. This strategy is particularly suitable for parties such as the Finnish Social Democrats (FSDP) or Japan's Liberal Democratic Party (LDP) which are faced by several smaller parties that can only form governments with disparate coalitions. The FSDP core following in the trade union movement look to it to act in its traditional role as the dominant party of the left committed to social spending and low unemployment. The LDP, on the other hand, has had to re-establish its high levels of loyal following, after corruption scandals undermined its traditional image. In Spain, in 1993, the leader—*Partido Socialista Obrero Español*/Socialist Party (PSOE)—was "compelled to develop a campaign which was primarily addressed at the mobilisation of its own electorate" (Castillo and Nieto 1994).

The problem for a leader in this strategy is that defence is seldom sufficient, especially when demographics erode the traditional base of support. In the context of Northern Ireland, for instance, the Ulster Unionist Party has occupied the position of leader for several decades. The proportion of the population to whom it appeals is in decline. It needs to consider a strategy of increasing market share rather than relying on defence. It may, therefore, think of targeting middle-class Catholics by suggesting that their interests are essentially similar to those of their traditional bourgeois Protestant supporters.

The sudden loss of leadership position is more likely to occur in the political market than its commercial equivalent. The verdict of the electorate is given suddenly and only periodically. In politics in general, it is continuity rather than change that is the most important characteristic. Nevertheless, the political market can be a volatile one.

These strategic approaches are underpinned by particular marketing instruments and variables. So, for the market leader to position itself as dominant/stable as well as innovative/responsive requires a particular blend of product (policies) and promotion (communications). Similarly, in defending its leadership position, it must consider the importance of the psychological price of a vote for itself or its opponents. For instance, the leader may wish to increase the electorate's perceived price of voting for another party by reference in its communications to that party's lack of governmental experience or inability to provide strong international leadership.

Challenger

Some of the best-known commercial organisations are viewed as challengers. Indeed, a classic case is Avis, whose "We try harder" campaign made a virtue of this position, with its inference of the leader being complacent. Effectively, such companies recognise that their market share is less than the leader's, and they pursue active, aggressive strategies with the aim of becoming leader. Unlike the follower discussed below, challengers do not adopt a conservative share-maintenance strategy. The challenger does not necessarily have to be the next biggest player after the leader. Rather, the distinguishing feature of the challenger is that it is a player that has chosen to attempt to depose the leader and has a realistic chance of so doing. There may be a number of challengers. Of course, the challenger does not have to attack the leader directly in order to gain the highest share.

The basic strategic objective of the challenger, though, is to attack. This can be done on three fronts. The aggressor can target the market leader directly in a high-risk but potentially high-payoff strategy, attack competitors of its own size, or attack small local and regional competitors.

In this analysis, the challenger in the Federal Republic of Germany was the *Christliche-Demokratische Union* (CDU). It managed to use its position in government to appeal to the new voters as the "party of the nation" and capture the greater share of the eastern vote at the post-reunification election. In doing so, it was continuing a tradition of direct attack. It had already broadened its appeal from the Catholic electorate, the core support for its prewar antecedent, into the Protestant community. Now, with increased secularisation, the party is once again assessing its strategic options. It had a 5% lead over the *Sozialdemokratische Partei Deutschlands* (SPD) at the national parliamentary elections of October 1994.

In some political markets, as in commercial markets, there may be no clear leader. Thus, for instance, France may be viewed as a market in which, to use Porter's terminology, several challengers may be "jockeying for position", albeit that for tactical reasons two of them—the *Rassemblement pour la République* (RPR) and the *Union pour la Démocratie Française* (UDF)—regularly choose cooperative approaches.

Attacking a competitor of its own size is the strategy dictated by electoral circumstance for some challengers. One example of a successful challenger is afforded by the Social Democratic Party (SPÖ) in Austria. In recent elections, it has effectively challenged the leading People's Party (ÖVP) by showing a "high degree of adaptability and, over time, has increased its speed in taking over policies from the ÖVP that seemed to have electoral potential" (Muller and Steininger 1994, p.8). Its position as leader seems confirmed after October 1994.

In many instances, the challenger adopts similar strategies to those that had previously been used by the leader when it first came to dominance. For example, the Greek New Democracy (ND) adopted the same strategy of a populist party platform and huge electoral rallies to challenge PASOK (Pan Hellenic Socialist Movement Party). Essentially, it has copied the marketing communication strategy of PASOK, although only with indifferent success.

The importance of a correct analysis is critical. The Labour Party in the Republic of Ireland came close to grief in the 1960s when, after minor electoral achievement, it felt itself to be on the verge of success and adopted strategies more akin to that of challenger than nicher. It eschewed coalition and other cooperative arrangements in favour of a broader attack on the two larger rivals: "The 1969 general election was supposed to produce the reward for the previous twelve years' effort to establish Labour as a major party. Instead, it proved a shattering disappointment. . . . [The results] demonstrated convincingly that the conditions were not yet ripe for a Labour breakthrough" (Gallagher 1988, p. 79).

The role of aggressive challenger may be more common in countries with the "first-past-the-post" electoral system because of the inequity in the votes-to-seats process. More proportional systems enable followers to survive or maintain their positions for long periods. This underlines again the importance of a thorough analysis of the distinct characteristics of the industry or context.

Head-on challenges are more likely where products are similar. A challenger offering policies broadly in line with those of the leader may have to characterise the bigger party as corrupt and/or incompetent. McKenzie (1963) suggested that British party politics could be characterised as a competition for political leadership. Some observers of the current competition between the two major British parties consider that the challenger, the Labour Party, has reduced policy differences between itself and the Conservatives so as to present itself as the more competent team.

"Back-door" strategies are often attractive for challengers. For instance, a political party may identify issues on the horizon which will become important and "brand" these early. The problem with this strategy is that, initially, it may appear that the challenger is out of step with public opinion. Once the issue does become central, its opponents may simply steal its ideas.

In fragmented or relatively new democratic systems, such as that in Spain, a challenger may progress by a "guppy" tactic of absorbing or targeting smaller parties. Thus the *Partido Popular* successfully moved in on the smaller parties to bring it much closer to the leader, PSOE. A guppy strategy may mean not taking share from the leader so the challenge may not be noticed immediately. It is particularly open to challengers not in government office who can, therefore, refashion their appeal with less constraint.

Perhaps the most spectacularly successful challenger in recent years has been *Forza Italia*, which in 1994 came from nowhere to take 21% of the vote and establish itself as the leader in the Italian market. Indeed, it is felt by many political observers to be less a political party and more a marketing vehicle for the ambitions of Silvio Berlusconi. It was a case of a new product establishing itself in a short space of time: "the brevity of the time available to establish itself in the electoral market place acted in its favour by legitimising it in the eyes of voters in a context in which the connotations of novelty was a positive electoral advantage" (Bull and Newell 1995, pp. 96–97).

Marketing instruments of particular use to challengers will vary according to the situation. In the case of SPÖ in Austria, it became a highly "adaptable" product. Communication or promotion needed to be subtle or held back by *Partido Popular* in Spain as it employed a guppy strategy; if it had announced or promoted its strategy too early, it would have damaged the potential of its approach to growth. Greek New Democracy, in a sense, employed the distribution strategies (accessing the market by means of huge rallies) of the market leader in support of its populist product adaptation.

Follower

Based on the premise that a strategy of imitation may be as profitable as one of innovation, the notion of a market follower has a particular appeal in certain circumstances. The expense of research and development, gaining distribution, and communications and selling is eschewed in favour of slipstreaming and copying the leader. This must be done at a level just below the leader's reactive threshold. More common in industries where differentiation possibilities are limited and price sensitivity is high, the position of the follower, with its highly stable market shares and acceptable returns, can be attractive.

This approach does not imply passivity—rather, it is a purposeful concentration, mainly on looking after the interests of existing customers. The follower cannot ignore the importance of maintenance strategies; it is very susceptible to attack from aggressive competitors, especially in the challenger role, and must develop some distinctive advantage in production costs, location, service or the like. Three broad strategies are identified: cloning, whereby the leader's advantages are copied assiduously (often illegally, as in the case of the counterfeit trade); imitating, whereby the leader's product is replicated but with enough differentiation to avoid retaliation; and adapting, whereby the follower adapts the leader's product and often sells in a different market to avoid direct confrontation. Japanese firms often engaged in such a strategy in several technological fields, later becoming challengers and, ultimately, leaders.

The *Freie Demokratische Partei* (FDP) in Germany has adopted a consistent follower strategy for a number of years. It has sought to maintain its pivotal electoral position through a strategy of clear self-definition, but without directly tackling the two larger parties. It relies a great deal on the personal popularity of its leading parliamentarians, and on cultivating the allegiance of its established following.

While the terminology of leader, challenger and nicher used here may be uncontroversial for the outside observer, few political parties would explicitly identify themselves as followers. They may, however, adopt such strategies in the name of protecting the interests of their traditional supporters, thus implicitly delimiting themselves within the political market. In the Republic of Ireland, for example, the Progressive Democrats appear to direct their appeal to the electorate as a whole. In fact, it is clearly aimed at an urban, middle-class market, which is thought to be sympathetic to its brand of European liberalism.

Followers in some political systems may be those who choose to nominate candidates in a restricted number of constituencies across the nation. Unlike nichers, who may define themselves in regional or issue terms, followers will generally have a national agenda but will recognise their limitations in not fighting across the board.

Followers are often large parties with stable market shares. Their strategy is to protect that share rather than challenge for leadership. They estimate that the dangers of an all-out attack outweigh the benefits. Followers must avoid alienating large numbers of traditional voters. Such a party may pay special attention to local networks and the quality of its local representation, but less to national slogans and aggressive advertising. Some electoral situations do not lend themselves to the broad-based competition despite the rhetoric of competition. A follower may be rewarded through the political system by cabinet appointments or other rewards of office—partly because it is *not* a challenger.

Followers, in adopting largely defensive strategies, are careful not to change their core product too radically, and they tend to avoid blatantly attacking opponents in the communications media. In a sense, their marketing communications are "below-the-line", with greater emphasis on local networking approaches rather than the national mass media.

Nicher

Rather than play the follower role in a large market, a firm can opt to be a leader in a small, well-defined market or niche. The key success factor of the niche player is that it specialises in serving the needs of the niche better than other, more casual, competitors. This enables it to charge a premium price, resulting in high margins rather than having to concentrate on developing high-volume sales. The main strategic tasks are to create, expand and defend niches. The major danger is that, in a dynamic and competitive environment or industry, the niche might either disappear or be invaded by a bigger, more resourceful, player determined to succeed. It is not uncommon for commercial companies to engage in multiple niching, rather than single niching, thereby avoiding the "all-eggs-in-one-basket" problem.

To be successful, some nichers in political markets have transformed themselves through radical strategic change. For example, the Austrian Freedom Party (FPÖ) "changed fundamentally in 1986 when [it] changed its leadership and political strategy, transforming itself into a protest party. As such, it is highly successful in attracting votes from both major parties" (Muller and Steininger 1994, p. 8). This is an example of a niche party attacking both the leader (ÖVP) and the challenger (SPÖ). The *Bloc Québecois*, on the other hand, has adopted a strategy of consolidation in a very defined part of the Canadian market in which it has displaced both leader and challenger. Another Canadian nicher, the Reform Party, concentrating in the two relatively prosperous provinces of Alberta and British Columbia, has also shown the potential of this strategy. The tension that exists in the strategy of nichers is well illustrated by the two French green parties; one, *Les Verts* presents a broad portfolio of policies and competes with challenger and followers directly; the *Génération Écologie*, on the other hand, adopts the strategy of a pure-issue movement (Ysmal 1994).

In Bavaria, the most distinctive and independent-minded of the German *Länder*, the *Christlich Soziale Union* (CSU), has pursued a successful role as nicher in national terms for forty years. The largest party in its own region, it has avoided direct challenges to its long-time partner, the CDU. It has used the localised benefits derived from frequent periods in coalition to resist attack from the national leader, the SDP.

Niche parties and candidates can be seen to use a range of marketing instruments to achieve their strategies. Highly focused product-positioning is at the heart of their marketing. Related marketing communication and promotion must precede and accompany such strategic directions. Indeed, product repositioning was clearly used by FPÖ in Austria in the example given above.

CONCLUSIONS AND RETROSPECTION

Since the time that this chapter was presented at the conference in 1995, much has changed in the international political landscape. Clearly the scenario regarding *Forza Italia* in Italy, as one instance, appears in hindsight anything but triumphant as time has passed. Similarly, the situation in Germany and other locations referred to here have changed in ways that have implications for political marketing. Indeed, such temporal dimensions merely underline the point that this kind of positioning analysis may provide a snapshot of a time rather than a moving view. This does not mean that the analysis is static, of course. The critical point of a dynamic strategic perspective is that historical and future scenarios are addressed, and so an ongoing, updated monitoring is central to appropriating value from this kind of approach (Lynch 2000).

The purpose of the chapter is to use a marketing framework to provide insights into party-political strategies. It repeats a point made elsewhere by the authors that marketing analysis, properly applied, can be useful in the area of politics, from public policy to electoral behaviour (Butler and Collins 1994, 1999). As Harris (1996) notes in his Editorial to a Special Edition of the *European Journal of Marketing*, the field is still under-researched, and so it requires a range of applications for new insights. Scammell (1999) usefully summarises the current political-science literature, though it is still argued here that political scientists place too much emphasis on the formal campaign period. Scammell's paper is particularly aimed at raising awareness of the importance of marketing as an approach at a strategic, rather than a tactical, level. O'Shaughnessy (1999) is keen to differentiate between political marketing and political propaganda. His argument would suggest an important focus on communications. In this case, however, the subject precedes any particular campaign or other communication and aims at the organisational or institutional positioning in the marketplace, with consequent suggestions for strategic directions. As such, it is undoubtedly strategic in its orientation.

The main conclusions are that parties generally operate in a strategic fashion that is analogous to commercial organisations; that strategy may not always be explicit, but it can be usefully discerned analytically; that strategic analysis and development must be sensitive to the distinctive characteristics of the political context; and that those who guide political parties may have access to strategies and tactics by considering analytical frameworks employed by commercial firms in analogous market positions. Newman's (1999) view that campaigns at all levels rely on increasingly sophisticated marketing techniques further forces research interests into analyses at a strategic level, rather than confining them to short-term, or merely operational, thinking and activity.

These conclusions are offered tentatively. There is an understandable reluctance on the part of any discipline to adopt the paradigm of another. Indeed, in the case of marketing and politics, the reticence is augmented by the generally prescriptive tone of much of the literature drawn from business. It is not the intention of the analysis presented here to do anything other than offer insights that might be heuristically useful. Certainly, there is no intention to promote the framework as some kind of alternative in the grand theory mode. Ultimately, votes are not a commercial currency and elections are not markets in the conventional sense. Political parties and their members may be uncomfortable with an analogy that they may consider trivialises the workings of democracy. Such views are an important constraint on the acceptability of the framework. Nevertheless, parties as organisations do compete for the attention of the public not only with each other but, often less successfully, with commercial, charitable and cultural enterprises. Messages about the new Ford Focus reach further than those for the new party manifesto. They may have something to gain from studying the *modus operandi* of business.

We must not be misled by the analogy of words. We use the word "parties" to describe the Republics of antiquity, the troops which formed round a condottiere in Renaissance Italy, the clubs where the members of the Revolutionary assemblies met, and the committees which prepared the elections under the property franchise of the constitutional monarchies as well as the vast popular organisations which give shape to public opinion in modern democracies. . . . Obviously, however, they are not the same thing. (Duverger 1959, p. xxiii)

Political parties are the vehicle for a stylised form of elite competition, but they only work if they are given the impetus of popular support. Most politicians acknowledge this by their actions.

NOTE

1. For an updated commentary on this and others examples, see the final section in this chapter, "Conclusions and Retrospection".

REFERENCES

Bowler, S., and Farrell, D. M. (eds.) (1992), *Electoral Strategies and Political Marketing*, New York, St. Martin's Press.

Bull, M., and Newell, J. (1995), "Italy changes course? The 1994 elections and the victory of the right", *Parliamentary Affairs*, vol. 48, no. 1, 72–99.

Butler, D., and Stokes, D. (1969), *Political Change in Britain*, London, Macmillan.

Butler, P., and Collins, N. (1994), "Political marketing: Structure and process", *European Journal of Marketing*, vol. 28, no. 1, 19–34.

Butler, P., and Collins, N. (1999), "A conceptual framework for political marketing", in B. I. Newman (ed.), *Handbook of Political Marketing*, Thousand
Oaks, Sage.

Castillo, P., and Nieto, L. (1994), "Spain", *European Journal of Political Research*, vol.
26, 423–429.

Denton, R. E., Jr. (1988), *The Primetime Presidency of Ronald Reagan*, New York,
Praeger.

Donovan, M. (1994), "The 1994 election in Italy: Normalisation or continuing
exceptionalism?", *West European Politics*, vol. 17, no. 4, 193–201.

Dunleavy, P. (1990), "Mass political behaviour: Is there more to learn?", *Political
Studies*, vol. 38, pp. 453–469.

Duverger, M. (1959), *Political Parties: Their Organisation and Activity in the Modern
State*, 2nd edition, London, Methuen.

Gallagher, M. (1988), *Political Parties in the Republic of Ireland*, Manchester, Manchester Press.

Harris, P. (1996), "Editorial", *European Journal of Marketing*, vol. 30, no. 10, 18–
20.

Harrop, M. (1990), "Political marketing", *Parliamentary Affairs*, vol. 43, 277–291.

Keman, H. (1994) "The search for the centre: Pivot parties in West European
party systems", *West European Politics*, vol. 17, no. 4, 124–148.

Kotler, P. (1994), *Marketing Management: Analysis, Planning, Implementation and
Control*, 8th edition, Englewood Cliffs, Prentice-Hall.

Lijphart, A. (1984), *Democracies: Patterns of Majoratarian and Consensus Government
in Twenty-One Countries*, New Haven, Yale University Press.

Luck, D. J., and Ferrell, O. C. (1982), *Marketing Strategy and Plans*, Englewood
Cliffs, Prentice-Hall.

Lynch, R. (2000), *Corporate Strategy*, 2nd edition, Essex, Financial Times/Prentice-
Hall.

Mackerras, M., and McAllister, I. (1994), "Australia", *European Journal of Political
Research*, vol. 26, 221–229.

Mauser, G. A. (1983), *Political Marketing: An Approach to Campaign Strategy*, New
York, Praeger.

McKenzie, R. T. (1963), *British Political Parties*, London, Heinemann.

Muller, W., and Steininger, B.(1994), "Party organisation and party competitiveness: The case of the Austrian Peoples Party 1945–1972", *European Journal
of Political Research*, vol. 26, 1–29.

Newman, B. I. (1999), "Foreword", in B. I. Newman (ed.), *Handbook of Political
Marketing*, Thousand Oaks, CA, Sage.

Niffenegger, P. (1989), "Strategies for success from the political marketers",
Journal of Consumer Marketing, vol. 6, no. 1, 45–51.

O'Shaughnessy, N. J. (1990), *The Phenomenon of Political Marketing*, Basingstoke,
Macmillan.

O'Shaughnessy, N. J. (1999), "Political marketing and political propaganda", in
B. I. Newman (ed.), *Handbook of Political Marketing*, Thousand Oaks, Sage.

Porter, M. E. (1980), *Competitive Strategy: Tools and Techniques for Analysing Industries and Competitors*, New York, Free Press.

Reid, D. M. (1988), "Marketing the political product", *European Journal of Marketing*, vol. 22, no. 9, 34–47.

Reif, K. (1985), "Ten second-order national elections", in K. Reif (ed.), *Ten European Elections*, Aldershot, Gower.

Scammell, M. (1999), "Political marketing: Lessons for political science", *Political Studies*, vol. 47, no. 4, 718–739.

Smith, G., and Saunders, J. (1990), "The application of marketing to British politics", *Journal of Marketing Management*, vol. 5, no. 3, 295–306.

Wensley, R. (1987), "Marketing Strategy", in M. Baker (ed.), *The Marketing Book*, London, Heinemann.

Ysmal, C. (1994), "France", *European Journal Political Research*, vol. 26, 293–304.

2

Social-Psychological, Economic and Marketing Models of Voting Behaviour Compared

John Bartle and Dylan Griffiths

> "The tone of a political campaign is strongly influenced by the attributes of the electorate, their political attitudes and their voting behaviour."
>
> Nimmo (1970, p. 19)

In order to understand the potential role and scope of political marketing, we first need to understand the nature of the electorate. This chapter outlines three models of voting behaviour drawn from three different academic disciplines: social psychology, economics and marketing. It examines the central assumptions of each model, their substantive conclusions about the forces that act upon the voter, and their implications for party strategy. This chapter suggests that while the social psychological and economic models are based upon very different models of man, in practice there are many similarities between them. These similarities are the inevitable result of the availability of good-quality data about the nature of the typical voter (Achen 1992). The consensus includes, *inter alia*, (1) that most voters have a relatively stable predisposition to vote for one party or another; (2) that this predisposition is not immutable, but responds to political experiences; and (3) that for most voters and most of the time, politics is remote from their everyday concerns.

The implication of this for political science is that many of the controversies about voting behaviour between the Michigan and economic approaches can ultimately be reduced to *empirical* questions. These relate to the most suitable way of measuring voters' predispositions and the responsiveness of such predispositions to current political debates. Other unresolved matters include understanding how information is given political meaning and how to model the interaction between long-term predispositions and newly acquired political information (Zaller 1992).

While the Michigan and economic models are sufficiently precise to be appropriate starting points for *ex post facto* explanation of voting behaviour, they are less than useful in terms of devising election campaigns to appeal to voters. In contrast, while political marketing models of voting behaviour are rather vague for the purposes of explanation, they can offer a great deal of practical assistance to politicians concerned with planning and implementing a campaign. This is, in no small measure, because they are not dogmatically committed to any single model of man. They also follow the implications of voter ignorance much further than the other two approaches, recognising the additional importance of generalised party images. The chapter concludes with appeals for political scientists to take marketing models much more seriously than they have done in the past.

THE SOCIAL-PSYCHOLOGICAL (MICHIGAN) MODEL

The Concept of Party Identification

The social-psychological (or "Michigan") model of voter behaviour treats the vote decision as an inherently complex one. The general explanatory approach of the model places more emphasis on "descriptive realism" than on abstraction *per se* (Campbell et al. 1960; Butler and Stokes 1974), identifying a wide range of potential explanatory variables and organising them into a logical "causal order" according to the stability of the explanatory variables and their "distance" from the vote (Miller and Shanks 1996). However, like all explanations, the Michigan model introduces a series of simplifying devices. The most important of these is the concept of party identification.

Party identification represents an enduring *emotional* attachment to a political party. It is not synonymous with formal membership of a party, or a person's voting record (Miller 1991). Voters may temporarily desert their party when propelled by "short-term" forces, such as unpopular policies or an attractive party leader. Moreover, unlike the vote, the "intensity" of identification varies from voter to voter. While some feel themselves to be "very strong Conservatives" or "very strong Labour", others feel a less intense identification (measured as "fairly strong" or "not very strong"). Increasing strength of identification is associated with a tendency to support one's party, to exhibit an interest in politics and to be politically informed (Campbell et al. 1960, pp. 142–144).

The importance attached to party identification is largely the result of its observed temporal stability. Much therefore depends on how the concept is measured. It is conventionally indicated by a willingness to describe oneself as "Labour", "Conservative" or "Liberal Democrat".[1] While others have suggested that this can be measured by observing voting records or measuring partisan attitudes, these methods are more properly regarded as indicators of partisanship (Miller 1976, 1991). A willingness to accept a party label is held to be the only measure of party identification that is fully compatible with the underlying theoretical model.

The Model of Man

In the Michigan model, the voter is held to be primarily a social animal who views the world in terms of a series of group memberships and loyalties. To identify with a group, like a social class, an ethnic group or a political party, is—in some sense—a simple extension of one's own ego (Miller 1976). Voters' identity with a political party is a part of how they describe themselves. The statement "I am Labour" is the equivalent of "I am a Catholic", "I am middle class" or "I am black". Like its economic competitor, the Michigan model uses a metaphor to help explain it: politics is analogous to religion, and the voter is analogous to a religious adherent (Miller 1976).

The Michigan approach stresses that for most people, most of the time, politics is peripheral to themselves and their families. Levels of political information, interest and attention are generally low. The attention that people pay to politics is sporadic and highly focused on general elections. One's party identity therefore serves to simplify an otherwise remote, complex and unintelligible world. Just as the religious adherent follows the symbols of their church, so too the identifier follows the symbol of party. In both cases the symbols suggest what is "good" and what is "bad". Moreover, just as theological leaders rather than adherents develop theologies, so party leaders rather than identifiers (Miller 1976) develop ideologies.

To understand the Michigan model and its relationship to the economic and marketing models, it is necessary to understand both the origins of a voter's party identification and its consequences. Like religious affiliation, one's party identity is formed by socialisation, the process by which people learn to which groups they belong and what the symbols of party mean. While changes in group membership might alter party identification (via class mobility, for example), opinion changes are held unlikely to do so (Achen 1992). In rare circumstances, during "cataclysmic events", party identification might respond to political forces (Campbell et al. 1960, pp. 145–150). However, since one's identity becomes fixed and less malleable with electoral experience, major shifts in partisanship are primarily located among the young or new voters who have not been socialised into the existing party system (Campbell et al. 1960).

The Michigan Model of Voting Behaviour

Given the fundamental complexity of political life and the expense of becoming politically informed on issues, voters in the Michigan model are, broadly speaking, "expressive" in nature. They are non-deliberative, non-calculating individuals who vote to assert their own self-image. Most party identifiers therefore simply vote in accordance with their identification. The model recognises that contemporary issues that are emphasised during the campaign itself will also influence some party identifiers. It is fully recognised that preferences relating to policy and party leaders, together with evaluations of the parties' competence, also influence vote decisions. However, it is suggested that the influence of party identification is such that only rarely do identifiers' opinions contradict their predispositions (Campbell et al. 1960, p. 133). Voters are subject to complex psychological pressures such as "persuasion" (adopting the policies and postures suggested by their party leaders) and "projection" (assuming that their party's view is synonymous with their own). They may observe and accept that their party's policy is different from their own yet go on to vote for that party—either denying the importance of that issue or placing some value on the party's commitment to principle. They may even accept that they differ from the party but go on to vote for it "out of habit" (Harrop and Miller 1987, p. 154). Thus, party identification has both direct and indirect effects on vote decisions.

Evaluation of the Michigan Model

This section evaluates the Michigan model from a particular perspective: its ability to provide an *ex-post facto* explanation of voting behaviour. Viewed from this perspective, party identification was—arguably still is—a brilliant simplification (Budge et al. 1976). It presents a plausible "model of man": voters who are neither fully informed nor completely ignorant and who need some way of understanding the political world. Its distinction between loyalists and floating voters fits in well with our intuitions. Unsurprisingly, therefore, it remains the dominant paradigm in political science.

The Michigan model is not without its faults, and four basic criticisms have been levelled at it. First, it is argued that party identification is itself subject to continual change from political forces (Crewe 1976; Clarke et al. 1995). The model draws too bold a distinction between long-term forces (affecting one's identity) and short-term forces (affecting one's vote only). Second, it is argued that the basic analogy at the heart of the model (the voter as "adherent") is inappropriate. The model places no theoretical restrictions on the ability of the party leadership to persuade its followers (Robertson 1976). The Michigan model also tends to minimise (perhaps because they are difficult to measure) the effects of deep-seated values (Scarbrough 1984). Third, whatever its theoretical attractions, it is difficult to measure party identification with any degree of accuracy. This is because the "root" question designed to trap party identification contains a reference to a political party, so that it invites "rationalisation": warping reports of one's identification to fit in with reported vote (Bartle 1999). Fourth, most Western nations underwent a process of "dealignment" from the early 1970s, so that the strength of party affiliations is much weaker than in the past. It is suggested that, while the model may have been applicable previously, increasing standards of education and a fracturing of the social structure meant that voters were more able to judge the parties on the basis of the issues and had less need of the psychological crutch of party identification (Dalton 1988).

The Michigan theorists' response to the first criticism has been to argue that although the strength of party identification is responsive to political issues, it is still very rare for voters to cross the boundary from one party to another or between party identification and non-identification. They have also produced measurement-error models suggesting that party identification is even more stable than previously thought (Green and Palmquist 1990, 1994). They have thus defended their assumption that the causal arrows predominantly run from party identification to issues, rather than vice-versa (Converse and Pierce 1992). In response to the second criticism, Michigan theorists have recognised that voters' values, either in the form of ideological position or policy-related predispositions, are indeed variables either logically prior to, or in some form of reciprocal relationship, with party identification. They have therefore revised their models accordingly (Shanks and Miller 1991). Turning to the third criticism, it has been conceded that there may be no perfect way to measure party identification (Miller 1991). However, they maintain that one's sense of identification exerts the strongest day-to-day influence on voting behaviour. It follows that the fourth criticism of party identification simply fails to distinguish between a decline in the strength of party identification and a decline in party identification *per se*. If the latter had occurred, then this would indeed have been damaging to the model, but dealignment is limited to a declining strength of party identification in Britain (Denver 1994, p. 54).

Some commentators have drawn the conclusion that the real issue is precisely how to measure voters' stable predispositions (Budge et al.

1976; Heath et al. 1994). Yet others have gone on to suggest that the concept is of little use in Western Europe, where socio-economic interests are related to ideological positions and the party system is so very different from the United States (Inglehart and Klingemann 1976; Thomassen 1976).

The Michigan Models and Party Strategy

Given the model of voter behaviour outlined above, what are its implications for a party that seeks to win votes and win elections? The Michigan model suggests that one can divide the electorate into three basic categories: "our" partisans, "their" partisans and "floating voters". Partisans can be subdivided according to the strength of their identification (ranging from very strong to fairly strong identifiers). These voters should not be targeted for conversion, but should be encouraged by their party to turn out. Floating voters, on the other hand (those who decline to accept a party identity and those who are "not very strong identifiers"), should be targeted for conversion. They are less fixed in their habits and might be persuaded by a successful campaign.

So far so good, but precisely who are these voters? What social locations do they occupy? The Michigan model suggests that voters who are cross-pressured by conflicting group memberships are likely to develop rather weak group loyalties. Thus, manual workers who own their own home, or who live in the South of England, are likely to be the classic floating voter according to this model (Butler and Stokes 1974). Similarly, managers in the public sector are likely to be subject to cross-pressures and become floating voters. Voters whose parents have mixed affiliations should also have rather weak party identities (Butler and Stokes 1974). Younger voters, who are not effectively socialised into the party system, are also likely to be susceptible to shifts in preference.

One immediate problem with this approach seems to be that many voters are likely to be subject to cross-pressures, so that it is not immediately clear that the Michigan model is useful in identifying target groups (Rose and McAllister 1986). Moreover, the young tend to pay little attention to election campaigns and are unlikely to be persuaded by them. Even if one can identify likely floating voters, how can the party contact them? In the absence of expensive national surveys, the local knowledge built up by political parties would seem to be the most reliable source of information. Party campaigns are based around the party organisation, reminding voters that there is an election, leafleting and generally mobilising pre-existing support. Such campaigns tend to lack a clear strategic focus.

Having established the existence of floating voters and the means of contacting them, how does the party persuade voters to support it? What principles, postures and policies should it adopt to secure their support? On this point, the Michigan model is silent. In fact, it is even worse than this: the Michigan model does not even suggest how one can motivate one's loyalists to turn out and vote! One is forced to conclude that because it ascribes such a minimal role to values and issues, and downplays the choice element of voting, the Michigan model is of limited use to the parties in guiding their strategies. The model suggests that campaigns merely reinforce existing attitudes, so that vote is, in effect, the product of prior socialisation, party identification and little else. The Michigan model may be a very good basis from which to build a *post-hoc* explanation of voting behaviour; however, as a heuristic for thinking about electoral campaigns, it is clearly uninformative. Yet is the economic model any better?

THE ECONOMIC (RATIONAL-CHOICE) MODEL

The Model of Man

The "economic approach" starts from a fundamentally different perspective to the Michigan model. Economic models apply the assumptions and methodology of neoclassical economic theory to what it likes to refer to as the "political market". Like the Michigan model, therefore, it is based on analogies: that parties can be modelled "as if" they were profit-maximising entrepreneurs and voters "as if" they were utility-maximising consumers (Downs 1957). Voters are regarded as "trading" their votes in return for favours (a higher standard of living) from the parties. Moreover, while the Michigan model is expressly concerned with descriptive realism, economic models tend to stress the benefits of parsimony and abstraction *per se*. For the economist, the ultimate test of any model is the extent to which it makes accurate predictions, not the realism of its assumptions (Friedman 1951).

The economists' model of man is portrayed as *"Homo economicus"*. *Homo economicus* is defined simply as a "rational" individual. More precisely, he is

1. *consistent* in his preferences;
2. *instrumental*: a vote is cast to affect policies—not to express identity;
3. *egoistic*: an individual casts his vote to optimise his own (or his household's) wealth or well-being;
4. *prospective*: a vote is cast to influence the future stream of benefits from the government, and the past has no bearing on voting choice except as a guide to the likely future performance of a party in government;
5. *an optimiser*: a voter will act to maximise benefits for a given level of costs, or minimise costs for a given level of benefit.

In the economic market, relative prices and income alone determine voters' buying behaviour. Habit, irrationality and errors are not features of *Homo economicus*.

Economic Models of Voting Behaviour

The economic model of voting behaviour follows logically from the assumptions about human nature at the heart of neoclassical economics. Voters will support whichever party is perceived as most likely to benefit them most. They therefore examine the promises of the parties in order to calculate an *"expected* party differential" that represents the difference between the utilities they expect from the two parties if they were elected to office. Voters may also compare the past performance of parties. This *"current* party differential" can be used as an alternative standard for the vote decision [though this is at odds with assumption (1) above]. Alternatively, the current party differential can be used to determine the credibility of the parties' promises (Downs 1957, p. 40). Parties that have kept their promises in the past will be more credible than those that have not.

Evaluation of the Economic Model

The rational-choice model has been criticised on several grounds. The most frequent grounds for criticism is the infamous "paradox of voting", which implies that rational individuals would not vote at all, since there is very little chance that their vote would alter the outcome (Brennan and Lomasky 1993). Economists also have difficulty in accounting for the stability of voters' preferences. The rational-choice lexicon appears to contain no simile for trust or loyalty (Fiorina 1981). More recently, however, economists have formulated explanations to account for the observed stability of preferences that are based on the proposition that, just as it is irrational to vote, so it is irrational to collect a great deal of information about politics. Voters are therefore "rationally ignorant" and use heuristics to simplify their world and reduce the cost of acquiring information. Some people therefore use their socio-economic reference groups vote to establish what is appropriate behaviour for "people like themselves". Others decide by comparing the parties' ideologies and supporting that party whose core principles come closest to their own (Downs 1957). The computation of this "ideology differential" means that it is not necessary to compare the detailed promises of the parties (Downs 1957, p. 96). Alternatively, voters may develop a "standing vote" that is only recalculated when some dramatic event causes voters to recalculate their predispositions, just as is implied by the Michigan model. In most elections, therefore, voters simply "decide not to decide" (Downs 1957, p. 85). Economists also now accept that once a predisposition is formed, it influences the interpretation of new information, as suggested by the Michigan model. However, they tend to assume that this aspect of partisanship is limited to issues for which voters have no other compelling evidence. Where the evidence suggests that "their" party is at fault, voters will respond accordingly.

Another exercise in drawing psycho-sociological conclusions from economic assumptions (methodological individualism and rationality) has been undertaken by Brennan and Lomasky (1993). Their argument draws a vital distinction between the political market and other consumer markets. In most markets, the consumer's choice is decisive (if I want Heinz baked beans, have the money to pay for them and someone is prepared to sell me that brand of baked beans, then I will have Heinz baked beans). However, in the political market a voter's preferences are not decisive (my getting the government I want is dependent on millions of other voters expressing the same preference). Thus, the instrumental value of my vote is (likely to be) vanishingly small; the only certain value of my vote is that it expresses something about me (my background, my group identity or my values). Voters can therefore afford to evaluate parties in terms of factors other than pure personal material benefit. Voters can afford to be altruistic and think of their country or of those less fortunate than themselves.

In summary, economic models place ideologies, policies and performance evaluations at the centre of voting choice. Economic models also chime with popular notions such as "pocketbook" voting. However, it is possible that voters do not choose which party to vote for in the same way as they choose which brand of breakfast cereal to purchase (the economic analogy may be simply inappropriate). Political information may be evaluated according to a voter's political bias, and a voter's opinions may be formed by their party identification, rather than vice versa. The process of electoral choice, even if it has some similarities to aspects of consumer choice in other markets, may be sufficiently different to render the market analogy more misleading than illuminating.

Implications for Party Strategy

Voters' decisions are largely based on their past experiences and their preferences about ideology, policies and leaders, together with assessments of the competence of the parties. While parties can do little to alter past experiences, they can use opinion polling to establish what positions and policies are supported by a majority of the electorate and can incorporate these into their manifesto. In a two-party system, this will lead parties to pursue the "median voter" if the electorate is normally distributed. The parties can also establish what consensual objectives are most valued by electorate (the quality of the National Health Service, the rate of inflation or unemployment) and explain how they will achieve those goals. In short, economic models suggest that election campaigns matter a great deal. Not only do they mobilise the parties' traditional supporters; they may actually convert others, since the distortionary effects of predispositions are relatively weak. Contrary to the Michigan model, there is a presumption that voters are changeable, even if they exhibit some degree of stability.

Hitherto, political science has borrowed from sociology, psychology and economics for its fundamental assumptions about the nature of voters. Although sociology, psychology and economics have provided insights into voting behaviour and provided the basis for much research in political science, the answers provided have been less than satisfactory. Has political science something to learn from marketing science?

MARKETING MODELS OF THE CONSUMER AND VOTER

The Model of Man

Marketing models have been developed in order to understand the buying behaviour of a "target market" and thus facilitate profitable exchanges (Kotler 1984). It is therefore revealing that most marketing models have rejected the assumptions of *Homo economicus* and instead have developed much broader theories of demand. Kotler, for example, argues that a buyer's choice is the "result of the complex interplay of cultural, social, personal and psychological factors" (Kotler 1984, p. 142). Marketing models accept that preferences can stem *both* from group identities (as in the Michigan model) and from perceptions of material interest (as in the economic models). They also recognise that variables such as voters' aspirations may also influence voting behaviour. Thus a party that carefully drafts its policy in order to ensure that the "median" voter is better off while richer voters pay more tax may well be punished by voters if they aspire to have higher incomes themselves. Variables such as voters' aspirations rarely figure in social-psychological or economic models, simply because they are difficult to measure. Marketing models' broader theory of demand therefore alerts us to the recurring problem of omitted variable bias (King et al. 1994).

Marketing models also recognise the influence of other explanatory variables, such as "lifestyle", which are again ignored by other approaches. They argue that just as consumers buy products to express the sort of person they are (or would like to be), so they might vote in order to express themselves. Thus, a middle-class manager might vote Labour to express solidarity with his working-class family, while a working-class voter may vote Conservative to express aspirations to upward mobility. Equally, however, consumers are capable of learning about a product (party) and altering their behaviour accordingly. While recognising the existence of brand (party) loyalty, marketing models recognise that sizeable changes in voters' evaluations will lead to a reappraisal of consumption patterns. This again fits in well with the Michigan approach's emphasis on the "cataclysmic change" that is required to shake party loyalties and the economic approach's suggestion that voters will respond to cheap information. Once one has broken free of the restrictive assumptions of *Homo economicus* and group-centred activity, one can give some recognition to the full complexity of influences on voter behaviour.

The Importance of Party Images

Marketers pay close attention to the detail of consumer behaviour, particularly the role of perceptions in influencing behaviour. It is believed that even the most well-informed voters may be affected by the subtle, subliminal messages from parties and their media allies. For Nimmo, the vital role of perceptions in voting behaviour is captured by the term "image":

To bridge the gap between what political scientists know about electoral behaviour and the notion that voters are consumers, a concept called the image is used. Image consists of the person's subjective understanding of things, i.e., of what he or she believes to be true about something, likes or dislikes, about it. This use of image parallels the definition of brand image in advertising and market research. As with brand images, political images do not exist apart from the political objects (or their symbolic surrogates) that stimulate political thoughts, feelings, and inclinations. In sum, an image is a human construct imposed on an array of perceived attributes projected by an object, event, or person. Thus, for instance, a candidate's image consists of how voters perceive him, perceptions based upon both the subjective appraisals made by the voters and the messages (utterances, attributes, qualities, etc.) transmitted by the candidate. (quoted in Newman 1994, pp. 91–92)

These arguments are very similar to those of Graham Wallas from earlier this century when he argued that parties were the centres of the voters' political world since they needed "something simpler and more permanent, something that can be recognised as being the same thing that was loved and trusted before; and party is such a thing" (quoted in Butler and Stokes 1974, p. 20).

By contrast, the "mainstream" Michigan and economic models have tended to downplay the importance of party images. This has largely been because political scientists (of whatever inclination) have tended to see elections as a choice determined by substantive affairs or a considered judgement about the performance of government. They have been reluctant to accept the role of vague impressions—this, despite the fact that there is considerable evidence to the effect that voters have little detailed information about party policies and have vague impressions of party performance. However, party images have also been underplayed because they are difficult to measure independently of vote choice, so that their causal status is problematic (Fiorina 1981). The closest to a model based on party images is that of Heath et al., but here again the emphasis is on political substance:

Our theory . . . is that it is also the "fit" between the voters' general values and their overall perceptions of what parties stand for—their general ideologies rather than specific policies—which affects how they vote and how strongly they are attached to a party. It is not the small print of the manifesto but the overall perception of the party's character that counts. If that character is seen to change, perhaps when a new team of leaders takes over, then support for the party will change too. (Heath et al. 1985, p. 107)

While this approach is plausible it excludes consideration of intrinsic benefits (such as simply registering one's identity as a party loyalist) and non-substantive factors (such as whether the party is considered extreme/moderate, united/disunited, capable of strong government/not capable of strong government, etc.). Thus, alone of all three approaches, marketing has taken the issue of images seriously. In this respect at least, the marketing approach fits in well with the language of the political campaigners themselves.

Marketing Models of Voting Behaviour

Given the complex determinants of consumer behaviour, any marketing model of the voter is likely to reflect a wide range of influences. Not surprisingly, marketing models, like Newman's model (1994, pp. 70–75), outlined below, reflects the influence of the other models. However, such models are not designed to offer *post-hoc* scientific explanations of voting behaviour but to produce a broad-brush framework within which parties and candidates can think about the development of party strategy. That is, these models are used for practical, rather than scientific, purposes of explanation. More generally, marketing models are just the starting points for the overall marketing strategy, which involves three distinct stages: (1) market segmentation, (2) targeting and (3) product positioning.

Market Segmentation

"Market segmentation" involves distinguishing types of consumer/ voter in the potential market according to their differing needs, wants and the marketing mix that is required to appeal to them (Kotler 1984, p. 251). Newman's model, for example, breaks down the electorate into five segments that can be the focus of the parties' "marketing strategy" (Newman 1994, p. 70). The first relates to the "functional value" offered to the voter, which broadly speaking represents the pursuit of utility income derived from having their preferred party in power. The second relates to the "social value" that stems from the importance of "group endorsements" and the benefits to parties of being associated with groups. This harks back to the Michigan emphasis on the importance of groups and the economic model's emphasis on "heuristics". The third represents the "emotional value" that relates to the "imagery" associated with and symbols conjured up by parties.[2] Alternatively, this may relate to the personality or charisma of a candidate or leader. The fourth segment relates to what Newman calls the "conditional value"—the assumed capacity of parties to deal with problems as they arise. This again takes in elements of the Michigan model (trusting one's own party) and the economic model (forming a rational evaluation, based on available evidence). The final "epistemic" segment represents the "novelty value" of a party or its appeal to voters' curiosity.

There are other, much more complex, means of segmenting the electorate. Voters can be segmented according to their demographic characteristics, geographically (e.g., marginal seats) or according to "psychographic" attributes like social class. Yet given that attitudes cannot necessarily be "read off" from a voter's socio-economic characteristics, a much more direct and effective method is to segment voters according to their attitudes (both positive and negative) towards the parties. Marketers therefore can take a sample of the electorate and ask them to assess the importance of various party characteristics. They can ask respondents to choose between either hypothetical or actual candidates on a number of dimensions (e.g., ideology, competence and image dimensions—caring, strength, change, etc.). They then use some form of either factor analysis or cluster analysis to identify target groups who share attitudinal characteristics (like centre-right ideology, great concern for competence and strong government, etc.), and on this basis they recommend suitable positions for the party to adopt.

There may be limitations to party responses. If the party is traditionally on the centre-right, one's analysis could take that fact as given and try to target those groups that might be swayed without abandoning its right-wing ideology.[3] Only after suffering a catastrophic defeat, or series of defeats, is a party likely to abandon its fundamental ideological character, because the reform process may cause some internal tensions within the party. Often, reform entails weakening the party's links with its "traditional" supporters and instead focusing on consensual "national-societal goals", rather than controversial ideological positions. "Segmentation" in socio-economic terms may be—in some sense—less necessary if there is a widespread consensus about goals and merely disagreement about the means to achieve those goals (Kirchheimer 1990).

Targeting

It might be objected that if we simply segment the market in this way, we have merely replicated the errors of the Michigan and economic models, since it is not certain that the targeted market is "worth" targeting. Yet, if our samples have been based on the characteristics of the electorate as a whole, the importance of each segment can be estimated. Marketers generally apply four practical questions in determining whether a market should be targeted:

1. Is the "purchasing power" measurable? In the electoral market, setting aside for a moment the problems caused by first-past-the-post systems, votes are of equal value.
2. Is the market "accessible", in the sense that we can we reach the target market by marketing instruments? For example, does that segment of the electorate read a particular newspaper, do they rely on national or local media?
3. Is the market substantial?
4. Is the market "accessible", in the sense that an effective programme can be designed to appeal to them (Kotler 1984, p. 262)?

This, of course, leads us to the final matter of "positioning".

Positioning

By mapping perceptions of where the parties and such groups stand, one can identify which groups can be most fruitfully targeted. Moreover, this process also begins to identify a likely positioning strategy. Positioning may be defined as either altering the product itself to cater for the market ("real positioning"), or altering perceptions of the product ("psychological positioning"). "Positioning is not what you do to a product. Positioning is what you do to the product in the mind of the prospect" (Kotler 1984, p. 273).

Methods such as "conjoint analysis" can be used to identify the importance that survey respondents attach to particular dimensions (Malhotra

1996). They can be asked to choose between a series of hypothetical candidates with certain characteristics. By observing their choices, we can calculate the importance that they attach to each characteristic and the "position" of the party can be modified accordingly. One interesting implication of this approach is that in repositioning themselves, parties might attract partisans from the other parties. For example, the British Labour Party has recently been quite successful in repositioning itself as "strong on law and order", mainly, it seems, by adopting the sound-bite "tough on crime and tough on the causes of crime". This may have attracted previous Conservative partisans, who supported the Conservatives because of its image as the "party of law and order". Thus, while the Michigan model is static, marketing focuses on the potential for change.

The practical use of this type of exercise is demonstrated by Mauser, who was appointed as adviser to the Democratic nominee in a Californian election (Mauser 1989). The Democrats were riven by divisions between those who wished to target the "floating voter" by moderating the candidate's policies, and those who would rather have been defeated on their "traditional" policies than compromise their principles. Mauser showed that identifying those issues and themes that were salient to the electorate and for which there was support for the Democratic position both within the party and among the electorate could accommodate both camps. The campaign appears to have had a substantial effect. The Democrats, who had previously been way behind in the polls, came very close to causing an upset. This emphasises that campaigns are often not simply about persuading voters to accept your position, but ensuring that certain issues are made salient in the campaign. The marketing approach recognises that often voters decide not on the basis of their preferences, but on what is made salient to them during the campaign.

CONCLUSIONS

All three approaches demonstrate considerable convergence in describing the nature of the electorate, albeit from disparate theoretical origins. This convergence is due to the fact that we have a great deal of high-quality data about modern electorates, and this generates a consensus about certain facts: the basic stability of voting behaviour, the capacity for change, and voters' relatively limited interest in, and knowledge of, political affairs (Achen 1992). Each model provides its own explanations of stability: the Michigan approach treats voters as having deep-seated emotional loyalties, the economic approach treats them as rationally responding to information costs and the marketing model treats them as habitual consumers. They also differ in the way that those predispositions are measured. The Michigan model directly asks voters

Crewe, I. (1976), "Party identification theory and political change in Britain", in Budge et al., *Party Identification and Beyond*, pp. 33–61.

Dalton, R. (1988), *Citizen Politics in Western Democracies: Public Opinion and Political Parties in the United States, Great Britain, West Germany and France*, Chatham, Chatham.

Denver, D. (1994), *Elections and Voting Behaviour in Britain*, 2nd edition, London, Harvester Wheatsheaf.

Downs, A. (1957), *An Economic Theory of Democracy*, New York, Harper & Row.

Fiorina, M. P. (1981), *Retrospective Voting in American National Elections*, New Haven, Yale University Press.

Friedman, M. (1951), *Essays in Positive Economics*, Chicago, Chicago University Press.

Green, D. P., and Palmquist, B. (1990), "Of artifacts and partisan instability", *American Journal of Political Science*, vol. 34, 872–902.

Green, D. P., and Palmquist, B. (1994), "How stable is party identification?", *Political Behaviour*, vol. 16, 437–466.

Harrop, M., and Miller, W. E. (1987), *Elections and Voters: A Comparative Introduction*, London, Macmillan.

Heath, A., Evans, G., and Jean, M. (1994), "The measurement of core beliefs and values: The development of balanced socialist/laissez faire and libertarian/authoritarian scales", *British Journal of Political Science*, vol. 24, 115–132.

Heath, A., Jowell, R., and Curtice, J. (1985), *How Britain Votes*, Oxford, Pergamon.

Heath, A., and Pierce, R. (1991), "It was party identification all along: Question order effects on reports of party identification in Britain", *Electoral Studies*, vol. 11, 93–105.

Hughes, C., and Wintour, P. (1990), *Labour Rebuilt: The New Model Party*, London, Fourth Estate.

Inglehart, R., and Klingemann, H. D. (1976), "Party identification, ideological preference and the left–right dimension among Western mass publics", in Budge et al., *Party Identification and Beyond*, pp. 243–276.

King, G., Keohane, R., and Verba, S. (1994), *Designing Social Inquiry: Scientific Inference in Qualitative Research*, Princeton, Princeton University Press.

Kirchheimer, O. (ed.) (1990), "The catch-all party", in P. Mair, *The Western European Party System*, Oxford, Oxford University Press, pp. 50–60.

Kotler, P. (1984), *Marketing Management: Analysis, Planning and Control*, 5th edition, London, Prentice-Hall.

Malhotra, N. K. (1996), *Marketing Research*, Englewood Cliffs, Prentice-Hall.

Mauser, G. A. (1989), "Positioning political candidates—An application of concept evaluations techniques", *Journal of the Market Research Society*, vol. 22, 181–191.

Miller , W. E. (1976), "The cross-national use of party identification as a stimulus to political inquiry", in Budge et al., *Party Identification and Beyond*, pp. 21–31.

Miller, W. E. (1991), "Party identification, realignment, and party voting: Back to basics", *American Political Science Review*, vol. 85, 557–568.

Miller, W. E., and Shanks, J. M. (1996), *The New American Voter*, Harvard, Harvard University Press.

Newman, B. I. (1994), *The Marketing of the President: Political Marketing as Campaign Strategy*, London, Sage.

Nimmo, D. (1970), *The Political Persuaders: The Techniques of Modern Election Campaigns*, Englewood Cliffs, Prentice-Hall.

Robertson, D. (1976), "Surrogates for party identification within a rational choice framework", in I. Budge, I. Crewe and D. Farlie (eds.), *Party Identification and Beyond: Representations of Voting and Party Competition*, London, Wiley, pp. 365–382.

Rose, R., and McAllister, I. (1986), *Voters Begin to Choose: From Closed Class to Open Elections in Britain*, London, Sage.

Scarbrough, E. (1984), *Ideology and Voting Behaviour: An Exploratory Study*, Oxford, Clarendon Press.

Shanks, J. M., and Miller, W. E. (1991), "Partisanship, policy and performance: The Reagan legacy in the 1988 election", *British Journal of Political Science*, vol. 21, 129–197.

Thomassen, J. (1976). "Party identification as a cross-national concept: Its meaning in the Netherlands", in Budge et al., *Party Identification and Beyond*, pp. 63–80.

Zaller, J. R. (1992), *The Nature and Origins of Mass Opinion*, Cambridge, Cambridge University Press.

3

Market Analogies, the Marketing of Labour and the Origins of New Labour

John Bartle

ECONOMIC MODELS OF VOTER AND PARTY BEHAVIOUR

I do not propose to examine the *rational*-choice approach in any detail in this chapter. Instead, I shall begin by simply noting some of its main attractions and one rather large omission. Chief among its appeals are its elegance and parsimony, which flow from the—not altogether unreasonable—belief that relatively simple assumptions can generate illuminating explanations of political phenomena. A more specific advantage is that the approach attempts to explain *both* voter and party behaviour. Ideally, one should show both how issues affected voters and how those issues were themselves shaped by politicians.

Noting the need to integrate studies of voter and party behaviour, however, also suggests one of the more obvious shortcomings of the rational-choice approach: the way in which it treats voters preferences as fixed. Advocates of an economic approach did not always make this assumption to politics. For example, Schumpeter, in developing his theory of the political entrepreneur, noted that Gladstone's "Midlothian campaign" energised the electorate in spite of the relative prosperity enjoyed by Britain under Disraeli's Conservative government. This led him to decry all theories that ignored the vital fact of leadership. He said that voters' "volitions do not, as a rule, assert themselves directly. Even if strong and definite, they remain latent, often for decades, until they are called into life by some political leader who turns them into political factors" (Schumpeter 1987, p. 270).

This chapter can merely offer reasonable evasions about the extent to which leaders can shape voter preferences, while recognising its potential importance and regretting that this area is under-researched. Clearly, the assumption that voters "cause" politicians to adopt certain policies, rather than vice versa, is a vital one that can be attacked. However, I would contend that it is a useful simplifying assumption and that critics of the rational-choice approach should provide alternative models of voter and party behaviour before rejecting it out of hand.

The following sections set out a rational-choice theory of party and voter behaviour—identifying the vital issue links of policy and performance. Later sections chart the effect of the issue theory of voting behaviour on Labour's campaign strategy. The final section calls into question the traditional psephological definition of an "issue" and suggests an amendment that takes account of "party image".

A BASIC RATIONAL-CHOICE MODEL
OF VOTING BEHAVIOUR

The earliest models of voting behaviour suggested that voting largely reflected voters' social origins. The Michigan model suggested that party identification was largely inherited from one's parents (Campbell et al. 1960; Butler and Stokes 1974). Once established, this identification was largely immune to the appeals of other parties. This in turn implied that parties were wasting their resources in attempting to persuade voters to their cause. Instead, they should seek to mobilise their voters by ensuring that their party got as much exposure as possible. Of course, this idea did not stop them from trying to persuade voters: "marketing" has been a feature of election campaigns since the introduction of universal suffrage (Wring 1994, 1995).

Over time, however, the social-psychological models of voting behaviour failed to account for observed patterns of voting behaviour, and attention turned to economic theories instead. These suggested that voters could be treated "as if" voters were utility-maximising consumers—just as parties could be treated "as if" they were profit-maximising entrepreneurs. Politicians therefore traded utility income (defined in terms of policies or performance) in exchange for votes. The basic problem for office-seeking parties therefore is to establish the link between what they do and how voters behave at the ballot box.

Extensive research into the nature of voter preferences is, therefore, the first part of a party's electoral strategy. In particular, they must determine the voters' responses to the issues on which the parties take positions. In an influential article, Donald Stokes (1963) distinguished between two types of "issue". "Position issues" relate to choices between controversial or ideologically based policy alternatives, such as the choice between "nationalisation vs. privatisation", "tax vs. spending", "membership of the EC vs. withdrawal", and so on. "Valence issues", on the other hand, relate to consensual objectives, where the only issue is which party is best able to produce those desired conditions. Since, in the pure economic model, parties treat the tastes and preferences of voters as fixed and rapidly shift to accommodate them, they adopt those policies preferred by the electorate. They also seek to convince voters that they—and they alone—can generate the desired conditions.

POLITICAL MARKETING

Having established the nature of the relationship between the voter and the parties in the economic models, I turn to an examination of the role of "political marketing". Newman has defined this as understanding the voter's needs and the development by the party of a product to meet those needs (Newman 1994, p. 8). In Newman's definition, it is intimately involved with "product definition" (i.e., is a part of the policy-making process). Ideally, continuous polling is used to monitor public opinion and to determine the position of the party. In turn the political "product" has two elements: (1) the platform of the party, which includes (a) its policies on controversial issues and (b) its competence in achieving consensual objectives, together with (2) the "image" of the party.

While 1 (a) approximates to Stokes's definition of a position issue and 1(b) resembles his definition of a valence issue, the second element of the party product has no obvious simile in the psephological lexicon. I argue later in the chapter that this represents a profound weakness with conventional "issue" models of voting behaviour.

Later sections examine the interplay between psephology understanding and party strategies over the period 1979–97. However, before I examine the period in detail, it is necessary to take a step back to examine the political experiences of Labour. Rather than examine the full expanse of postwar history, I start at the period during which Labour seemed to be the "natural party of government" and chart its decline in public esteem.

PARTY MOTIVATIONS

In order to account for the evolution of party strategies, it is necessary to provide models of both voter and party behaviour. Moreover, to explain party behaviour, it is important to make certain assumptions about the motivations of politicians. Without such assumptions, what follows would amount to little more than a description—a recital of the events and development, without explaining them.

Economic theories of voting behaviour assume that parties act "as if" they were profit-maximising producers. Politicians seek office not to produce a better society, but for the rewards of office that accrue to themselves—income, status and power. The basic assumption, therefore, is that, "parties formulate policies in order to win elections, rather than win elections in order to formulate policies" (Downs 1957, p. 36) So, just as production of goods is incidental to the pursuit of profit, so the satisfaction of voters needs is incidental to the politician's pursuit of office (Schumpeter 1987, p. 282). In a perfect political market, the "competitive struggle for the vote" between parties ensures that consumer sovereignty prevails (i.e., that voters obtain the policies and outcomes that they desire).

SHORT-RUN DEVIATIONS FROM OFFICE SEEKING

Clearly the rational-choice model of party behaviour is highly abstract and, in some sense, unrealistic. It is certainly not my intention to suggest that this model is valid at *all times* and in *all places*. However, I do maintain that the pursuit of office represents a useful *long-run* approximation. The general tendency of parties is to respond to voter preferences. I therefore adopt the assumption of office-seeking behaviour in my explanation of recent developments in the Labour Party. However, the assumption must be qualified in the short-run, because:

1. Parties *do* have other objectives—primarily of an ideological nature. They attempt to reconcile these with the pursuit of office. Moreover, those within the party who do not have strong office-seeking objectives either:

   (a) tend to reject the market analogies on which the model is based, or

   (b) believe that the party should not take the distribution of preferences as given, and that it should persuade or educate the voters to accept its ideology.

The implications of both arguments is that, in the long run, the best vote-winning strategy is simply to set out one's beliefs and try to convert voters via moral leadership. In some sense, therefore, this strategy does not represent a denial of the office-seeking assumption; rather, it purports to offer a virtuous strategy for electoral success.

2. Parties may be uncertain how to pursue office, because the relationship between what they do and voter behaviour may be unclear, ambiguous or controversial. How do parties establish what voters' preferences are?[1] Imperfect information is a problem since:

   (a) it can lead to the adoption of incorrect strategies, and

(b) acquiring perfect (or even adequate) information may be prohibitively costly.

Moreover, uncertainty increases the number of problems, because:

(a) There are competing models of voting behaviour—and competing interpretations of those models—making the accommodation of voter preferences problematic.
(b) It could be argued that information about past relationships between party outputs and voter behaviour are irrelevant under new circumstances.
(c) It is also misleading to treat a political party as a unified actor with one goal. "Factions within the party may have different goals. Activists tend to be more ideological than the leaders" (May 1973). If they enjoy a policy-making role within the party, or are necessary for mobilising support, then leaders are constrained from ruthlessly pursuing office.

OFFICE SEEKING AS A LONG-RUN TENDENCY

Given these hurdles to an office-seeking strategy, what, then, is the relationship between the long-run tendency to vote maximisation and short-run variations from it? It is simply this: parties are not stupid. Given certain assumptions about voter behaviour, parties that fail to accommodate voter preferences will eventually cease to be political parties. Once support falls below a certain level, voters will cease to believe that it can win and activists will desert it. Parties therefore learn from their mistakes. Thus, taking each of the points raised above in turn:

1. If it becomes clear that the attempt to reconcile ideological and electoral goals is impossible, or voters are resistant to ideological persuasion, then ideology will "give way" to the office-seeking strategy. The speed at which the party reacts is an important empirical question, requiring detailed historical analysis—but the direction of change is governed by office-seeking motivations.
2. Information is never so prohibitive as to preclude an office-seeking strategy (cf. Budge 1994). The information feedback from election results is a cheaper source of information. Thus, successive election defeats, together with opinion-poll evidence, spurred Labour to reform. It has learned, by a process of elimination, that the source of its defeat lies deeper than either a poor campaign or an unpopular leader, or even unpopular policies—it lies within the party itself.
3. Factions *are* important, but several forces tend to push effective power into the hands of the leadership:
   (a) Electoral campaigns are now subject to severe media scrutiny, and therefore parties must be united. Any difference of opinion between

party leaders will be dissected and magnified. Given that there are assumed to be large electoral costs connected with disunity, this sharpens the need for the party to speak with one voice—the leader's. Consultation on policies would also lead to inflexibility. Parties recognise this, and, within reasonable limits, the leader will get his (or her) way on policy issues.

(b) Campaigns tend to emphasise the role of leaders. Any leader who has policy forced on him by the party organisation would continually look defensive (Bean and Mughan 1989). To that extent, an internally democratic organisation might be a barrier to electoral success (Michels 1968).

(c) Given that activists are also in politics to achieve something, even the most committed activists are likely to respond to repeated defeats, reasoning that if they get rid of unpopular policies then they can implement their more popular policies.

(d) Activists are less essential to political parties, now that leaders can reach the electorate directly via the electronic media (cf. Seyd and Whiteley 1992).

(e) Finally, Mackenzie suggested that the real force shifting power to the party leadership was the acceptance of the rules and conventions of the governmental system (Mackenzie 1955).

In sum, what had initially appeared to be a highly abstract model of party behaviour emerges as a plausible working assumption that parties tend to seek office by accommodating voter preferences. Moreover, given the ingenuity of most political entrepreneurs and the inherent flexibility of ideologies, leaders can often effect the most fundamental ideological reorientation, stressing that circumstances have changed while their ideological values have not.

Thus, the debate about change within a political party takes place at two levels. The first stresses the electoral imperative, while the second attempts to reconcile an old and new ideology. In this way, the electoral imperative can be sanctified by ideological revisionism. Both activists and voters can be kept content. In most cases, however, we assume that it is the electoral tail wagging the ideological dog. Indeed, what was remarkable about such debates in the Labour Party in the late 1980s was that the need for reform was always cast in electoral terms. With a few rare exceptions (e.g., Hattersley 1986), there was no attempt by the Labour leadership to reconcile their policy reforms with fundamental principles.

Having established party motivations, I now turn to examine Labour's recent history. I provide a brief description of events and examine the reasons given for its electoral success and failures. In doing so, I hope to show how Labour slowly "learned" about the electorate and responded accordingly.

HAROLD WILSON
AND THE LABOUR GOVERNMENT, 1964–70

The Labour Party had lost three successive general elections in the 1950s and appeared to be in danger of terminal decline. In 1960, a pamphlet entitled *Must Labour Lose?* suggested that growing affluence among the working classes and a dislike of nationalisation was placing Labour support under strain (Abrams and Rose 1960). Labour's "cloth-cap" image was said to be out of step with the aspirations of many voters. To the delight of all those who enjoy poking sociologists in the eye, however, Labour went on to win four out of five general elections!

Labour's electoral success in 1964 and 1966 was largely based on the claim that Labour was an efficient manager of the economy (Crewe and King 1994). Harold Wilson argued that Labour understood how the system worked and how it could be improved. He promised to promote the "white-hot heat" of the technological revolution and to shake away the last vestiges of a class system that held back talent and economic growth. Yet Wilson also paid careful attention to his relations with the media and public opinion. Indeed, one of the very things that appeared to make Labour modern (and thereby play down the cloth-cap image) was its use of communications techniques. Mark Abrams, one of the authors of *Must Labour Lose?*, was appointed by the National Executive Committee as the party's pollster, in order to monitor trends in public opinion in the run-up to the general election, while Wilson himself paid careful attention to his relations with the media and cultivated contacts with journalists (Wring 1994). The outcome seemed a vindication of the approach. Labour's modern campaign, but above all its putative economic performance, carried Labour to power.

Set against these high expectations, the reality of the 1964–70 Labour governments was disappointing. While many of its social reforms (the legalising of homosexual relations and the creation of the Open University) had lasting benefits, Britain's economic performance was little less than average. Unemployment rose. The pound was devalued. The number of days lost through unofficial industrial action rose dramatically. When the economy finally turned around, Wilson called an election— partly on the basis that Labour had solved the country's balance-of-payments problems.

Of all these events, I suspect (suspect but, alas, cannot prove) that the devaluation of sterling in 1967 had profound effects on Labour's image. Labour governments had been associated with devaluation in 1931 and 1948, but Wilson had pledged that he would not follow suit. Labour had imposed curbs in public expenditure and controlled pay in an effort to support the pound. However, when push came to shove, the pound was devalued and all the pain appeared to have been for nothing.[2] Moreover, for once Wilson's public-relations skills deserted him. His "pound in your pocket" broadcast only added salt to the public's wounds. Devaluation was a simple case of a central government policy being smashed for all to see—even if they could not understand its precise effects. It severely dented the party's reputation as an economic manager. Labour's subsequent defeat at the 1970 general election appeared to be a classic case of an electorate punishing a party for economic performance.

POLITICAL COMMUNICATIONS AND THE LABOUR PARTY

Wilson's "canny" style of politics left its mark on Labour. In particular, political communications fell into disrepute. Frustration with Labour's alleged failures in office reinforced existing suspicions of politician communications and "gimmickry". What role Wilson envisioned for political marketing was uncertain, but his ideas about communications were of a short-term, "seat of his pants" variety—putting a favourable spin on events. Both Wilson and Labour became associated with short-term political fixes and the avoidance of tough but necessary decisions.

Beyond the immediate response to Wilson's style, there were deeper reasons for Labour's suspicion of marketing. First, the type of person associated with marketing (professionals) has always aroused intense suspicion among some party members. Second, marketing was associated with promoting capitalism. Thus, even when the middle class took over much of the party in the late 1970s, marketing was looked on with intense suspicion. Third, if policy were simply a response to voter preferences, then the policy-making role of the trade unions and individual members would be reduced. What would be left for party members to do—other than organise raffles and support the leadership? Finally, with its emphasis on discovering the needs and desires of voters, marketing delivered an unwanted message to the party: that many of its policies were desperately unpopular. Thus, the failure to market Labour over the period 1970–83 arose from a wilful desire to implement socialism—no matter how unpopular parts of that programme were. Merely to suggest listening to the electorate was to define oneself as being to the right, so that marketing became part of the broader battles within the Labour Party.

1974: LABOUR RETURNS TO OFFICE

Edward Heath's Conservative government too faced severe economic problems. Their experiment with laissez-faire economics resulted in rising unemployment. The government's Industrial Relations Act was effectively vetoed by the trade unions. An embarrassing U-turn on economic policy did little to help the Conservatives' reputation as economic managers. The miners' strike in 1974 culminated in a "three-day week". In the resulting general election of February 1974, Harold Wilson returned to office, having polled fewer votes than the Conservatives. In the exceptional follow-up election of October 1974, Labour gained a fragile majority of three—polling just over 40% of the vote. Labour had won largely on the basis that it could work with the unions. Economic failure seemed to push the electoral pendulum, as Conservatives and Labour played musical chairs in the House of Commons.

To some on the left, Labour's victory in 1974 seemed to confirm that it could still win elections on a left-wing platform. In opposition, Labour had swung sharply to the left. The party's programme of 1974 promised a massive expansion of the public sector, further nationalisation, the introduction of planning agreements, the repeal of all the Conservatives' anti-union legislation and a massive increase in public spending. Amid frantic policy-making, Labour gave little thought as to how such policies could be presented to the public. Policy evolved in the cosy vacuum of party committees insulated from electoral concerns. Labour seemed to be operating in the short-run—deviating from office seeking. Yet victory in 1974 was proof to the political activists that they had no need for political marketing and could win on a radical manifesto.

In reality, between 1970 and 1974 Labour's vote fell—but not by as much as the Conservatives'. Viewed in hindsight, it was fortunate that in 1974 Labour had to compete with a discredited government. When a more credible opponent appeared in the guise of Margaret Thatcher, Labour found itself on the wrong end of the largest swing since the war.

Having established some of the deeper causes of Labour's problems, I now examine the reasons given for Labour's four most recent defeats—noting both the party's response to their prior defeat and the electorate's response to their new strategies. I show that, over the period 1983–97, Labour has acted in the manner suggested by the rational-choice model—gradually learning from its defeats and adjusting its strategy accordingly. In the end, the party has done what it thought necessary to achieve office. As I show, however, the model on which they based their strategy was fundamentally flawed by a failure to recognise the importance of "party images".

THE 1979 GENERAL ELECTION: THROWING THE RASCALS OUT

It can be argued that Labour's defeat in 1979 simply reflected the electorate's negative evaluation of the government's economic performance. Unemployment had risen again over the period 1974–79, while inflation often rose in tandem. Public spending had initially spiralled out of control and then was sharply cut under the terms of a loan from the

IMF, causing prolonged disputes with public-sector workers. The loan itself appeared to symbolise Labour's inability to pursue an independent economic policy. Strict control of the money supply and a rigid incomes policy controlled inflation but eroded the standards of living of many traditional Labour voters.

In the 1970s Labour had acquired an "unenviable reputation for economic and industrial mismanagement" (Newton 1992, p. 131). This was especially true after the "Winter of Discontent"—a series of particularly bitter industrial disputes (King 1981). Their opponents skilfully exploited the image of events at one cemetery, where the dead remained unburied. It hardly mattered that such events were exceptional—they were potent *symbols* of Labour's failure. It seems likely that the Winter of Discontent not only sealed the fate of the Labour government, but had profoundly symbolic effects on the electorate—effects that were to resonate with voters years later, as they pondered their prospects under a future Labour government (Gould 1998b).

A DESIRE FOR A CHANGE OF DIRECTION?

Some commentators have attributed a greater role to the party's policies in accounting for the 1979 defeat. As early as 1977, Crewe and his colleagues had identified a "major haemorrhaging of support for the party's basic tenets"—its policies on nationalisation, trade unions and the welfare state" (Crewe et al. 1977, p. 152). Crewe argued that, by 1974, there was an "ideological chasm" between the party and many of its supporters and that Labour's problems lay "not in its record, but in its *enduring* principles" (Crewe 1981, p. 297, emphasis added).

In addition to this ideological disjuncture, some specific Conservative policies, supported by the electorate, but opposed by Labour, damaged the party. This was especially true of the proposals to introduce legislation to control the unions, sell council houses to their tenants, introduce a short sharp shock for young offenders and cut direct taxation (Crewe 1981). On this interpretation, therefore, the 1979 defeat reflected much more than the electorate's rejection of the performance of the Labour government. Mrs Thatcher had not only captured the electors' pocketbooks; she had captured the "mood of the times" as well. This was captured in Callaghan's confession to an aide during the 1979 campaign:

There are times, perhaps once every thirty years, when there is a sea change in politics. It does not matter what you say or do. There is a change in what the public wants and approves of. I suspect that there is now such a change and it is for Mrs Thatcher. (Donoghue 1987, p. 191)

While there was therefore something profoundly wrong with Labour's campaign platform in 1979, Labour was to make matters worse—much worse—in the next four years. The left, which gained control of many trade unions (and thereby of the Annual Party Conference) were greatly disappointed with Labour's record on nationalisation, the welfare state, unemployment and the EEC. These angry voices accused the Labour government of betrayal (Crewe and King 1995). They said that Labour had lost because it had failed to deliver socialism, though, as Crewe had shown, there was no evidence for this allegation. For the period 1979–83, the Downsian assumption of office seeking is scarcely an appropriate tool for analysis. The party fell under the control of ideologically motivated factions.

THE 1983 GENERAL ELECTION:
ALL REWARD AND NO PUNISHMENT?

If voters do simply punish a government for economic performance, then the 1983 result might be thought to represent something of a puzzle. Mrs Thatcher was re-elected with a majority of over 140 seats in the House of Commons, despite presiding over a massive rise in unemployment, the collapse of much of British manufacturing industry and unprecedented levels of real interest rates. At first glance it seems perverse to suggest that she won the election as a result of macroeconomic success. Yet in spite such a record, however, it is possible to weave a "performance theory" of the election result. The severe deflation eventually resulted in low inflation, which, when coupled with reductions in direct taxation, resulted in moderately rising living standards for the contented majority who remained in work (Galbraith 1993). Low inflation and declining interest rates also led to rising personal financial expectations and, it seems, a recovery in Conservative fortunes (Sanders et al. 1987).

For psephologists, the 1983 general election remains controversial. Some, like Norpoth, suggest that unemployment did have a negative effect on Conservative support but this was offset, at least in part, by a "Falklands factor" (Norpoth 1991). Others, like Sanders et al. (1991), suggest that any Falklands effect was short-lived and that unemployment was of little relevance to voters. They assign more credit to the gradual rise in personal financial expectations that occurred in the wake of Geoffrey Howe's 1982 budget. While the debate about the magnitude and length of any Falklands factor remains unsettled, there is an altogether more obvious cause of Labour's defeat in 1983—its policies.

THE LONGEST SUICIDE NOTE IN HISTORY

Labour entered the election campaign with possibly the most left-wing manifesto in the party's history. Over the period 1979–83, the left worked feverishly at producing policy—endless streams of policy poured forth from the massive policy-making committees, sub-committees and advisory groups. Little or no thought was given to how all these policies could be sold to the public, or how competing demands could be reconciled (Kellner 1985). Amid this confusion, Labour even decided it could do without the professional services of its own pollster—Bob Worcester. He only started polling again in February 1983, just four months before the election, and thus was unable to influence the formulation of policy in any way (Mitchell 1983)!

The resulting manifesto was memorably described by Gerald Kaufman as "the longest suicide note in history". It proposed withdrawal from the European Community (EC) and (effectively) a siege economy, unilateral nuclear disarmament, the repeal of all the Conservatives' trade union legislation, comprehensive state intervention, and—perhaps the most breathtaking example of lunacy of the period—the compulsory repurchase of council houses sold to their (largely working-class) tenants. These policies were unpopular even among its own supporters (Crewe 1985). Moreover, few in the shadow cabinet believed in the manifesto, so that divisions and splits became the main news of an otherwise dull campaign. The image was that of a party in chaos, one that could not govern itself, let alone the country.

Curiously, in view of the general lack of organisation, the 1983 campaign did contain one small, but important, innovation. For the first time, Labour acquired the services of a professional advertising agency, John Wright & Partners. Yet this innovation came too late, and their client fundamentally handicapped the agency: it was denied access to Labour's market research, so that it was always shooting in the dark (Wring 1994, p. 20). More importantly, the policies themselves were unsaleable. The agency, which had been given no role in the policy-making, could hardly be blamed for the resulting defeat.

To add to its policy woes, the Labour leader, Michael Foot, was perceived to be weak and eccentric—quite unsuited to be prime minister (Bean and Mughan 1989). The party was slowly emerging from beneath the black cloud of a bitter civil war, which had led a group of former cabinet ministers to form the Social Democratic Party (SDP). Two constitutional changes—the mandatory reselection of MPs and the election of the leader through an electoral college, gave the trade unions and activists increased influence within the party—when many voters viewed both with suspicion. The campaign itself was a shambles and served only to emphasise divisions and Labour's unfitness to govern. The Conservative Party scarcely needed the shine of the Falklands War to defeat Labour—that factor merely helped to sink the SDP/Liberal Alliance.

Viewed in this light, the question becomes why didn't Labour lose *even more* disastrously? There are, I believe, two reasons. First, there was a kernel of truth in the social-psychological model of voting behaviour. Labour had retained the *emotional* loyalty of many voters. Their attitude could be summarised as, "I don't like its policies. I don't like its performance. I think the Leader is dreadful. But I am Labour, so I will vote Labour." Whether such support could be sustained indefinitely is doubtful, however. Secondly, the first-past-the-post system insulated Labour from the full effects of its loss of votes. Despite winning a mere 2% more of the popular vote than the Alliance, Labour had 180 more seats— giving it both a false sense of security and a much-needed breathing space.

1983–87: UNITY, DISCIPLINE AND KINNOCK

In the autumn of 1983, Labour elected a new leadership team—Neil Kinnock and Roy Hattersley. Kinnock could not interpret his victory as a mandate for a major reform of policies. Moreover, being a man of the left, he was reluctant to jettison policies such as unilateralism and withdrawal from the EC. The lessons that he drew from the 1983 defeat were that, if he could unite his warring party, discipline the entryist groups such as "Militant" and nudge the party to accept a *slightly* more moderate policy package, then a repeat of the disaster of 1983 could be averted—and, just possibly, Labour might recover just enough votes to win. His victory speech at the 1983 Party Conference resonated with appeals for unity and discipline (Leapman 1987).

Other than appealing for unity, there seemed little idea about how to avoid further disaster. The hard-won policy victories of the left were not going to be surrendered until it was clear that there was no other way forward. Moreover, Kinnock calculated that any policy change would divide the left of the party. In this way, both Michael Foot and the 1983 campaign became convenient explanations of Labour's defeat, and Labour postponed addressing the fundamental problems of policy and image.

In the meantime (and somewhat ironically in view of Kinnock's appeals for unity) the four years from 1983 to 1987 were spent enforcing internal discipline, beginning the process of reforming the party's Byzantine structures (Shaw 1993). In 1984, Kinnock tried to introduce one member one vote for the selection of parliamentary candidates, but he was defeated. This defeat only served to emphasise his weakness and Labour's reluctance to change. Support on the party's governing National Executive Committee (NEC) was initially hard won—and at a cost to Kinnock's credibility with the electorate (Hughes and Wintour 1990). He could not be assured of support on the NEC until the "soft left" (like David Blunkett and Michael Meacher) had become detached from the more extreme "Bennite left". Slowly, however, such members of the NEC began to appreciate the electoral burden that groups like Militant imposed on Labour, and they supported Kinnock's action against groups like the Liverpool City Councillors (Leapman 1987). By the end of the 1980s, the leadership gained almost total control of the party machinery.

The shift in policy terms over the period 1983–87 was slight—so slight indeed that few voters may have noticed it. Labour accepted council-house sales. The first recognition of the need for markets emerged, and hostility to membership of the EC was replaced with a grudging acceptance. Yet unilateralism remained a potent symbol of Labour's leftist stance. Moreover, in its language the party appeared to remain attached to declining industries, public-sector unions and the protection of minorities. The notion that Labour could take power with the help of a "coalition of minorities" impeded reform and—almost by definition—excluded those who defined themselves as part of the "majority" (Gould 1998b). In a secret memorandum, leaked to the press, Patricia Hewitt conceded that, "The gays and lesbians issue is costing us dear among the pensioners, and fear of extremism and higher taxes is particularly prominent in the GLC area" (Leapman 1987, p. 19).

MEDIA COMMUNICATIONS
AS A POLITICAL MARKETING STRATEGY

In 1985, the Labour Party decided to replace Nick Grant as the Head of Press, Publicity and Advertising. During the 1983 election, the unfortunate Mr Grant had been forced to report to a forty-strong campaign committee—resulting in chaos (Kellner 1985). Gradually such organisational matters were addressed, and Labour leaders identified the need for an effective communications strategy. Some, like Robin Cook, had been impressed by the way in which the Conservatives and Saatchi & Saatchi had marketed Mrs Thatcher during the 1983 campaign (Wring 1994). There was a general feeling that Labour could improve its image by adopting similar techniques. However, the scope for marketing was always limited to presentation alone, and no policy-making role was contemplated. Yet again, the belief that the Conservatives had won elections because they were simply more effective in campaigning prevented substantive policy reform.

Because of the concern with presentation, the decision was taken to create the new post of Director of Communications. However, the new position did not carry with it input into policy-making. This was reflected in the personal manifesto that the successful applicant, Peter Mandelson, presented to the NEC. According to him, Labour's communications strategy involved: (1) ensuring that Labour's message was encapsulated in memorable phrases, (2) producing attractive campaign materials, (3) improving press and broadcasting contacts and relations, (4) targeting priority seats and mobilising the whole party and (5) projecting a united and able leadership team (Mandelson 1988, p. 15). Mandelson's role fell far short of being integrated with policy-making, because considerations of intra-party power were never far away. While Mandelson's selection heralded a revolution in Labour's media relations, his manifesto must have been most welcome to those who feared that communications advisers would have too much influence on policy formation. Labour insiders kept the communications strategy at arms length from policy-making.

Following his appointment, together with Philip Gould, Mandelson established the Shadow Communications Agency (SCA) in February 1986. This gave outside professionals a direct input into the ongoing media-relations revolution. Initially, the SCA had little direct role in the development of party policy, but it oversaw a transformation in Labour's reputation for professionalism in media circles. It advised Labour leaders on appearances, performance in front of the camera and even the memorable phrases to use when attacking the government. It began to identify policy areas of Labour strength, such as the health service and the environment, by convening focus groups. This supplemented quantitative opinion poll data, which was now continually collected. Labour launched its *Freedom and Fairness* campaign in early 1986, to promote its policies on housing, pensions, education, the environment and law and order. The harmonious red rose replaced the class-laden symbol of the red flag, so that, all in all, Labour's corporate image had improved dramatically (Franklin 1994).

Labour's new-found professionalism had paradoxical consequences, however. Since the professionalisation of the party was not coupled with substantive policy change, it was often viewed, both within and outside the party, as a cynical attempt to fool voters that the party had changed (Franklin 1994). The new professionalism became equated with the slick and superficial. This clearly suggested that there were limits to the benefits derived from improved political communications alone (Hughes and Wintour 1990, p. 56).

THE 1987 GENERAL ELECTION CAMPAIGN

By the 1987 general election, Labour was better prepared to campaign, but the "product" remained much as before. The SCA, together with Campaigns Co-ordinator Bryan Gould, fought what was thought by some a brilliant campaign. The party effectively set the agenda throughout, though it was forced onto the defensive on the issues of defence and taxation. Having started the campaign level-pegging with the SDP/

Liberal Alliance in the polls, Labour ended with a 9-point lead. The more telling fact, however, was that Labour remained some 13 points behind the Conservatives. Good communications was the difference between coming second and coming third. The product (policies and perform-ance) seemed to be the difference between coming first and coming second.

The absence of any real policy change had played its part in the decision to fight a presidential campaign—focusing on the merits of Neil Kinnock. Hugh Hudson made a Party Election Broadcast—quickly dubbed by the media, "Kinnock—the movie"—that proved successful in boosting his personal ratings. He emerged with his reputation en-hanced—but Labour gained a mere 3%, up to 31%. Yet, despite losing badly, his *personal* position was secure. There was a realisation, however, that the excuses had run out—and that there was no alternative to policy reform. However, before I examine Labour's response, it is again neces-sary to examine those issues that caused Labour's defeat.

THE ELECTORAL IMPLICATIONS OF THE LAWSON BOOM

The 1987 general election again emphasised that Labour suffered from a credibility gap on economic issues. The period 1983–87 had been one of relatively high growth, low inflation and high, but gradually falling, unemployment. Furthermore, where inflation was present, in the form of house-price inflation, this merely increased the money wealth of the voters and their ability to borrow more cheap money. The added dash of direct-tax cuts added further fuel to the "Lawson boom" and the voters' sense of economic well-being—the so-called feel-good factor. Having noted that "an expanding economy is the most generally accepted for-mula for economic success", the Nuffield study argued that the Con-servatives were regarded as more likely to increase general living standards (Butler and Kavanagh 1988, p. 268). The crucial factor, how-ever, was that those who thought that their personal circumstances had improved were more likely to defect to the Conservatives. Put quite simply, the Conservatives had convinced enough people that their standard of living had improved and that it would continue to do so.

LABOUR POLICIES AND THE 1987 GENERAL ELECTION

The election postmortems suggested that two policies in particular had harmed the Labour Party in the 1987 campaign: defence and taxa-tion. Until Neil Kinnock made a "gaffe" during an interview, when he implied that the best that Britain could do was to render a Soviet *occupa-tion* impossible (thus implying that Labour would not deter them in the first place), defence had not been a major issue. Rather than affect the

Labour vote directly, it is quite possible that it was thought to reflect Labour's general image of *unfitness to govern*. The election campaign also revealed inconsistencies in Labour's taxation policies. These were picked over by a hostile press and helped to reinforce a widespread fear that taxes would rise drastically under Labour—a view that was helped by the uncosted nature of many of Labour's earlier promises and constant criticism of Conservative cuts in public spending. Conservative charges about Labour profligacy were made all the more effective by the fact that they were plausible.

REDESIGNING THE PRODUCT: THE POLICY REVIEW

To some extent, Labour needed the 1987 defeat. Until then, the party could ascribe its 1983 failure to an unpopular leader, party divisions and a poor campaign. These factors were absent in 1987, but Labour had still lost. It was acknowledged that Labour's media-friendly image was not enough:

Some . . . in the Party assert that Mrs Thatcher cannot be defeated by rehabilitating Labour's respectability through slick PR and distancing from the "loony left". *I could not agree more.* These are necessary, not sufficient, conditions for success. What we stand for and what we will actually do for people are the additional qualifications for success. (Mandelson 1988, p. 13; emphasis added)

Shortly after the 1987 defeat, Kinnock launched the *Labour Listens* campaign—a series of public meetings at which Labour politicians sat and listened to the concerns of ordinary people. In fact, these meetings merely served as a PR ploy and provided the internal justification for policy change. Clearly, the aim was simply to become what it had always been until the madness of the early 1980s—a European "social democratic" party (Smith 1993).

A second step was to take policy-making out of the divisive and quite labyrinthine procedures of the Annual Party Conference, by establishing seven Policy Review Groups (PRGs) staffed with both NEC and shadow cabinet members. This helped to ensure internal support for the reforms and represented a conscious step away from traditional policy-making forums that damaged Labour's image. Each PRG received reports from the SCA and the Political Intelligence Officer on public attitudes to Labour. Eric Shaw suggests that, "No significant development of policy was considered without the most careful attention to likely public response" (Shaw 1993; see also Webb 1992). However, there can be no doubt that the real spur to action had been the election defeat itself and that most Labour leaders had a clear idea of the necessary reforms. At last, slowly—and initially uneasily—policy-making and marketing were becoming integrated, as effective policy-making power passed back from the Annual Conference to the leader.

Labour's new policy statements—*Social Justice and Economic Efficiency*, in 1988; *Meet the Challenge Make the Change*, in 1989; *Looking to the Future*, in 1990; and *Opportunity Britain*, in 1991—were published amid a great fanfare of trumpets. These were presentationally stylish. In policy terms, they represented an acceptance of the market economy and of a great deal of the recent trade union legislation, enthusiastic endorsement of the EC (particularly its social policies) and support for education and training. The "challenge" and the "change" in the second document referred not the electorate, but to the party itself. The desire to oust the Conservatives burned so deeply that eventually even the unilateralist policy was finally abandoned.

IMPROVING PERCEPTIONS OF LABOUR'S ECONOMIC COMPETENCE: A TALE OF SEAFOOD

If there were some truth in the performance theory of voting, policy change alone would be insufficient to gain Labour office. Paralleling the policy reforms, therefore, Labour made strenuous efforts to court industry and portray itself as a party that could work with business. The shadow Treasury ministers made regular visits to the City to explain Labour policy and listen to their concerns. As the Lawson boom soured and turned into recession, they found their ideas received with interest. Margaret Beckett, the shadow chief secretary to the Treasury, continually stamped "As resources allow" on every Labour utterance and gained an unrivalled reputation for financial orthodoxy. The bank-manager style of Smith was well received by financiers, and the party's conversion to membership of the European Exchange Rate Mechanism (ERM) for a time meant that the two were in an unholy alliance against the Conservative government. Smith's "prawn-cocktail" offensive showed dividends as Labour began to shed its reputation for economic profligacy. Michael Heseltine pleaded with Smith to "spare the prawn" in the House of Commons, but this "joke" merely served to underline Labour's new-found respectability.

TURNING THE CORNER AND PREPARING FOR OFFICE

Throughout this period (1987–92), Labour leaders spoke candidly about "removing the barriers to voting Labour". Encouragingly polls suggested that people were prepared to pay "higher taxes" for "better public services", but the Labour leadership also paid close attention to quantitative opinion research that showed that Labour still suffered from an image as a high-tax party. "Moderation", "prudence" and "common sense" became new entries in the lexicon of Labour Party spokespersons.

An examination of opinion polls in 1989 shows that Labour was increasingly viewed as a credible political party. In part, this was no doubt due to the unpopularity of the poll tax, the usual mid-term effects, Mrs Thatcher and the recession, but there was additional evidence that Labour's policy review was noticed and approved of by the voters. A poll in the *Independent* showed that 27% of the electorate thought that "Labour [had made] big changes for the better", as opposed to only 6% who thought that it had "changed for the worse" (Kellner 1989). However, 59% of voters felt that Labour had "not changed for better or worse". A poll in the *Daily Telegraph* showed that, without prompting, 22% of voters said that "Labour was becoming more moderate", 19% gave its change of policy on defence a favourable mention, 14% said it was "more united", and 10% commented on Kinnock's improved performance. Labour still lagged behind the Conservatives on the economy (King 1989). Overall, it was felt that Labour had much to be happy about.

By early 1992, the party had become united and disciplined. Policymaking was finally under the control of the leader. The product appeared to be right. The marketing and the communications were excellent. Yet Labour lost the election that year. It appeared that theories of issue voting had it wrong. But had they?

THE 1992 CAMPAIGN: THE INITIAL ASSESSMENT

Policies and the 1992 General Election

At the 1992 election, Labour enjoyed substantial leads on policies relating to "social issues" such education, pensions, the National Health Service and the environment. It also enjoyed a lead on the issue of unemployment. Moreover, in the wake of the end of the Cold War, defence ceased to be an issue. In terms of pure policy reasons for not voting Labour, the list was short. To be sure, the polls suggested that Labour was still not trusted over taxation and inflation—but even this had not suggested that Labour would lag a full 9 points behind the Conservatives.

THE CONTINUING PROBLEM OF ECONOMIC COMPETENCE

If policies seemed to be in Labour's favour, what about the economy? In 1992 the Conservatives could not rely on the "feel-good factor", which had been thought so important to them in 1987. The long-awaited economic recovery mysteriously failed to materialise—a fact that profoundly altered the Conservatives' own marketing strategy. Rather than point to their own success, they had to argue that, whatever their own failings, it would be much worse under Labour (Barry 1994). In particular it was said that both taxation and inflation would rise—the so-called double whammy. Repeatedly, Conservative politicians hammered home the allegation, "You Can't Trust Labour". This strategy seems to have worked. By the end of the campaign, the only policy areas of importance on which the Conservatives enjoyed an advantage were taxation and inflation. The Nuffield study concluded that, "In spite of what the public was saying until Election Day, the 1992 election result seems to reflect however furtively and reluctantly a classic pocket book outcome in the classic mould" (Butler and Kavanagh 1992, p. 268).

Labour seemed to have done all that it could to develop a product in terms of policies and economic competence that voters had told pollsters they wanted. But the product was rejected again. Two beliefs gained ground. First, Britain had become a "nation of liars", professing a willingness to pay higher taxes for better services—a kinder society—but sneaking off to vote for lower taxes in the privacy of the polling booth. Second, Neil Kinnock had cost Labour the election because of his lack of prime ministerial *gravitas* (Crewe and King 1994).

JOHN SMITH'S LABOUR: ONE MORE PUSH

In the immediate aftermath of the 1992 defeat, Labour seemed to have accepted the above assessment of the 1992 defeat. Without pausing for breath, it reacted to form—conservatively—and elected John Smith, the architect of its tax plans, as its leader (McSmith 1994). The assumption appears to have been that by electing the affable bank manager, Labour would remove the final stains of its tax-and-spend past. Smith's own style seemed to reassure the party that if they simply sat back and "played the long game", by harrying an increasingly beleaguered Major government, victory would be at hand. "One more push" became the *de facto* strategy.

And that was almost the limit of Labour's introspection—the party's product was to remain the same. The Policy Review had adopted very nearly all the policies that psephologists had thought necessary. Smith established the Social Justice Commission—giving it a remit to examine all matters of tax and spending—but this was very much tinkering at the edges of policy. Labour became even more firmly disciplined not to commit itself to costable expenditure. There was one further internal reform—the removal of the trade-union bloc vote at a dramatic conference in 1993. However, there was no suggestion that Smith would have continued with the process of internal reform. Smith was altogether too comfortable with many of the symbols of "Old Labour" and thought that

Labour needed to unite. In spite of the high personal esteem in which many "modernising" Labour MPs held Smith, there was a growing frustration with Labour's apparent inertia (Gould 1998b).

When Smith died in May 1994, the enormous outpouring of grief resulted not only from the loss of a great man, but also from the realisation that, without Smith, the "one-more-push" strategy was untenable. There was no leader of equal stature—no pillar of prudence able to push on. It was therefore time to reassess the 1992 defeat. The bout of introspection that had been postponed in 1992 could no longer be avoided. Why had the Labour Party performed so poorly in election after election? What was it about Labour that turned voters off?

THE 1992 GENERAL ELECTION: A REASSESSMENT

Blair's electoral strategy is based on a radically different interpretation of the 1992 general election from the one offered above. Lost beneath the economic account of Labour's defeat is a more subtle explanation— an explanation that is alluded to elsewhere in the Nuffield study: "the election still appeared to have turned on fear of Labour" (Butler and Kavanagh 1992, p. 227).

Kinnock had learned from Labour's defeat in 1983 that unity, discipline and a good campaign were requirements of victory. In 1987, he had learned that fundamental policy reform was also necessary. True, the Policy Review had signalled a return to 1970s social democracy. However, that sort of programme had been rejected even in 1979—both the world and the electorate had moved on. Moreover, Kinnock made the error of treating the party's policies or its performance as the product— that is, both he and the psephologists ignored the second part of the product: the party's "image".

This notion of party image is venerable, going back as far as 1906.[3] It found echo in *Must Labour Lose?* with its dire warnings about Labour's "cloth-cap image". In 1987, Bryan Gould had warned the party that, "it's not our policies they don't like—it is us" (Hughes and Wintour 1990, p. 128) while Peter Jenkins acidly remarked after 1992 that Labour lost "because it was Labour" (Butler and Kavanagh 1992, p. 278). The 1992 result merely underlined that the Labour Party was simply not trusted. Labour lost because of its image, which can be defined as "the subtleties which are extraordinarily hard to catch on paper, but which nevertheless provide a better guide to the party's behaviour" (Marquand 1990, p. 197; see Jenkins 1988, p. xvi)

This theory of party image should not be confused with image in any trivial sense. It has *nothing* to do with Tony Blair's haircut, the replacement of the "red flag" with the "red rose", Mandelsonian "spin doctors".

The very use of the word "image" can suggest something artificial and ephemeral. "Party image" is the very opposite of this. It is the experience and record that the party has accumulated. Marquand argues that it is this—what he calls the "ethos" of Labour, its language, fundamental character and symbols—that has greatly damaged the Labour Party.

There is a theoretical basis for the theory in rational-choice and Bayesian decision-making theory. Politics is uncertain, and, given its importance, a degree of trust between party and voter is essential. Given the complexity of party policy and assessments of likely performance, it is understandable that voters ask simply, "Do I trust Party X?" Neither issue voting nor rational choice generally has considered trust when devising party strategies. Yet to any "outsider" considering voting behaviour, the importance of such considerations would be readily apparent.

WHAT DO VOTERS BUY: POLICIES OR PARTY?

The essential point to note is that the "product" of a party, then, is not like "cornflakes"—it is more like a specialist financial or legal service. Increasingly, such products are marketed on the basis that the people who are selling the product are trustworthy, independent and have an incentive to provide the best product. Where the product requires an essential element of trust, then the reliability of the person selling the product is highly relevant. Thus, when assessing a policy it is often impossible to separate the policy from the party (cf. Heath et al. 1985, p. 92).

Over time, Labour had lost the emotional sympathy of great swathes of the electorate. Once these were lost, they became difficult to regain. The symbols of devaluation, the industrial chaos in the Winter of Discontent and high taxation could be drawn upon by its Conservative opponents at any time. Thus, what made the Conservative "double whammy" so effective in 1992 was not simply the slogan itself, but the fact that it exploited voters' latent fears—fears that were based on *real* experiences.

For Marquand, the explanation of Labour's electoral decline is necessarily cast in terms of something that is nebulous and impalpable. The lesson for psephology is clear: the theoretical distinction between policy and performance may be irrelevant to the voter who decides how to vote on the basis of synoptic evaluations of a party's image. Rose suggests that the problem may not be that political scientists have too little data but that we have far too much—because "in a General Election voters do not develop a reasoned approach" (Rose 1974).

This puts public concerns about Labour's economic competence in a different light. Gamble suggests that voters *instinctively* think that the

Conservatives were better able to manage the economy (Gamble 1993, p. 61). The use of the word "instinctive" suggests a highly complex response on the part of the voter, one that formal models fail to pick up. Moreover, it suggests that symbols shape reactions long after they have ceased to be current issues. It is therefore misleading to argue that Labour lost because it was not trusted on the economy. Labour lost because it was not trusted, "full stop". Labour's internal review of their 1992 defeat came to a similar conclusion: that economic issues were merely *symbolic of a broader fear* about the degree to which Labour policies would threaten individual personal circumstances—especially during a recession" (Timmins 1992).

NEW LABOUR: THE PARTY AS PRODUCT

Tony Blair's task was more than the production of a new set of policies or proving that he could run the economy better than the Conservatives. He could change policies, he could improve Labour's competence, but he *could not* rewrite Labour history. Instead, he had to restore the voters' trust in Labour—by placing as much distance between itself and the negative associations of "Old Labour". He needed to create an image of "change" and "modernisation", just as Wilson did in 1964. He therefore removed some of the symbols of "the past"—such as Clause IV—that were cherished by party members. Viewed in this light, therefore, Blair's relatively comfortable victory in the vote to remove Clause IV was further proof of the power of the office-seeking model.

Another part of the Blair strategy is the language he uses. He is very "inclusive"—emphasising that Labour is a national party with something for everybody. He claims to speak on behalf of "middle England", "the middle class", "the victims of crime", "the unemployed", "industry" "small business" and "one nation". The defence of minorities is placed firmly in the context of community and responsibility, so that he avoids setting the party in opposition to "majorities". He emphasises "New Labour" at ever opportunity—signalling a clear break with the past. He also never uses the word "socialism" where the word "fairness" will do.

Blair has also identified certain aspects of life, such as law and order and job security, that are of deep concern to voters. Like Schumpeter's political entrepreneur, he has simply transformed Labour's image on the "law-and-order" issue. Traditionally, Labour has been regarded as "soft" on law and order, while many of its voters have been authoritarian. In its language, Labour appeared to be more sympathetic to the criminal than the victim and more concerned about civil rights than securing convictions. Indeed, the very fact that Blair talks about crime as an important issue represents a fundamental shift. Equally, he has identified job security as an important issue, rather than focusing on the narrower issue of unemployment. His is a deeply majoritarian language.

EPILOGUE

Labour has continued to emphasise the distinction between "Old" and "New Labour", distancing itself from the unions (promising "fairness not favours") and embracing a dynamic market economy. Power has been increasingly centralised in the party leadership, and dissenters sidelined or disciplined. In government, Labour has constantly eschewed "Old Labour" policies where they have been perceived to have failed (Rawnsley 1995). Moreover, the "long campaign" in the year running up to the 1997 election itself focused on the essential issue of "New Labour". Was it Old Labour in disguise? Was it a new, innovative party? Alternatively, was it a new party with new dangers (Butler and Kavanagh 1997, p. 35)? Labour's victory seemed to suggest that most voters thought that Labour was a new, moderate and responsible party, though at least one of Labour's advisers emphasises that many voters remained uncertain all the way through the campaign and that many decided to vote Labour only at the last moment (Gould 1998a).

However, it is clear that other events contributed to Labour's landslide. The Conservative government's reputation for economic competence was severely dented by their forced exit from the ERM in September 1992, making it easier for any Labour Party (either New or Old) to compete (King 1998; Sanders 1994). Subsequent divisions over Europe, sleaze and the leadership election of 1995 all served to portray the Conservatives as fundamentally divided and unfit for government. Labour itself hammered home the message of betrayal with its allegations of "22 tax rises", "Enough is enough" and assertion that "Britain deserves better".

Whether "New Labour" or the ERM crisis contributed most to Labour's landslide remains an open question, but Labour leaders appeared convinced of the importance of party images. Their advisers have continually emphasised the need to rebuild trust between political leaders and citizens, to carry out their modest promises and to continually monitor reactions to the parties. Their Conservative opponents have tried to mimic some of Labour's organisational innovations by increasing power at the centre under the guise of extending democracy (Conservative Party 1998). However, they have shown limited sign of reviewing their policies or reassessing their image as an anti-public services, low-tax, financially incompetent and uncaring party. It may be that one legacy of the Thatcher era is to land the Conservatives with a rigid ideology that inhibits change. Until the Conservatives engage in a fundamental review, the party may find itself unable to challenge the electoral dominance of New Labour.

NOTES

1. See Budge (1994) for a discussion of party strategies in the light of radical uncertainty.

2. This process seems to have repeated itself twenty-five years later during the ERM crisis.

3. Graham Wallas, for example, argued that parties were the centre of the voters' political world since they needed, "something simpler and more permanent, something that can be recognised as being the same thing that was loved and trusted before; and party is such a thing" (quoted in Butler and Stokes 1974, p. 20).

REFERENCES

Abrams, M., and Rose, R. (1960), *Must Labour Lose?* London, Penguin.

Barry, P. (1994), *The Impact of Tory Electoral Advertising in 1992*, Unpublished BA Dissertation, University of Essex.

Bean, C., and Mughan, A. (1989), "Leadership effects in parliamentary elections in Australia and Britain", *American Political Science Review*, vol. 83, 1165–1179.

Budge, I. (1994), "A new spatial theory of party competition: Uncertainty, ideology and policy equilibria viewed comparatively and temporally", *British Journal of Political Science*, vol. 24, 443–467.

Butler, D., and Kavanagh, D. (1988), *The British General Election of 1987*, Basingstoke, Macmillan.

Butler, D., and Kavanagh, D. (1992), *The British General Election of 1992*, Basingstoke, Macmillan.

Butler, D., and Kavanagh, D. (1997), *The British General Election of 1997,* Basingstoke, Macmillan.

Butler, D., and Stokes, D. (1974), *Political Change in Britain: The Evolution of Electoral Choice*, London, Macmillan.

Campbell, A., Converse, P., Miller, W., and Stokes, D. (1960), *The American Voter*, New York, Wiley.

Conservative Party (1998), *The Fresh Future*, London: The Conservative Party.

Crewe, I. (1981), "Why the Conservatives won", in H. R. Penniman (ed.), *Britain at the Polls, 1979: A Study of the General Election*, Washington, D.C., American Enterprise Institute.

Crewe, I. (1985), "How to win a landslide without really trying: Why the Conservatives won in 1983", in A. Ranney (ed.), *Britain at the Polls, 1983*, Washington, D.C., American Enterprise Institute.

Crewe, I., and King A. (1994), "Did Major win? Did Kinnock lose? Leadership effects in the 1992 British General Election", in A. Heath et al., *Labour's Last Chance? The 1992 Election and Beyond*, Aldershot, Dartmouth.

Crewe, I., and King, A. (1995), *SDP: The Birth, Life and Death of the Social Democratic Party*, Oxford, Oxford University Press.

Crewe, I., Sarlvik, B., and Alt, J. (1977), "Partisan dealignment in Britain 1964–1974", *British Journal of Political Science*, vol. 7, 129–190.

Donoghue, B. (1987), *Prime Minister: The Conduct of Policy under Harold Wilson and James Callaghan*, London, Macmillan.

Downs, A. (1957), *An Economic Theory of Democracy*, New York, Harper & Row.

Franklin, B. (1994), *Packaging Politics: Political Communications in Britain's Media Democracy*, London, Edward Arnold.

Galbraith, J. K. (1993), *The Culture of Contentment*, London, Sinclair Stevenson.

Gamble, A. (1993), "The Labour Party and economic management", in M. J. Smith and J. Spear (eds.), *The Changing Labour Party*, London, Routledge.

Gould, P. (1998a), "Why Labour won", in I. Crewe, B. Gosschalk and J. Bartle (eds.), *Political Communications: Why Labour Won the General Election of 1997*, London, Frank Cass.

Gould, P. (1998b), *The Unfinished Revolution: How Modernisers Saved the Labour Party*, London, Little, Brown and Company.

Hattersley, R. (1986), *Choose Freedom: The Future for Democratic Socialism*, London, Penguin.

Heath, A., Jowell, R., and Curtice, J. (1985), *How Britain Votes*, Oxford, Pergamon.

Hughes, C., and Wintour, C. (1990), *Labour Rebuilt: The New Model Party*, London, Fourth Estate.

Jenkins, P. (1988), *Mrs Thatcher's Revolution: The Ending of the Socialist Era*, London, Pan.

Kellner, P. (1985), "The Labour campaign", in A. Ranney (ed.), *Britain at the Polls, 1983*, Durham, NC, Duke University Press.

Kellner, P. (1989), "Labour regains credibility, but fails to convince on the economy", *The Independent*, 16 September.

King, A. (1981), "Politics, economics and the trade unions", in H. R. Penniman (ed.), *Britain at the Polls, 1979: A Study of the General Election*, Washington, D.C., American Enterprise Institute.

King, A. (1989), "How the voters see Labour's new look", *The Daily Telegraph*, 28 November.

King, A. (ed.) (1998). *New Labour Triumphs: Britain at the Polls*, Chatham, Chatham.

Leapman, M. (1987), *Kinnock*, London, Hyman.

Mackenzie, R. (1955), *British Political Parties*, London, Heinemann.

Mandelson, P. (1988), "Marketing Labour: Personal reflections and experience", *Contemporary Record.*

Marquand, D. (1990), *The Progressive Dilemma*, London, Heinemann.

May, J. D. (1973), "Opinion structure of political parties: The special law of curvilinear disparity", *Political Studies*, vol. 21, 135–151.

McSmith, A. (1994). *John Smith*. London: Orion.

Michels, R. (1968), *Political Parties: A Sociological Study of the Oligarchical Tendencies of Modern Democracy*, New York, Free Press.

Mitchell, A. (1983), *Four Years in the Death of the Labour Party*, London, Methuen.

Newman, B. I. (1994), *The Marketing of the President: Political Marketing as a Campaign Strategy*, Beverley Hills, Sage.

Newton, K. (1992), "Caring and competence", in A. King (ed.), *Britain at the Polls 1992*, Chatham, Chatham.

Norpoth, H. (1991), "The popularity of the Thatcher Government: A matter of war and economy", in H. Norpoth, M. S. Lewis-Beck and J. D. Lafay (eds.), *The Calculus of Consent*, Ann Arbor, University of Michigan.

Rawnsley, A. (1995), "Blair's devil is in the detail", *The Observer*, 5 March.

Rose, R. (1974), *The Problem of Party Government*, London, Penguin.

Sanders, D. (1994), *The Economy, Political Forecasting and the Marketing of UK Political Parties*, Paper presented to the Conference on Political Marketing, The Judge Institute of Management, March.

Sanders, D., Ward, H., and Marsh, D. (with Fletcher, T.) (1987), "Government popularity and the Falklands War: A reassessment", *British Journal of Political Science*, vol. 17, 281–313.

Sanders, D., Ward, H., and Marsh, D. (1991), "Macroeconomics, the Falklands War and the popularity of the Thatcher Government: A contrary view", in H. Norpoth, M. S. Lewis-Beck and J. D. Lafay (eds.), *The Calculus of Consent*, Ann Arbor, University of Michigan.

Schumpeter, J. (1987), *Capitalism, Socialism and Democracy*, London, Unwin.

Seyd, P., and Whiteley, P. (1992), *Labour's Grassroots: The Politics of Mass Membership*, Oxford, Clarendon.

Shaw, E. (1993), "Towards renewal? The British Labour Party's policy review", *West European Politics*, vol. 15, 112–132.

Smith, M. J. (1993), "Understanding the politics of catch-up: The modernisation of the Labour Party, *Political Studies*, vol. 42, 708–715.

Stokes, D. (1963), "Spatial models of party competition", *American Political Science Review*, vol. 57, 368–377.

Timmins, N. (1992), "Labour delivers election verdict: Internal report blames defeat on deep-seated public mistrust", *The Independent*, 18 June.

Webb, P. (1992), "Election campaigning, organisation transformation and the professionalisation of the British Labour Party", *European Journal of Political Research*, vol. 20, 267–288.

Wring, D. (1994). *From Mass Propaganda to Political Marketing: The Transformation of the Labour Party*, Paper presented to the Elections, Public Opinion and Parties Conference at Cardiff, September.

Wring, D. (1995), *Political Marketing and Intra-Party Power: Perspectives on Labour "Old" and "New"*, Paper presented at the Conference on Political Marketing, the Judge Institute of Management, Cambridge, March.

4

Kirchheimer's Catch-all Party: A Reinterpretation in Marketing Terms

Stephan C. M. Henneberg and Stefan Eghbalian

Thirty years ago Otto Kirchheimer, a political scientist, published an article under the title "The Transformation of the Western European Party System" (Kirchheimer 1966: hereafter TRANS). In it he analysed the ways "major European parties [function] as transmission belts between the population at large and the government" (p. 177). A central part of his analysis was the identification of a new kind of political party with unique characteristics and an innovative strategy (Wolinetz 1991). He named this party type the "catch-all party" because of its electoral approach. This study became very influential in political science and serves nowadays as a well-established concept in the research on party development and election campaigning (Katz and Mair 1995; Wolinetz 1979, 1991).

However, this chapter does not adopt a mainstream political scientist's methodology but follows the concept of political marketing. Therefore, the question is: what has the "historic" concept outlined in TRANS to do with the recently emerging discipline of political marketing? In particular, one should remember that when TRANS was published in 1966, political marketing did not exist as a research area (see Introduction herein); even the term "political marketing" was coined for the very first time years after Kirchheimer's publication. The relationship between catch-all parties and modern marketing and campaign technologies still seems to puzzle some political scientists (Kavanagh 1995, pp. 173–176). However, it can be argued that Kirchheimer described organisational behaviour that is more than just related to what nowadays is called "political marketing management" (see chapter 5 herein). TRANS contains terms and a theoretical framework that seem very modern.

Indeed, we argue in this chapter that Kirchheimer used a proto-political marketing concept that covered nearly all aspects of a political marketing strategy for political parties. His analysis can be interpreted as describing the transformation of party strategies from a "selling" to a "marketing concept". In order to elucidate these points, we reinterpret Kirchheimer's original article by using marketing terms and methods. However, we also argue that a political marketing approach based on mass standardisation, as Kirchheimer characterised his catch-all party in TRANS, has now been superseded by a more advanced marketing strategy, which might be named "political customisation". Therefore, the catch-all party will eventually be superseded by the "customised party".

UNDERSTANDING POLITICAL MARKETING

Research in political marketing is still in its infancy, although recently more and more studies have adopted this perspective of looking at phenomena of political competition.[1] However, the context of the explanandum of political marketing has not been defined in a clear-cut way; most studies have implicit assumptions about the research object but do not elaborate this (Wortmann 1989). Hence, it is important to make clear what one understands under the concept of political marketing.

Political marketing is concerned with the use of marketing instruments, strategies and concepts by actors in the political sphere. Political marketing instruments can be communication instruments (e.g. mail shots, party political broadcasts) or product instruments (e.g. "packaged" products, image generation); political marketing strategies involve segmentation and targeting approaches, and so forth, while political marketing concepts are, for example, about voter or ideology orientation. All levels are underpinned by political marketing research, the intelligence gathering and dissemination function. This definitorial approach focuses mostly on the behavioural aspects of managerial use of political marketing management. A definition of political marketing on a more theoretical level uses systematic abstraction: political marketing seeks to establish, maintain and enhance long-term voter relationships at a profit for society and political parties so that the objectives of the individual political actors and organisations involved are met. This is done by mutual exchange and fulfilment of promises[2] (Henneberg 1996).

Here political marketing is not characterised according to behavioural activities in the political market, but the definition utilises the exchange paradigm of the "generic concept of marketing" (Hunt 1991; Kotler 1972). Therefore, marketing concepts and theories are legitimately applicable to any exchange process. One can argue that the distinct explanandum of marketing theory is the exchange itself, which is not restricted to simple transactions of goods but also applicable to abstract exchanges of ideas, emotions, services, and so on (Bagozzi 1974, 1975; Hunt 1976, 1983, 1991; Kotler 1972; Kotler and Levy 1969). Political marketing can be subsumed under this wider definition of exchange (Bauer et al. 1995; Kotler and Andreason 1991; O'Shaughnessy 1990). Although the political exchange process is more complex than most commercial exchanges, the underlying isomorphism (structural similarity) of both markets allows an analogous use of marketing management philosopies in the political sphere (Henneberg 1995, 1996; Newman 1994; see also chapter 5 herein). Henceforth, the above definition of political marketing and its implications on the use of marketing theory will be the guideline of the following reinterpretation of TRANS.

KIRCHHEIMER'S ARTICLE—CONTENT AND RECEPTION

TRANS was published shortly after Kirchheimer's death in 1966 in an edited book by J. LaPalombara and M. Weiner, which contained chapters by other such eminent but diverse scholars as H. Daalder, D. A. Rustow, S. Rokkan and I. Wallerstein.

Kirchheimer's contribution, TRANS, started with an assessment of the "load concept" in different European party systems. This concept was proposed by LaPalombara and Weiner (1966) in the same volume. In general, Kirchheimer was concerned with the organisation of the integrating links between government and the electorate and the changes of party structures, strategies and systems in time. In the first section of TRANS, the success— but more often the failure—of parties in fulfilling this integrative function is analysed, using the examples of Britain, France, Italy and Germany. Kirchheimer's conclusion was that, especially after the First World War, mass parties were "neither capable of nor interested in integrating [their] members into the existing political community" (p. 182). TRANS then follows up on this conclusion in the second section, which is devoted to an analysis of the mass-integration party. Kirchheimer argued that there were several reasons for the failure of the mass-integration party to fulfil the integrative function. First, other political actors were not willing to admit a mass party, based on cleavage divides, into the political market as a full member. This behaviour especially restricted Socialist mass parties. Second, these other players (bourgeois parties) failed "to advance from parties of individual representation to parties of integration" (p. 183). However, this rejection of transformation, but also the refusal by the bourgeois parties to allow transformed parties to play their proper integrative role, was only a temporal phenomenon. The main analysis in TRANS starts with the conclusion: "Yet after the Second World War the acceptance of the law of the political market became inevitable in the major Western European countries. This change in turn found its echo in the changing structure of political parties" (p. 184).

The concept of "catch-all parties" comes into play in the third section of TRANS. Kirchheimer identifies two aspects of the transformation process of party systems in Western Europe: first, old-style bourgeois parties became a dying species; second, mass-integration parties changed their competitive strategy and structure towards a catch-all approach. The driving force behind this transformation can be identified in a weakened cleavage structure. However, in TRANS there is a reluctance to identify specific rules or determinants for this transformation process. It focuses more descriptively on the catch-all party's characteristics and on limiting factors. The fourth section of Kirchheimer's analysis is concerned with the integration potential of the catch-all party. Leader and party image as well as party differentiation perform vital integrative functions. However, the voter loyalty towards a catch-all party is intrinsically weak because of its general characteristics. Therefore, Kirchheimer also analyses the interplay with a source of permanent clientele, the interest groups. Examples of the integrative process after the Second World War are given in the fifth section of TRANS, while the last section deals with the catch-all party's general contribution to the functioning of the party system. Kirchheimer identifies the mass mobilisation of voters in the leadership-selection process as the main contribution of catch-all parties that is providing a link between the electorate and the government.

TRANS is one of the most influential and widely cited articles in political science on the question of party and party-system development. It has become a classic and is acknowledged today as predicting most characteristics of the current people's party correctly. Gordon Smith (1989) stated that "the essential features of Kirchheimer's formulation of the people's party correspond to the character of most large West European parties" (p. 159). However, the argument of TRANS has been evaluated and scrutinised several times, and some criticism of the concept has occurred. Nevertheless, this criticism was not so much a qualification of Kirchheimer's argument but an enlargement and an elaboration thereof. Wolinetz (1979) stresses, for example, the fact that the concept of catch-all strategies should be adopted by all successful parties because of its competitive advantage. Parties that fail to adopt should become insignificant; hence, the party systems should become less fragmented. However, the exact opposite happened. Wolinetz concluded that the adaptation of catch-all strategies is only successful in party systems in which the voter's attachment is weak. Those countries (West Germany, France, Austria) were characterised by discontinuities in their development. Smith (1989) made the point that the catch-all party, rather than being more stable than other parties, has an inherent stability problem.

Although Smith's "people's party" draws on traditional support bases, it also uses classical catch-all techniques to broaden its electoral horizon. This requires a constant effort to renew the party's initial base thus making it vulnerable. Mair (1989) also stresses the vulnerability of the new party type. He argues that the weakened attachment of voters without clear ideological orientation made voters more promiscuous in their electoral behaviour. Competition should become more intense; hence, no support base can be stable (at least not between parties that compete in the same segment of the political spectrum).

Some aspects of these evaluations of the catch-all thesis are discussed later under the keyword "customisation". At this point it suffices to conclude that Kirchheimer's concept is one of the pillars of modern political science in the analysis of parties. It has proven to be a robust theory in the last 30 years and was a reference point for many studies on the electoral behaviour and organisation of parties as well as analyses of the development of party systems.

KIRCHHEIMER AND MARKETING TERMS

TRANS is reinterpreted, in the following, from the particular perspective of political marketing This new way of analysing political competition has proven fruitful in looking at phenomena in the political sphere that are difficult to get to grips with using "mainstream" political-science theory. Nevertheless, political marketing is only one way of looking at TRANS, but it is a new and thought-provoking approach. However, it can and will be argued here that this specific political marketing approach had (unrecognised) predecessors in political science—for example, the proto-political marketing concept implicitly stated in TRANS.

Before the details of the tools and strategies of political marketing management, outlined by Kirchheimer, come under scrutiny, it can prove helpful initially to analyse how far Kirchheimer used the terminology of economics and management studies to underline his argument in TRANS. In fact, an astonishing affinity to economic terms can be noted, obviously fostered by the impact of Downs's (1957) study. The terms "political market" or "political competition" are virtually ubiquitous in TRANS (e.g., pp. 183, 184, 186, 188, 192). This alone is an indication of Kirchheimer's thinking in an economic framework, because the underlying market analogy has widespread implications. In a nutshell, the same concepts and tools can be used to analyse political and commercial competition (see chapter 2 herein). Furthermore, a market is nothing else but a (sometimes abstract) trading place for exchange processes. By referring back in general to the definition of political marketing (see above), this implies that marketing theory can be applied to political markets in a rigid way and specifically to the discussion in TRANS.

Kirchheimer did not stop there. In addition to the market and competition analogy, he also used generic conceptual terms of marketing in his
analysis. One obvious example in TRANS is the equation of parties with
major brands (p. 192). The brand concept is enlarged by the discussion of
the importance of "brand differentiation" (p. 192), a critical concept of
product policy in a marketing mix (Kotler and Armstrong 1996; Mercer
1992). Parties of a catch-all kind, therefore, play roles analogous to
"highly standardized articles of mass consumption" (p. 192).

KIRCHHEIMER AND THE MARKETING CONCEPT

One should not overemphasise the use of marketing terminology. Of
more importance is an analysis of the catch-all concept itself and its
relationship with marketing theory, which serves as a reference concept.
Therefore, this reinterpretation starts with a brief summary of marketing
management concepts. We then proceed by analysing the evidence for
our thesis that there is a proto-political marketing concept underlying
the argumentation in TRANS by providing proof on a conceptual, strategic and instrumental level (see Fig. 4.5 for the structure of a normative
political marketing concept).

The marketing concept as it now stands is the result of a gradual
development of marketing management philosophies, which have been
shaped by the changing demands of market and societal characteristics.
Marketing philosophy itself has reacted to developments in the markets from supply-side domination to demand-side orientation. Those
markets were increasingly satiated and highly competitive as well as
characterised by a greater sophistication of consumers. The best-known
conceptualisation of the development of marketing management is that
by Kotler (Kotler and Armstrong 1996). Kotler proposed a four-stage
model. Besides the earlier stages of the *production* and the *product concept*,
the *selling concept* can be characterised as shown in Figure 4.1a.

Underlying this selling philosophy is an "inside-out" perspective. The
assumption is that consumers will not buy a firm's products unless they
are pushed into it by large-scale selling and promotion activities. These
motivate the consumer to buy. The aim is to sell what the firm produces,
not what the consumer desires. Bad consumption experiences cause
(according to this concept) only short-term dissatisfaction but have no
negative long-term effects on intentions to repurchase the product/
brand. Therefore, this philosophy is inherently inward-oriented: it starts
with the firm, focuses on existing products and potentials of the firm
("how can we sell our products?"), uses aggressive push-instruments
and tries to maximise sales volumes (Kotler and Armstrong 1996).

This concept seems crude and in most cases is suboptimal: dissatisfied
consumers, whose desires have not been taken into consideration, do not

(a)

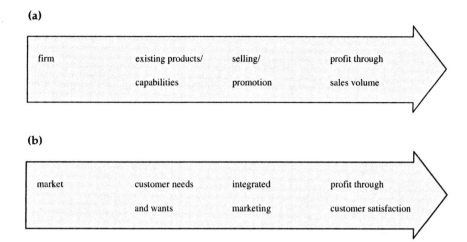

(b)

Figure 4.1. Marketing management philosophies: (a) the selling concept; (b) the marketing concept.

buy the same product again and, in addition, engage in negative word-of-mouth activities. Consequently, companies that follow this concept are very vulnerable because new entries into the market, if serving the consumer better by providing superior benefits, can cause drastic changes of the market positions (market leaders can lose their position overnight). This concept is diametrically opposed to the *marketing concept*, which has customer-orientation as its core element (see Fig. 4.1b). It follows an "outside-in" perspective—that is, it starts with the needs and wants of the customers in the market and asks how these can best be satisfied. Only by delivering the desired benefits more effectively than competitors will the company reach optimal profits and a stable position in the market. Therefore, the means to achieve this aim are very complex, comprising a whole variety of (mainly pull-) instruments that work together in an integrated way, directed by a marketing strategy (Houston 1986; Kotler and Armstrong 1996; O'Shaughnessy 1988).

Just how far can one adopt these concepts to the characteristics of the political market and distinguish distinct political marketing management philosophies? Is there something that can be called a *political selling concept?* We argue that such a concept does exist and that it summarises strategies that most political parties and candidates implicitly or explicitly follow. It can also be argued without too much oversimplification that this concept is one of the reasons of *"Politikverdrossenheit"* (moroseness with politics), disengagement with politics (less voter involvement), the increase of "low politics" (i.e. extra-parliamentary activities), the decreasing strength of party identification among individual voters, and so forth (Bauer et al. 1995; Sainsbury 1990). The theoretical starting point for a transfer of marketing thought into the political sphere has been established in the generic concept of marketing, as described before. It is now necessary to discuss the content of such concepts. The *political selling concept* has been vividly described by a marketing scientist emphasising that

the selling concept [is also] practiced in the non-profit area. A political party, for example, will vigorously sell its candidate to voters as a fantastic person for the job. The candidate works in voting precincts from dawn to dusk—shaking hands, kissing babies, meeting donors, and making speeches. Much money is spent on television advertising, posters and mailings The candidate's flaws are hidden from the public because the aim is to get the sale, not to worry about consumer satisfaction afterwards. (Kotler and Armstrong 1996, p. 16)

It seems clear that such a *political selling strategy* is short-termed and has negative effects in the long-run on party/candidate performance but also on the credibility and legitimacy of the party system itself. The focus on a fixed ideological and programmatic world view ("how can we sell our ideology") causes parties to neglect voter's wants and alienates them. Ideological rigour is seen to dominate, not the benefits of the voter. On the instrument level, social-propaganda techniques and isolated-communication approaches prevail (see Fig. 4.2a).[3] Party-system insta-bility and revolutionary shifts of the electorate's voting behaviour, as in Canada in 1993, can be explained by the long-term effects of party strategies built on this concept. It normally takes only incremental changes of the market structure (e.g. the entry of new players) for the old conceptual basis to become obsolete.

On the other hand a normative *political marketing concept* is founded on voter-orientation (see Fig. 4.2b). It takes into account the electorate's needs and wants and tries to achieve a high level of satisfaction. This is opposite to the inward-oriented "ideology-satisfaction" of the *political selling concept*. In comparison the *political marketing concept* is not inher-ently elitist like the *selling concept*, but seems to be better suited to an egalitarian or also plebiscitarian approach (O'Shaughnessy 1990; Scammell 1995). The different conceptual characteristics also have con-sequences on the instrumental level. A political marketing concept will not simply use promotional tools nor will it engage in social propaganda of any form (O'Shaughnessy 1990, 1996). Integrated marketing ap-proaches—that is, a marketing-mix concept as part of a political market-ing management strategy—will be used.[4]

This *tour de force* through two basically antagonistic approaches of political strategy can give only a brief description of their main charac-teristics. However, it provides the theoretical foundation of an analysis

(a)

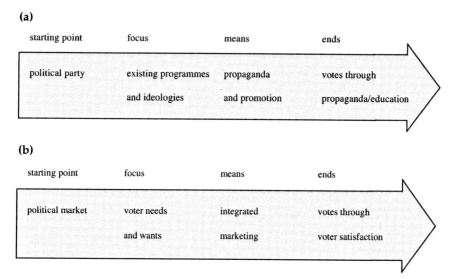

(b)

Figure 4.2. Political marketing management philosophies: (a) the political selling concept; (b) the political marketing concept.

of Kirchheimer's catch-all approach. Kirchheimer's description of a transformation of political parties from mass-integration to catch-all parties is arguably an example of the change from a *selling* to a *marketing concept* in the non-profit area. Mass-integration parties are mainly class or religion based—that is, determined by one of the dominant cleavage structures of the party system. One consequence of this is an ideology focus of the parties, an "inward-orientation". The party and its ideology as well as the subsequently formed subculture around it are the starting points for political rationalisations like the electoral strategy. The party is not there to serve voters or the electorate; it serves its vision of a better world, expressed in a party ideology. Effectiveness in the electoral market is not the main strategy: a broader, all-embracing political endeavour is at the heart of the mass-integration party's rationale.

TRANS describes the mutation of this party type into a party with political marketing tendencies. This transformation was inevitable for Kirchheimer because it meant "the acceptance of the law of the political market" (p. 184). Kirchheimer's catch-all party has "immediate electoral goals" (p. 185), it is "turning more fully to the electoral scene" (p. 184) and becomes an electoral agent. Ideology or the party itself is not the main focal point any more. Ideology is seen as, to use the famous phrase, "baggage" (p. 190) which needs to be thrown overboard. The aim is to appeal to the electorate and accommodate their interests by providing a matching political programme (TRANS, p. 186). The concept of voter-orientation is inherent in the statement that "the democratic catch-all party [. . .] must continue to express widely felt popular concerns" (p. 189). It has to "tak[e] up grievances, ideas and problems developed in a more searching and systematic fashion elsewhere in the body politic" (p. 198). The proximity of Kirchheimer's catch-all party and the political marketing strategy on conceptual and strategy level is evident. Catch-all parties must achieve flexibility and manoeuvrability in the electoral market and must be "led" by the voters, not lead them.

KIRCHHEIMER AND MARKETING STRATEGY

The outside-in perspective of the catch-all party becomes clear when one looks at the underlying support function of any (political) marketing strategy: the intelligence process, named (political) marketing research. It is defined as "the systematic and objective identification, collection, analysis and dissemination of information for the purpose of improving decision-making related to the identification and solution of problems and opportunities in marketing" (Malhotra 1996, p. 8). Marketing research (political) is the linkage function between the company (party) on the one side and consumers and the public (voters and society) on the other (Kotler and Armstrong 1996). Voter-orientation as the core element of a *political marketing concept* must be based on knowledge about the preference structure of the people (or the target segment). In addition, the ramifications of different marketing means can only be predicted via knowledge about the market, about competitors' and voters' behaviour. Therefore, a *political marketing concept* is impossible without political marketing research. On the other hand, a *political selling concept* does not need a full-scale political marketing research function, at least not at a strategy level. Most important is an efficiency control of the push-policies at the instrumental level. TRANS hints at political marketing research as an essential tool for a catch-all party and its *political marketing concept* on several occasions. For example, Kirchheimer discusses the expressive function of the catch-all party and states: "The party would atrophy if it were no longer able to function as a relay between the population and governmental structure" (p. 189). This "relay" can only be an information function like political marketing research. The party is also characterised in TRANS as a "carrier of messages [. . .] that are at least partially in accord with the images, desires, hopes and fears of the electorate" (p. 190). How can a political party, if it does not want to follow elitist and ideological concepts, find out about these "images, desires, hopes and fears" if not by using political marketing research (Worcester 1996; Wortmann 1989)?

Coming to the strategic elements of political marketing one can distinguish three elements (see Fig. 4.5): a political party has (1) to segment the entire market and consequently (2) target one, several or all segments. Furthermore, (3) it has to take care strategically of vital ("generic") functions in order to succeed and survive as an organisation in the long run.[5] The segmentation and the targeting concept are interrelated, and therefore they will be discussed together (Dibb et al. 1994). In commercial marketing strategy, the market can be segmented (clustered) into broad classes according to buyer characteristics. These characteristics can be geographic, demographic (e.g. age, income or life cycle), psychographic (class, lifestyle or personality) or behavioural (benefits sought, user status or loyalty) (Dibb et al. 1994; Kotler and Armstrong 1996; O'Shaughnessy 1988; Smith and Saunders 1990). This segmentation approach does not fulfil a function *sui generis* but facilitates a targeting strategy—that is, it "reveals [. . .] market-segment opportunities" (Kotler and Armstrong 1996, p. 249), which are consequently evaluated (according to size/growth and attractiveness). This evaluation (together with internal objectives and capabilities of the company) provides the input for decisions about the target segments (i.e. the homogeneous set of buyers that the company decides to serve) and the targeting strategy.[6]

Exactly the same elements have to be fulfilled in political marketing management. The electorate has to be segmented into clusters with homogeneous characteristics. Subsequently, political parties have to assess these segments' attractiveness and the party's potential to meet the voters' preferences (Collins and Butler 1996; Newman 1994). Segmentation and targeting concepts are at the core of TRANS. One might even argue that Kirchheimer is talking in TRANS about nothing else but a change of targeting strategies of political parties. Mass-integration parties served a clearly divided market. The demarcation line (segmentation characteristics) were the cleavage divides; particularly salient were religious and class cleavages (Lipset and Rokkan 1966). The class structure, the most powerful separator, determined two market segments with homogeneous preferences: bourgeois parties served the "right" segment, socialist parties the "left". Therefore, the targeting strategy came naturally to the parties: they served one of the two subsegments (TRANS, pp. 182–185). In marketing terms, this is a concentrated-target strategy (Dibb et al. 1994; Kotler and Armstrong 1996). No attempt is made to accommodate any preferences from voters beyond the strict segmentation line (see Fig. 4.3a).

The transformation from mass-integration to catch-all parties, as Kirchheimer described it, is primarily a change in targeting strategy, triggered by changes in the market structure. Both approaches are, however, mass-standardisation approaches. The "harder class lines and more sharply protruding denominational structures" (p. 184) weakened after the Second World War; the old segmentation approach was not valid any more "since [it] deter[red] segments of a potential nationwide

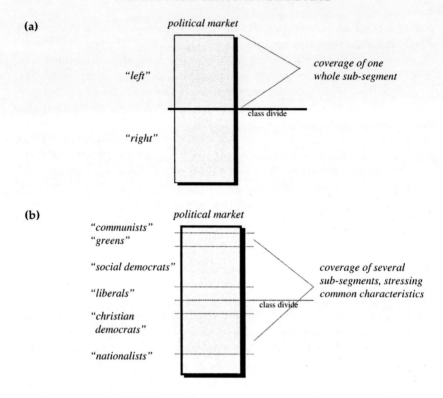

Figure 4.3. Targeting approaches of political parties: (a) concentrated approach (mass-integration party); (b) undifferentiated approach (catch-all party)

clientele" (p. 185). Kirchheimer concluded that "under present conditions of spreading secular and mass consumer-goods orientation, with shifting and less obtrusive class lines, the former class mass parties and denominational mass parties are both under pressure to become catch-all peoples' parties" (p. 190).

Hence, more subsegments emerge that are, however, less distinguishable. The catch-all party tries to adapt to this by an innovative targeting strategy: not concentrated, but undifferentiated targeting is the appropriate means (see Fig. 4.3b).[7] With a fragmentation of preferences, the segments become smaller. A large political party, therefore, must target more than one (in extreme cases, all) segments with their political offer. Kirchheimer therefore stated that the catch-all party's "potential clientele is almost limitless" (p. 186). What are the characteristics of an undifferentiated targeting strategy? Kotler describes it as follows: "Ignore market segment differences and go after the whole market with one offer. The offer will focus on what is *common* in the needs of consumers rather than on what is *different*" (Kotler and Armstrong 1996, p. 250, emphasis in original). Compare this to the following statement in TRANS:

If the [catch-all party] cannot hope to catch all categories of voters, it may have a reasonable expectation of catching more voters in all those categories whose interests do not adamantly conflict. Minor differences between group claims, such as between white collar and manual labor groups, might be smoothed over by vigorous emphasis on programs which benefit both sections alike. [. . .] Even more important is the heavy concentration on issues which are scarcely liable to meet resistance in the community. National societal goals transcending group interests offer the best sales prospect for a party intent on establishing or enlarging an appeal previously limited to specific sections of the population. (p. 186)

The similarities of the targeting approaches of commercial and political marketing are apparent.[8]

The third element of a political marketing management strategy is concerned with the generic functions that a party has to serve by providing adequate behavioural responses. At a strategic level, it has to be decided in general what the specific standards for these functions are. Here a match between functional goals and other aspects like corporate (party) culture and philosophy has to be achieved (Henneberg 1996a, 1996b).

Kirchheimer did not identify generic functions in a marketing sense (however, he refers to the traditional party functions identified by political scientists; TRANS, pp. 188–189). Nevertheless, implicitly he was concerned in TRANS with a very important aspect of the product function, which can be called "strategic-product positioning". The product function of political marketing management is restricted because the political offer is only partly marketing-relevant. Another part is fixed in the short-run and cannot be influenced by marketing management. This is due to rigidities imposed by a party's ideology and history. If a party breaks too abruptly with its past or if it "leapfrogs", it loses credibility. However, credibility is the most important selling asset for a service. The political offer shares many characteristics of a service, hence credibility of the offer is extremely important (Newman 1994).[9] Fickle political behaviour, therefore, harms the party. Having said that, sometimes it is necessary to break with an unsuccessful past that hinders future success and to drastically "re-position the political offer in the voter's preference space". One example for such a risky move is the transformation of Labour to New Labour under Tony Blair. Strategic decisions about the optimal long-term positioning of the political product/party as part of

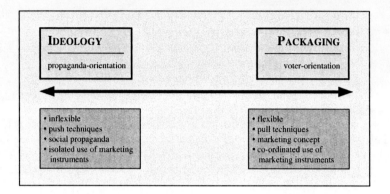

Figure 4.4.   Strategic-product positioning (Henneberg 1996b)

the product function can be done on a continuum that resembles different orientations and also different marketing management philosophies (Henneberg, 1996b) (see Fig. 4.4).

An offer can either be more on the ideological side (with the implication of restrictions for marketing activities) or more on the packaged side with marketing backing. However, these poles are not absolute. A party has to find the right location within this spectrum. Therefore, "today [politics] is not only driven by political ideology but also by marketing" (Newman 1994). The transformation from mass-integration to catch-all parties is represented by a shift to the right of the strategic-product positioning continuum. Such a shift is also directly connected to the new target strategy. Undifferentiated targeting needs a different product offer from the conventional cleavage-determined offer of concentrated targeting. Kirchheimer specifically dealt with the rigidities that limit the party's freedom to use positioning strategies freely. He stated in TRANS that "in some instances the catch-all performance [read: the freedom of strategic re-positioning] meets definite limits in the traditional framework of society (p. 185). He gives an example by showing that the ideology of the Italian *Democrazia Cristiana*, which was determined by the religious cleavage, its "doctrinal core" (p. 185), inhibits it from introducing targeting strategies that "appeal to the anticlerical elements of the population" (p. 185). "Thus tradition and the pattern of social and professional stratification may set limits [. . .] to the party's appeal" (p. 186). A shift to the right of the product continuum is not possible. Additionally, he discusses the prospects for the German SPD and British Labour Party for repositioning on the "packaged" side. Here, Kirchheimer perceives no structural rigidities that would inhibit careful long-term repositioning and an undifferentiated targeting approach,[10] because "there is enough community of interest between wage-and-salary earning urban or suburban white- and blue-collar workers and civil servants to designate them all as strategic objects of simultaneous appeals" (p. l86).

Underlying the conceptual and strategic changes described in TRANS are organisational implications. The political marketing organisation is a kind of framework, it embellishes the political marketing strategy with an organisational hold and allows the allocation of resources for implementation of activities. TRANS stresses the development towards a strengthened top leadership in the catch-all party, which goes together with a downgrading of the influence and importance of the grass-roots members and activists (TRANS, p. 190). The targeting and strategy changes coincide with a shift towards a top-down approach of organisation (Mair 1989). This can be interpreted as a tendency following an attempt of professionalisation of the political marketing management and the electoral approach in general. Eventually, this should foster a kind of functional party organisation (Kotler and Armstrong 1996; Newman 1994; Panebianco 1988).

EVALUATION OF KIRCHHEIMER'S PROTO-POLITICAL MARKETING CONCEPT

Summarising the evidence given in the last two sections, it does not seem too overambitious to conclude that Kirchheimer was way ahead of his times when he wrote TRANS. His concept of catch-all parties as a new kind of election- and power-oriented organisation, building on a new targeting method and other deduced strategic and conceptual consequences, shows remarkable similarities to a (normative) political marketing management approach. A reinterpretation of TRANS in marketing terms elucidates Kirchheimer's skill in anticipating an electoral strategy that only in time became fully visible and comprehensible and only nowadays has been consequently implemented by some European parties and American presidential candidates.

However, it is time to piece together all the elements and ask how far TRANS covers the entirety of the marketing approach towards political management. A normative model of political marketing management will serve as a benchmark model for this assessment (see Fig. 4.5).[11] This model shows that political marketing management can be seen as the interplay of three elements: the core consists of the conceptual base, the strategy level and the marketing instruments. As we have argued above the concept of political marketing is based on organisational voter-orientation. This is implicitly acknowledged in TRANS, although not made explicit in a conceptual way. At a strategy level, where internal capabilities are matched with external relationships (Mintzberg and Quinn 1996), TRANS covers the segmentation and targeting concepts extensively. However, generic functions are neglected. Although the

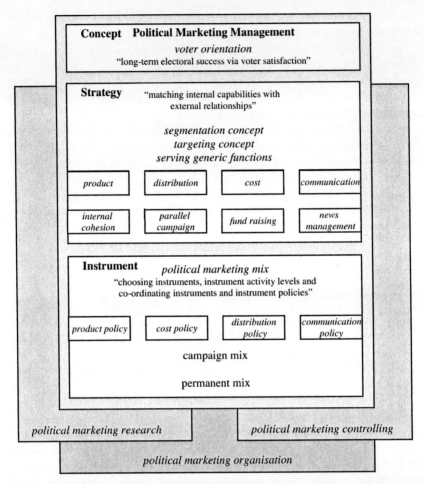

Figure 4.5. Political marketing management, structural model (static)

product function via the discussion of the strategic positioning problem has been discussed by Kirchheimer, there is only one other function from the total of eight generic functions (Henneberg 1996b) that he hints at: the parallel-campaign function is dealt with implicitly by stressing the importance of cooperation with interest groups (TRANS, pp. 192–193). All other essential functions were not part of Kirchheimer's analysis. The same is true at the instrumental level of the core. The four main instrument policies (instrument groups) do not lie at the heart of TRANS. Hence, Kirchheimer mentioned only one instrument explicitly: brand (image) differentiation as a means of achieving product positioning (TRANS, p. 192). All other instruments are not discussed. Furthermore, the political marketing mix concept remains unmentioned—that is, the need for choosing instruments and their activity levels as well as coordinating them. Also unrecognised goes the duplicity of political marketing mix activities of a catch-all party, which comprise an underlying *permanent marketing mix* plus an additional *electoral campaign mix* (a promotional mix in marketing terms) (Blumenthal 1982; Henneberg 1996b).

The second element of political marketing management besides the core are the *integrative functions*, mainly political marketing research and political marketing controlling (Newman 1994). Both have ramifications on strategy as well as to the instrumental level. As argued above, TRANS deals with political marketing research, although it is not discussed in full depth. However, the controlling function is not mentioned in TRANS.

Third, core and integrative functions manifest themselves in an *organisational structure* (Panebianco 1988; Wortmann 1989). TRANS does not really touch upon this, though some isolated statements show that Kirchheimer was aware of the ramifications of the transformations at the conceptual and strategic level for the organisational structure.

Kirchheimer's catch-all concept covers most of what can be described in today's marketing terms as political marketing management. Although TRANS has, from a modern marketing-scientist's view, some shortcomings, especially in its treatment of political marketing instruments, it must be seen in its entirety as the first proto-political marketing concept.

KIRCHHEIMER TODAY—THE CUSTOMISED PARTY

The analyses in TRANS are more than thirty years old, and most aspects of Kirchheimer's study have been proven correct, subject to some minor qualifications (Wolinetz 1991; see above). Although TRANS can be seen as a proto-political marketing concept it is interesting to analyse whether his catch-all approach is still valid as a superior electoral strategy from a normative marketing point of view. To set out the task in marketing terms: is the *political marketing concept*, partly described in TRANS and visualised in Figure 4.2b, still the underlying state-of-the-art concept of today's professional parties?

If one looks at the development of marketing management theory, there has been an increasing emphasis on the shortcomings of the traditional marketing concept, especially its reactive nature. Although customer orientation is still the core element, society's well-being is also considered. The (possible) conflict between the wants of consumers or target markets and the long-term well-being of society has to be resolved by responsible marketing. This is not an act of altruistic motives but the search for an even more profitable strategy that is not only aimed at customers and the company owners, but is broadened to a stakeholder

(a)

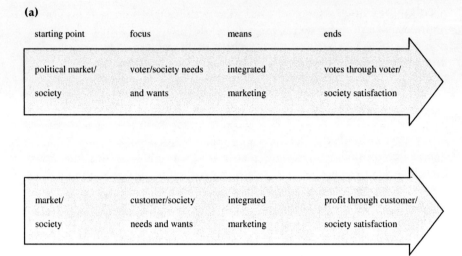

Figure 4.6. Advanced (political) marketing management philosophies: (a) the restricted political marketing concept; (b) the societal marketing concept.

approach (Houston 1986). This rationale builds the foundation of the *societal marketing concept* (Kotler and Armstrong 1996; O'Shaughnessy 1988) (see Fig. 4.6b).

By the same token, the traditional *political marketing concept* is suboptimal for the party as well as for society. An unrestricted, irresponsible use of the political marketing concept might lead to demagogy. Public opinion[12] as the only guiding principle results in a "follower" mentality. While the *political selling concept* is too monolithic, the *political marketing concept* can be too fickle and without a backbone for a long-term optimal strategy. Societal well-being needs a long-term perspective and a general framework. Therefore, a *restricted political marketing concept* seems more appropriate from a normative stance (see Fig. 4.6a and the definition of political marketing above). Not only the wants of the voters but also societal needs are guidelines for the competitive behaviour of political parties. The concept is "restricted" insofar as it focuses on more than the immediate target groups. However, this does not mean a revival of ideology-orientation as one might be tempted to believe. If one looks at this concept in more detail, it becomes clear that, on the contrary, the societal needs can be incorporated into politics via a general framework concept that is able to learn—that is, the political offer is stable but not monolithic like an ideology, responsive but not educational. Although one may still call these frameworks "ideologies", they have more similarities to corporate cultures of competitive organisations. In this sense, they can be called "image ideologies". These are behavioural and intellectual guidelines for the party that give the electoral efforts a certain hold by interacting with people's values and preference systems.[13] This new kind of image ideology, though different from ideological concepts of the mass-integration party, reflects its heritage, bringing credibility to the political offer and legitimacy to the political competition. However, the *restricted political marketing concept* does not mean a shift to the ideology-orientation side of the strategic-product positioning continuum (see Fig. 4.4), because image ideologies are a strategic marketing means and inherently intertwined with a packaging orientation.

Connected with the restricted political marketing concept is a new targeting strategy that is different from the undifferentiated catch-all approach (see Fig. 4.3b). Market fragmentation has now reached a degree of atomisation. It becomes more difficult to appeal to a sufficient part of the electorate with vague and common-grounded offers (valence-issues) that stress inter-segmental societal goals. Such a leader strategy loses out against niche-market suppliers, which cater specifically for the benefits of the few (see chapter 1 herein). These can offer political products specifically designed for a small preferential segment.[14] The fragmentation tendencies of most European party systems show that new party entries into the electoral market indeed take place with increased frequency and cause a more volatile political system.[15] These tendencies are contrary to what Kirchheimer himself anticipated when he was talking about the inevitable success of catch-all parties, which would have caused a concentration tendency. However, it is in line with other aspects of his argument, mainly the de-ideologisation of parties which allowed minor parties to express new issues and anti-establishment resentments (Wolinetz 1979). Later writers on the phenomenon of the catch-all party stressed its vulnerability as an essential point (Mair 1989; Smith 1989). For such a new-market situation, an undifferentiated targeting is not appropriate any more for large parties. The old mass-standardisation approach of mass-integration and also catch-all parties (be it as part of concentrated or undifferentiated targeting) must be succeeded by a customisation via a differentiated-product offer. Marketing theory speaks in this context of "micro-marketing" (Kotler and Armstrong 1996). A differentiated approach involves targeting several distinct target markets not with only one offer and one political marketing strategy (standardisation), but with several separate offers and political marketing strategies (customisation) for each target market (Kotler and Armstrong 1996; Webster 1994) (see Fig. 4.7).

The normal way to achieve this in commercial marketing is to create different product lines—that is, products and strategies that are specific to the needs of a certain customer segment. For example, Toyota, a car manufacturer that essentially served the middle-class car market, introduced the new brand Lexus in order to compete in the upper-class

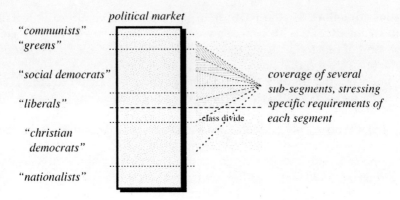

Figure 4.7. Differentiated targeting approach of parties

market (in marketing terminology of the Ansoff matrix, a so-called product development; Mercer 1992, p. 298). Political parties cannot do the same. Labour cannot form a new additional product line with the name "Green Labour" in order to attract the niche-segment of green voters. Political parties have to live with the fact that they are one organisation, one brand and one image ideology. However, there is space for differentiation and development within this broad framework. A political targeting approach can contain several different "political offers"—for example, one with emphasis on green topics for green voters, one with emphasis on health care and pensions for elder voters, one on free-market values for achievers, and so forth. Each "programme" has a marketing strategy tailored to suit the segment group it is targeted for. A means of delivering these programmes efficiently is, for example, channel segmentation and communication-media selection (Mercer 1992). The art is to integrate these differentiated programmes and activities under a party umbrella into a cohesive whole. This means living with potentially conflicting political offers (e.g. pro-environment versus pro-competition issue stands/candidates). Hence, the political marketing mix, with its coordination function, becomes even more important. Such conflicts have to be resolved in a responsible manner according to the party's corporate culture (its image ideology) (Henneberg 1996b). However, if such an integration is possible, the customised party is able to exploit the ever more competitive political market and to give the electoral competition stability and long-term credibility. In addition, the customised party regains the ability proactively to structure the electoral market, a capability inherent to mass-integration parties but lost with the adoption of undifferentiated targeting by the catch-all party (Mair 1989). Although Kirchheimer's catch-all party is not dead, the market demands on political marketing management have moved on. Kirchheimer's "ideology-over-board" approach towards flexibility proves short-sighted in the new political environment. Only a customised and responsible political marketing approach can perhaps serve nowadays as a means for larger people's parties to survive.

CONCLUSION

A reinterpretation of Kirchheimer's study about transformational processes of political parties and party systems, using the distinct methodology of marketing theory, provides insight beyond traditional political-science understanding. TRANS can be seen to be mainly concerned with political parties' responses to changing characteristics of political markets. With more volatile voters and less clear-cut cleavage divides, Kirchheimer showed that a successful electoral strategy must abandon the concentrated targeting approach and embrace undifferentiated methods. This new "catch-all" approach has further implications. It goes together with a systematic re-orientation of the party from a political selling concept towards a (proto-) political marketing concept. The party's approach becomes more voter-oriented; marketing means are used flexibly in an integrated way, guided by strategic considerations and market intelligence information.

However, from some points of view, such a reinterpretation of TRANS and the use of marketing methodology for the analysis of electoral behaviour of parties might not seem viable. It could be argued that although marketing theory sheds new light on political activities, this does not complement political science, because the two disciplines are methodologically different. However, "Candidates [and parties] are being marketed, and the sooner we all realize and understand how it is happening, the sooner we can begin to work and make sure that marketing is used in a way that helps strengthen the political process" (Newman 1994, p. 145). Therefore, political marketing analyses are necessary because they can provide additional leverage for understanding political phenomena. Nevertheless, as has been shown, there is a certain overlap between the disciplines, exemplified by Kirchheimer's concept of catch-all parties which has strong leanings towards a political marketing approach. These overlaps can be utilised by political scientists in order better to understand political behaviour and motivation. Such an approach also has implications at the aggregate level. Wolinetz states that "needed for a deeper understanding of party system change is a clearer understanding of how parties appeal to voters and respond to changing political markets" (1991, p. 125). Exactly this problem can be explained by using concepts of political marketing strategy like segmentation theory.

Having said that, political marketing management activities are dynamic, according to market characteristics. Therefore, the new model of the customised party has been developed that qualifies the catch-all model. Its differentiated, customised approach is better adapted to recent developments in European and American party systems and, additionally, highlights the more demanding coordinational and operational prerequisites associated with them. Future research, especially empirical case studies, are necessary to determine the specific characteristics of the customised party in different party systems.

NOTES

This chapter is a revised version of a paper that one of the authors [S.E.] presented at the Second Conference on Political Marketing, University of Cambridge, March 1996. J. Bartle (University of Essex) provided invaluable criticism.

1. For an overview and a categorisation of research in political marketing, see the Introduction and chapter 5.

2. This definition is political-party oriented. However, it can also be used for any other political actor. Other definitions of political marketing are rare, see Scammell (1995, pp. 5–9), Harrop (1990, p. 277) or Farrell and Wortmann (1987, pp. 298–299).

3. For other descriptions of the *political selling concept*, see Smith and Saunders (1990).

4. Cf. the slightly different definitions of political marketing management philosophies in Wring (1995) and Newman (1994).

5. Cf. Newman (1994) for a different approach towards political marketing strategy.

6. Interesting to mention in this context is the critique of some political scientists who study political marketing activities: they question the effectiveness of segmentation and targeting approaches (e.g. Harrop 1990, pp. 282–284). However, they overlook the resource allocation function inherent in these strategic decisions as well as the problem of customised political marketing activities (see below).

7. Some political scientists see the development of political marketing determined by media and technology developments (Harrop 1990). Market change has been overlooked as an independent variable in many cases.

8. This discussion of different targeting approaches is mirrored in the concepts of "position-issues" and "valence-issues" (Stokes 1963). Our thanks to J. Bartle for highlighting this.

9. Marketing scientists never understand the simple equation of a political offer with "washing powder". This analogy, mainly used by journalists and political scientists as an argument against the "unethical use of marketing techniques in the political sphere", is a very crude argument because the marketing for a fast-moving consumer good (like washing powder) has to be totally different from that of a service (Bauer et al. 1995). If one wants to argue against political marketing, one should compare it, for example, to the marketing of professional services.

10. Nevertheless, this does not imply total flexibility. "Real estate interests or independent agricultural properties" cannot be accommodated in a reasonable way (TRANS, p. 186).

11. For a model of political marketing in a candidate-centred party system see Newman (1994) and Reid (1988).

12. Public opinion is notoriously difficult to operationalise: for example, one only needs to think of the problem of short-term versus long-term public opinion, target group opinion versus general opinion, etc.

13. The "image ideology" approach is similar to political science concepts grounded in the discussions about the essence of ideology as a reaction to the "end of ideology" debate of the 1960s (Wolinetz 1979).

14. However, they normally cannot offer any reasonable expectation of implementing these offers. Their chances of governing are negligible, therefore, these groups sometimes prefer to compete in the segment of "low" politics—that is, the non-electoral market for interest groups.

15. It is questionable whether this increased competitiveness also works over cleavage lines (Bartolini and Mair 1990).

REFERENCES

Bagozzi, R. P. (1974), "Marketing as an organized behavioral system of exchange", *Journal of Marketing*, vol. 38, 77–81.

Bagozzi, R. P. (1975), "Marketing as exchange", *Journal of Marketing*, vol. 39, 32–39.

Bauer, H. H., Huber, F., and Herrmann, A. (1995), "Politik-Marketing", *Der Markt*, vol. 34, 115–124.

Bartolini, S., and Mair, P. (1990), *Identity, Competition and Electoral Availability*, Cambridge, Cambridge University Press.

Blumenthal, S. (1982), *The Permanent Campaign*, New York, Simon & Schuster.

Collins, N., and Butler, P. (1996), "Political marketing—Considerations on research issues", in S. C. Henneberg, N. O'Shaughnessy and S. Eghbalian (eds.), *Proceedings of the Second Conference on Political Marketing*, Judge Institute of Management Studies, Cambridge University.

Dibb, S., Simkin, L., Pride, W. M., and Ferrell, O. C. (1994), *Marketing, Concepts and Strategies*, Boston/London: Houghton Mifflin.

Downs, A. (1957), *An Economic Theory of Democracy*, New York, Harper & Row.

Farrell, D. M., and Wortmann, M. (1987), "Party strategies in the electoral market: political marketing in West Germany, Britain and Ireland", *European Journal of Political Research*, vol. 15, 297–318.

Harrop, M. (1990), "Political marketing", *Parliamentary Affairs*, vol. 43, 277–291.

Henneberg, S. C. (1995), "The political market—Does it exist?", in S. C. Henneberg and N. O'Shaughnessy (eds.), *Political Marketing—Evolving Science or Maturing Art? Conference Proceedings*, Judge Institute of Management Studies, Cambridge University.

Henneberg, S. C. (1996), "Marketing for political parties—Generic functions and instruments", in S. C. Henneberg, N. O'Shaughnessy and S. Eghbalian (eds.), *Proceedings of the Second Conference on Political Marketing*, Judge Institute of Management Studies, Cambridge University.

Houston, F. S. (1986), "The marketing concept: What is it and what is it not", *Journal of Marketing*, vol. 50, 81–87.

Hunt, S. D. (1976), "The nature and scope of marketing", *Journal of Marketing*, vol. 40, 17–28.

Hunt, S. D. (1983), "General theories and the fundamental explananda of marketing", *Journal of Marketing*, vol. 47, 9–17.

Hunt, S. D. (1991), *Modern Marketing Theory: Critical Issues in the Philosophy of Marketing Science*, Cincinnati, South-Western Publishing.

Kavanagh, D. (1995), *Election Campaigning: The New Marketing of Politics*, Oxford, Blackwell.

Katz, R. S., and Mair, P. (1995), "Changing models of party organization and party democracy: The emergence of the cartel party", *Party Politics*, vol. 1, 5–28.

Kirchheimer, O. (1966), "The transformation of the Western European party system", in J. LaPalombara and M. Weiner (eds.), *Political Parties and Political Development*, Princeton, Princeton University Press, pp. 177–200.

Kotler, P. (1972), "A generic concept of marketing", *Journal of Marketing*, vol. 36, 46–54.

Kotler, P., and Andreason, A. R. (1991), *Strategic Marketing for Nonprofit Organizations*, Englewood Cliffs, Prentice-Hall.

Kotler, P., and Armstrong, G. (1996), *Principles of Marketing*, Englewood Cliffs, Prentice-Hall.

Kotler, P., and Levy, S. J. (1969), "Broadening the concept of marketing", *Journal of Marketing*, vol. 33, 10–15.

LaPalombara, J., and Weiner, M. (1966), "The original development of political parties", in J. LaPalombara and M. Weiner (eds.), *Political Parties and Political Development*, Princeton, Princeton University Press, pp. 3–42.

Lipset, S. M., and Rokkan, S. (1966), "Cleavage Structure, party systems, and voter alignments: An introduction", in S. M. Lipset and S. Rokkan (eds.), *Party Systems and Voter Alignments*, New York, Free Press, pp. 1–64.

Mair, P. (1989), "Continuity, change and the vulnerability of party", *West European Politics*, vol. 12, 169–187.

Malhotra, N. K. (1996), *Marketing Research*, Englewood Cliffs, Prentice-Hall.

Mercer, D. (1992), *Marketing*, Oxford, Blackwell.

Mintzberg, H., and Quinn, J. B. (1996), *The Strategy Process*, Englewood Cliffs, Prentice-Hall.

Newman, B. I. (1994), *The Marketing of the President*, Thousand Oaks, Sage.

O'Shaughnessy, J. (1988), *Competitive Marketing*, Boston, Unwin Hyman.

O'Shaughnessy, N. (1990), *The Phenomenon of Political Marketing*, Basingstoke, Macmillan.

O'Shaughnessy, N. (1996), "Social marketing and social propaganda: A critical difference?", *European Journal of Marketing*, vol. 30, no. 10/11, 62–75.

Panebianco, A. (1988), *Political Parties: Organization and Power*, Cambridge, Cambridge University Press.

Reid, D. M. (1988), "Marketing the political product", *European Journal of Marketing*, vol. 22, no. 9, 34–47.

Sainsbury, D. (1990), "Party strategies and party–voter linkage", *European Journal of Political Research*, vol. 18, 1–7.

Scammell, M. (1995), *Designer Politics,* Basingstoke, Macmillan.

Smith, G. (1989), "Core persistency: change and the 'People's Party'", *Western European Politics,* vol. 12, 157–168.

Smith, G., and Saunders J. (1990), "The application of marketing in British politics", *Journal of Marketing Management,* vol. 5, 295–306.

Stokes, D. (1963), "Spatial models of party competition", *American Political Science Review,* vol. 57, 368–377.

Webster, F. E., Jr. (1994), *Market-Driven Management,* New York, Wiley.

Wolinetz, S. B. (1979), "The transformation of Western European party systems revisited", *West European Politics,* vol. 2, 4–28.

Wolinetz, S. B. (1991), "Party system change: The catch-all thesis revisited", *West European Politics,* vol. 14, 112–123.

Worcester, B. (1996), "Political marketing: The application of market research instruments for political marketing", in S. C. Henneberg, N. O'Shaughnessy and S. Eghbalian (eds.), *Political Marketing. Conference Proceedings,* Judge Institute of Management Studies, Cambridge University.

Wortmann, M. (1989), *Political Marketing—A Modern Party Strategy,* PhD thesis, Florence, European University Institute.

Wring, D. (1995a), "Political marketing and intra-party power: Perspectives on Labour, 'Old' and 'New'", in S. C. Henneberg and N. O'Shaughnessy, *Political Marketing—Evolving Science or Maturing Art? Conference Proceedings,* Judge Institute of Management Studies, University of Cambridge.

5

Understanding Political Marketing

Stephan C. M. Henneberg

"[W]e see a chance to systematise the existant [*sic*] literature under the marketing concept thus addressing the deficiencies of the political science literature which is still an arbitrary collection of unrelated subjects."

Wortmann (1989, p. 311)

"[It] is necessary for marketing as a discipline to present its insights and analytical perspectives in a 'political-science-user-friendly' fashion."

Butler and Collins (1996, p. 32)

Political marketing acts as the guiding theory in the development of a model voting behaviour with managerial implications. Much has been said about the use of marketing tools and techniques in the political sphere. By now, there exist numerous studies on the topic, written by political scientists, marketers, communication specialists, and so forth. Nevertheless, political marketing as a concept is rather new and still very much in flux. It is therefore inappropriate to use political marketing as the theoretical base for a discovery and interdisciplinary approach without explicating what exactly is meant by this juvenile concept. Political marketing is often misused in analyses of political activities as a journalistic "buzzword", a fashionable term that is so familiar that it does not need substantiation or conceptual discussion. Although a recent assessment of publications counted no less than 350 academic sources on political marketing in the period 1990–1996 (Henneberg 1995b; see also final section in this chapter), it is astonishing that even seminal texts do not provide definitional or conceptual clarifications of the essence or the scope of political marketing (Henneberg 1996b; Lock and Harris 1996). It has to be acknowledged that the most recent publications are located in the sphere of the *theory of political marketing management*—that is, they are managerially relevant by either analysing existing marketing-management practices or prescribing them. Furthermore, it is interesting to notice that there is a clear-cut "division of labour" in publications and research foci in the sense that most political scientists specialise more in descriptive studies—that is, on analyses of marketing activities as shown by political actors (prominent examples are Bowler and Farrell 1992c; Franklin 1994; Jamieson 1992b; Kavanagh 1995b; Scammell 1995). Marketing scientists, on the other hand, anchor their research more in the normative management theory. Here, the "optimal" use of marketing strategies and instruments in the political sphere is prescribed (e.g. Mauser 1983; Newman 1994a; O'Shaughnessy 1990a; Smith and Saunders 1990; Wangen 1983; Wortmann 1989). It remains questionable whether this structure is fruitful for a new interdisciplinary research area. At this point, it suffices to state that the lack of attention shown for grounding research in the area of the *theory of political marketing* seems to be troubling (Henneberg 1995b).

The present chapter, on conceptual aspects of the phenomenon of political marketing, introduces an anchor point for this book of readings by drawing on existing research in the area of political marketing, but predominantly by providing an integrated concept using and developing established marketing theory. It therefore follows the rationale outlined in Wortmann (1989).[1] As guidelines for such a fundamental analysis of political marketing, one can use the following six principles which have been derived from a qualitative and quantitative assessment of the existing political marketing literature (Henneberg 1995b). Political marketing should be seen as a:

- holistic phenomenon;
- permanent phenomenon;
- theoretical phenomenon;
- international phenomenon;
- interactive problem;
- ethical problem.

A holistic approach is necessary in order to counteract the existing tendencies (especially by political scientists) to restrict the scope of analysis to communication instruments (Butler and Collins 1996). These do not only simplify the variety of instruments available in the political marketing mix but ignore non-operational—that is, strategic—elements of political marketing, or, as Wortmann (1989) puts it: "thus, political parties' acting is mainly seen in its communicative function while the fact is neglected that political communication is only one part of political acting" (p. 8).[2] This holistic element also includes broadening the range of relevant actors to all players in the political market, rather than limiting the interest just to political parties (Lock and Harris 1996). Such a holistic approach to political marketing is still lacking in research, and Reid's conclusion, made in 1988, still stands about ten years later: "there appears to be a dearth of published research which treats it [i.e. political marketing] in a holistic way" (Reid 1988, p. 34). Political marketing is, furthermore, permanent—that is, it is not restricted to the short and intensive period of political campaigning. Today, it is used on an ongoing basis, even for governing purposes (Blumenthal 1982; Kavanagh 1995b; Newman 1995b; Scammell 1994). The theoretical aspect of research in political marketing has been pinpointed above: the essence of the research object must be clarified as a starting point. This also includes a demarcation of political marketing from similar research topics—for example, political propaganda (O'Shaughnessy 1996b). Furthermore, political marketing has international implications: it is not an isolated phenomenon but occurs with differing intensity in all democratic countries (Bowler and Farrell 1992c; Thurber and Nelson 1995). Therefore, a concept of political marketing must include candidate-centred as well as party-centred party systems in any existing form.[3] Differing political marketing activities can also be seen as cross-fertilising themselves—for example, the use of the "Clinton-concept" by Blair in the 1997 general election, or the "export" of political marketing consultants (one example is the work of American consultants in Latin America, in France and recently in Britain) (Mauser 1983; Scammell no date). Lastly, political marketing has an interactive and an ethical dimension. Interactivity refers to the systemic process of political management, which has to be viewed holistically in order to be appreciated fully. It is an exchange-based understanding that demands a dynamic perspective. Ethical questions of political marketing are extremely important because the impact of political marketing activities on the democratic process are under-researched and need clarification. However, this clarification must be grounded in a sound theoretical understanding of the basics of political marketing and the effects of political marketing management, be it at a strategic or instrumental level (Fowler 1995; Lock and Harris 1996; O'Shaughnessy 1989/90, 1990a). Otherwise such "criticism" deteriorates into mere "witch-hunting" or "anti-marketing propaganda" (Bauer 1995; Mauser 1983).

THE CONCEPT OF POLITICAL MARKETING MANAGEMENT

"Political marketing is now clearly woven into the fabric of British politics. It has been adopted by right and left of the spectrum, trade unions, pressure groups and charities."

Scammell (1995, p. 269)

"Almost all politicians *use* marketing techniques and ideas, but very few wish to admit it openly."

Mauser (1983, p. 3, emphasis in original)

Political Marketing: A "New" Phenomenon

Political marketing came into existence as a new phenomenon of political activities. It is now a seemingly ubiquitous element of political life. When Tony Blair created "New Labour" (i.e. repositioned the party), when Bill Clinton used new information-dissemination channels (cable-TV shows) in order to communicate directly with target voters, or when the German Neo-Communists used sarcasm as their main political "ideology" in order to transform the political competition, all these activities can be understood as comprising political marketing elements (in these examples product/image management, channel and targeting strategy, and communication strategy, respectively). There is a scholarly consensus that political marketing has changed the political sphere (Franklin 1994; Jamieson 1992a, 1992b; Kavanagh 1995b; O'Shaughnessy 1990a; Scammell 1995), without a clear understanding of the essence and the mechanism of this change. Several detailed studies have highlighted the influence of the marketing perspective on campaigning in different countries and times (e.g. Scammell 1991, 1994 for the British Tories, in particular the Thatcher era; Kavanagh 1995b; Rallings 1995, Wring 1995a, 1995b, 1995c for British Labour; Arnold 1995 for the Liberals; Newman 1994a, 1995b, Popkin 1995, Wattenberg 1995 for the US Democrats under Bill Clinton). Synonyms like "media democracy" (Franklin 1994) or "Americanisation of politics"[4] (Field 1994) are commonly used in order to describe this phenomenon. Furthermore, it has been equated with an expression of the postmodern characteristics of our times (Axford and Huggins 1995; Axford et al. 1996). Alas, others argue that what is now called political marketing has always existed (Lock and Harris 1996). Similar instruments to marketing have always been engaged in every historic political struggle. Therefore, these scholars argue, political marketing is only a new name for an established way of political competition. It is indeed striking to notice many "modern" aspects of political competition in descriptions of historic political campaigns (Jamieson 1992a; Kavanagh 1995b; O'Shaughnessy 1990a [especially chapt. 2],

1996b; Scammell 1995; Wring 1996a). Nevertheless, this view must be qualified. It has often been pointed out that the overlap between the use of propaganda or crude communication instruments on the one hand and the concept of political marketing on the other is only a superficial one (O'Shaughnessy 1996b; Scammell 1995). Even today, not every new communication gimmick demonstrates the employment of political marketing instruments. As O'Shaughnessy puts it: "for the term 'political marketing' to have any descriptive value it must replicate most of the processes involved in consumer marketing—research, advertising, personal selling, product management and so on—and this would make it an almost exclusively post-Second World War phenomenon" (1990a, p. 17).

Scammell (1995) adds to these characteristics strategic management intent and the use of the perspective of a consumer/voter-orientation as constituent elements of political marketing. These elements have only recently been introduced into the tool-kit of political management (Wangen 1983). Hence, political marketing as a concept "represents a qualitative change in the nature of 'state of the art' campaigns" (Harrop 1990, p. 286) or, to use the oft-cited words of Kotler: "Campaigning has always had a marketing character. The 'new methodology' is not the introduction of marketing methods into politics; but an increased sophistication and acceleration of their use" (1982, pp. 461–462).

In order to get to grips with the elements of this new quality—that is, its sophistication—it is helpful to "reconstruct" the development of (political) marketing in a phase model before one can "deconstruct" the fundamentals of political marketing. Wring (1995a; see also Rallings 1995) has proposed a model of the development of political campaigning, mirroring commercial-strategy developments in the consumer-goods markets, which is based on earlier concepts by Shama (1973, 1976) (see Fig. 5.1, left-hand side). In a first phase of electioneering, a "mass-propaganda" approach prevails. Intensive promotion and publicity approaches are the main instruments used. The conceptual-orientation is towards the candidate. Availability of opinion research and mass media, especially television, introduces a second phase—that of "media campaigns"—with a sales-orientation: the emphasis is now on market segmentation and targeting via sophisticated advertising, following a consumer-orientation. The last phase, that of "political marketing", is even more based on market research and a total management of the whole political offer—that is, a strategic and managerial understanding of the marketing of politics in a market-orientation (Wring 1995a, 1995b).

Of course, this concept shows considerable overlap with Kotler's phase model of marketing's development, which has been used directly by Newman (1994a) (see Fig. 5.1, right-hand side). Mass propaganda can be equated with a product perspective, media campaigning with a sell-

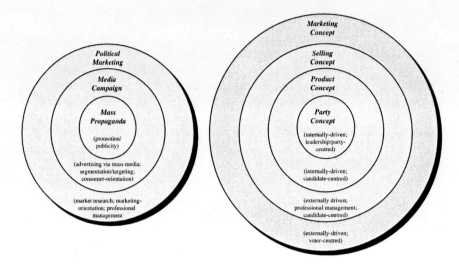

Figure 5.1. Phase models of political marketing (after Wring 1995a and New-man 1994a).

ing concept, and modern political marketing practice with the marketing perspective of commercial organisations (Kotler 1972; Kotler and Andreason 1991; Kotler and Armstrong 1996; Smith and Saunders 1990). It is assumed generally today that political campaigning and political management has progressed to the level of the political marketing perspective in most Western countries and that many, if not all, actors in the political market follow this conceptual orientation (Newman 1994a, 1994b, 1996; O'Shaughnessy 1990a; Scammell 1995; Wring 1995a). In the next sections, this view will be contested and qualified by, first, scrutinising the essence of the political marketing concept, and second, analysing the macroelements, microelements and auxiliary concepts of political marketing management.

Political Marketing: Fundamentals and Definitions

At the core of any attempt to understand the phenomenon of political marketing are, of course, definitional exercises. At the same time, herein lies one of the main shortcomings in research in political marketing. Although somewhat developed as a discipline, definitions of political marketing are rare to find (Henneberg 1996c; Lock and Harris 1996), even in seminal texts on the subject. However, this must not serve as an excuse for neglecting this crucial element, especially not for a study that takes political marketing theory as its major theoretical anchor.

Political Marketing: A Definition

A definition of political marketing is, of course, bound to definitions of marketing in general, due to its link with marketing theory (Hasitschka 1995; for a general discussion of the development of marketing definitions see Mercer 1992). The following discussion provides an overview of definitional attempts of political marketing in seminal texts. However, most scholarly contributions do without explicit considerations of the scope and essence of their research field. Implicit assumptions dominate over overt and concise clarification.

Definitional attempts can be distinguished broadly along two dimensions: nearly all definitions of political marketing focus, first, on the exchange concept underlying the political activity and, second, on the political marketing activities themselves. Hence, differentiations along these two dimensions allow for a classification of different definitions. The exchange dimension, applying modern marketing theory, can be characterised by a continuum between transactional exchange and a relationship approach (Berry 1995; Grönroos 1990, 1995; Zeithaml and Bitner 1996). On the other hand, the activity dimension distinguishes definitions that are focused mainly on the instrumental level—that is, the operational side of political marketing (like the different political marketing mix instruments)—and those with a more holistic (i.e. strategic) perspective (incorporating political-marketing-strategy questions like targeting, positioning or voter-retention approaches). These two dimensions are used here as illustrations of different definitions of political marketing in four studies judged influential for the development of the discipline (see Fig. 5.2).

Farrell and Wortmann (1987), in a comparative analysis of party strategies, come close to defining political marketing by stating:

The political market is a system of exchange in which two or more actors each possess "something-of-value" which can be traded. The "sellers" offer representation to their "customers" in return for support. [. . .] The exchange occurs at election time when, to ensure maximum revenue, the sellers market themselves through an application of directed promotional activities. They market their particular styles of representation and specific intentions for government as a "product" which comprises party image, leader image, and manifesto proposals or selected issues.

The marketing exercise consists of a strategy in which a product is designed with close attention to market demands. Market research surveys the market, allows it to be segmented into homogeneous groupings of customers; and indicates potential targets. The seller has four types of instruments at his disposal with which to influence these targets: product policy, communication, policies distribution, and pricing. The marketing strategy aims to apply, with the aid of marketing research, the optimum "mix" of these instruments. (p. 298)

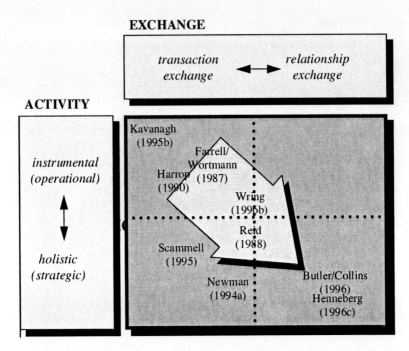

EXCHANGE

ACTIVITY

Figure 5.2.   Definitional attempts of political marketing in context.

Farrell and Wortmann (1987) continue by defining the four policy elements of political marketing. However, any attempts at getting to grips with the strategic elements they mention in the quotation above, as well as with the "mix problem" itself, are absent from their study. In terms of the two dimensions under discussion here, the main emphasis is on the following aspects: operational elements prevail over a truly holistic view, and a traditional exchange definition as a transaction is used.

Another definitional attempt can be found in Harrop (1990). He also stays very closely with conventional definitions of marketing:

The formal definition of marketing is that it involves facilitating exchanges between an organisation and its environment. For our purposes, however, we can break marketing down into two simple dimensions: strategy, which involves providing things people want, and promotion, which is selling the things you have decided to provide. [. . .] Thus the study of political marketing is not simply an investigation of promotional activities such as press advertisements; party political broadcasts and election addresses. It is a much broader area, covering whether where and how a party positions itself in the electoral market. (p. 277)

What is interesting in the above is the somewhat flawed use of the concept of "promotion" as well as the limited understanding of "strategy" in a management context. A classical "follower-mentality" of marketing seems to be advocated (Dickinson et al. 1986). Altogether this definition seems to resemble the commonly used classification of strategic versus operational levels of marketing. Unfortunately, Harrop's study does not do justice to the strategic elements of political marketing as well as their implications for the concept itself. Its characteristics are therefore predominantly operative, though noticing the implications of the strategic level. The exchange characterisation remains transaction-oriented.

Wring (1996b) produces a more modern approach towards marketing by defining political marketing as:

the party or candidate's use of opinion research and environmental analysis to produce and promote a competitive offering which will help realise organisational aims and satisfy groups of electors in exchange for their votes. (p. 5)

A real development in this definition is the implicit reference to relationship approaches of marketing by "voter satisfaction". Wring also subsequently analyses some strategic elements of political marketing management as well as discussing the marketing mix problem.

Newman does not give a concise definition but a model description of political marketing (1994a, picture p. 12). From this model it is clear that he incorporates instrumental as well as strategic considerations (from strategy intelligence to formulation and implementation). However, the exchange concept does not embrace a relationship approach, although the discussion of voters' loyalty has some prominence in his study.

It is more difficult to grasp the implicit understanding of political marketing in some seminal articles. Reid (1988), for example, focuses very much on strategic elements of political management and does also question a purely transactional understanding of the exchange process without formulating a full-scale relationship approach. Another influential study, by Kavanagh (1995b), is concerned more with communication and media aspects of campaigning and remains very much in the political scientists' tradition of looking at political marketing. This is also underlined by the limited use of the exchange concept, even in its traditional form, as a system of isolated transactions. Scammell (1995) stresses the holistic approach towards marketing. However, in her treatment of the political exchange process, on the other hand, she follows mainstream political scientists' interpretations. The influence of recent developments in marketing theory can be seen in Butler and Collins' (1996) study of strategic aspects of political marketing. Holistic and relationship-oriented thinking dominates their analysis.

Altogether, these definitional attempts and implicit assumptions lead to an interesting pattern (see Fig. 5.2). Two aspects spring to mind: first, there is a tendency, over time, to incorporate more holistic aspects of political marketing into the analysis as well as a development towards relationship definitions of the underlying exchange process (Kavanagh 1995 has to be seen as an outlier). Second, while most political scientists' understanding of political marketing can be found in the top-left quadrant (the "traditional" approach) of Figure 5.2, that of marketing theorists can be found in the bottom-right area. This division demonstrates the grounds for misunderstandings between the two "mother-disciplines" of political marketing regarding the essence of the research object. However, one has to back Butler and Collins who state that: "[I]t is pointless to berate political scientists [. . .]; rather, we should acknowledge fault on both sides. [. . .] it is necessary for marketing as a discipline to present its insights and analytical perspectives in a 'political-science-user-friendly' fashion" (1996, p. 32). Therefore, a definition of political marketing should follow state-of-the-art marketing, without forgetting the need to elucidate its meaning and implications to political scientists. This also means incorporating and conciliating the research traditions of political science.

One main aspect of innovation in marketing theory is the so-called market network or relationship approach, sometimes named the "Nordic school of marketing" (Easton 1995; Henneberg 1997; Wensley 1995). It has severe implications for the understanding of the essence of marketing, embedded in an innovative definition of marketing (J. O'Shaughnessy 1995). This approach is followed through here for the field of political marketing. Relationship marketing differs from standard interpretations of marketing (e.g. Dibb et al. 1994; Mercer 1992) in that it stresses the following new characteristics:

- A relationship, a kind of partnership, between the market players is advocated. This includes a commitment-and-trust exchange as the underlying attitudinal foundation of the relationship (Morgan and Hunt 1994).
- A long-term perspective that shifts the emphasis from one-off transactions to continuous exchange, which can go a long way beyond the originally intended primary exchange (Grönroos 1995).
- An acknowledgement of the objectives of all involved players (individual actors or organisations, but also societal goals influenced by externalities of the primary exchange) (Kotler and Armstrong 1996).
- Mutual benefits of the exchange relationship and the delivery of promises (Bitner 1995).

Following a definition of commercial marketing by Grönroos (1990), all these elements can be bound together in a formal analytical definition of political marketing (Henneberg 1996c):[5]   .

Political marketing seeks to establish, maintain and enhance long-term voter relationships at a profit for society and political parties, so that the objectives of the individual political actors and organisations involved are met. This is done by mutual exchange and fulfilment of promises.

This definition, here especially targeted at the exchange processes between parties and voters (i.e. the electoral market), can be generalised in order to fulfil the demands of a holistic approach, incorporating all political activities:

Political marketing seeks to establish, maintain and enhance long-term political relationships at a profit for society, so that the objectives of the individual political actors and organisations involved are met. This is done by mutual exchange and fulfilment of promises.

The scope of this definition embraces governmental political marketing and interest-group political marketing as well as that of political parties and candidates. It furthermore gets to grips with the permanent character of political marketing, acknowledging its theoretical and international implications by, first, leaving the instrumental level out of the definition by focusing only in general on strategic objectives ("establish, maintain and enhance . . .") and, second, by not limiting the applicability to a specific political situation. Interactivity features prominently with the introduction of the rationale of a "relationship exchange", while ethical problems are acknowledged via the stress on societal responsibility. As can be seen from Figure 5.2, this definitional attempt (Henneberg 1996c) follows the general development of political marketing definitions towards more holistic and relationship-oriented interpretations. Together with Butler and Collins (1996), it forms the latest attempt of transferring marketing-theory innovations into the subdiscipline of political marketing.

However, political marketing is comprised of more than discussions of definitions. In order to grasp its essence, an analysis of fundamental concepts underlying the rationale of political marketing and its managerial application follows.

Fundamental Concepts of Political Marketing

One fundamental element of political marketing—that is, its reference to an underlying exchange process—has been mentioned above. It needs, however, further elucidation because it is often claimed that the exchange process is in fact the underlying explanandum of marketing which separates it from other disciplines like economics (where a "market" constitutes the basic research object) (Hunt and Morgan 1995).[6] A major development in the theoretical content of this marketing exchange process was the inclusion of "ideas" as objects of exchange in addition to products and service. This broadened the scope of the marketing concept considerably and was the foundation of social and non-profit marketing. For an exchange to take place, it is generally assumed that four conditions have to be fulfilled:

- two players must participate (these may be individuals/groups, or organisations);
- each player must possess something of value (a product, service or an idea) that at least one other player desires;
- each player must voluntarily be willing to exchange the value belonging to him for the value in the belonging of another player;
- last, the players must be in contact in order to facilitate the exchange of values (Dibb et al. 1994; White 1986).

The exchange is guided by the so-called law of exchange, which states that an exchange only happens if all involved parties receive something which they perceive to be of greater value than that which they traded-in for it (Wortmann 1989). Exchange theory, based on a sociological understanding of transactions (e.g. Heath 1976; Homans 1961), has been developed, especially by Bagozzi, into a distinct concept underlying marketing theory (Bagozzi 1974, 1975, 1978, 1995; White 1986).

Another structural concept of political marketing that is often referred to is the voter-orientation of this managerial approach. It is mentioned unanimously by political scientists and marketing theorists in their discussions of the essence of political marketing (Bauer et al. 1996; Collins and Butler 1996; Newman 1994a; O'Cass 1996; O'Shaughnessy 1990a, 1996b; O'Shaughnessy and Wring 1994; Smith and Saunders 1990). Scammell concludes that "[t]his emphasis on the 'consumer', the voter, and the satisfaction of consumer wants, differentiates political marketing from earlier forms of political salesmanship: . . . even [from] the use of commercially derived techniques" (1995, p. 8). However, further elucidation is clouded by the use of the original marketing concept of "customer-orientation". The implications of the political competition with voters (or citizens) as the "consuming" part of the exchange process have rarely been explicitly treated. Whether, for example, the different goal functions of consumers and voters influence the philosophy of an outside-in perspective remains unclear.

Consumer-orientation is defined as an understanding of the needs and wants of an organisation's target customers (actual or potential) as a basis for the creation of offerings (J. O'Shaughnessy 1995)—that is, the organisation must be "oriented towards satisfying the needs of its customers" in order to be successful (Dickinson et al. 1986, p. 18). The concept of voter-orientation for political parties would mean acquiring knowledge about the needs and wants of their voters—that is, about the "public opinion"—and consequently facilitating an offering that satisfies this preference structure.[7] Furthermore, a preconception about segmentation and targeting regarding the entirety of voters is also part of the definition. However, this definition of consumer- (voter-)orientation is a very limiting concept of (political) marketing (Newman 1996), be it in its "soft" or "hard interpretation" (J. O'Shaughnessy 1995, p. 8). It has been argued that consumer-orientation in its traditional interpretation is flawed—for example, by a simplistic "follower-mentality", a dominance of consumer wishes. This creates a very static market without many breakthrough-product innovations (process innovations and product differentiations would prevail) as well as difficulties for the companies to find a unique selling proposition and therefore a strategic and sustainable competitive advantage in the market (Day 1997b; Dickinson et al. 1986). This mirrors partly the confinement of a "fit-strategy" of the organisational industrial-economy school (Porter 1996)—that is, an optimal organisational positioning in the market according to external restrictions. Modern "stretch-strategies", built on internal capability development, allow more flexibility in an organisation's market approach (Bourgeois 1996; Hamel and Prahalad 1996). Furthermore, a mix of internal and external strategy orientations is now perceived to be the most promising approach in strategic management (Day 1997a, 1997b). Consequently, customer-orientation must be understood more proactively prior to becoming a foundation of "stretch-approaches" of dynamic strategic management.[8] Thus, it must consist of a matching exercise of customer/voter needs and the internal capabilities of the relevant organisation, a more bidirectional approach to strategic marketing which supplements the predominant outside-in perspective with an inside-out one.

One initial way to enlarge and "modernise" the customer-orientation concept is by integrating it into the larger context of a marketing-orientation. This concept, which was revived during the 1990s, is one of the key concepts of recent research in marketing (Greenley 1995; Wensley 1995; for a comprehensive conceptual criticism see Dreher 1994). The concept of a marketing-orientation embraces a customer-orientation (outside-in view) as one element, supplemented by a competitor-orientation (inside-out view) and the component of interfunctional coordination (Narver and Slater 1990).[9] Kohli and Jaworski, in a slightly different operationalisation of a marketing-orientation nevertheless also include a "customer focus" as one of the pillars of their concept (Jaworski and Kohli 1993; Kohli and Jaworski 1990). This is in line with the "received view" of the marketing concept. A marketing-orientation therefore tries to remedy the problems of the "tunnel vision" of a pure customer-orientation by putting it into a wider context of the whole market as well as the intra-organisational sphere (Andreasen 1993; Wensley 1995). The repercussions of marketing-orientation for the concept of political marketing are

plentiful. Furthermore, a proper understanding of marketing-orientation is necessary for an appreciation of ethical aspects of political marketing. It suffices here to point out that voter-orientation in its classical form
would open up fears of populistic politics, a dictatorship of the fickle
opinions of the masses (Birch 1993; Jamieson 1992b). In politics, parties
and candidates always have been guided by an ideology—that is, an
idea of creating public well-being. These ideas have been implemented
more often than not via political leadership—that is, a top-down approach—which also includes the "education" of the voters. Furthermore, it can be shown that, in fact, leadership is one of the most
important traits of political figures in the eyes of the voters. Tocqueville
has summed up this aspect in his inimitable way:

What I call great political parties are those more attached to principles than to
consequences; to generalities rather than to particular cases, to ideas rather
than to personalities. Such parties generally have nobler features, more gener-
ous passions, more real convictions, and a bolder and more open look than
others. (1994/1848, p. 175)

Therefore, a pure voter-orientation brings with it the accusation of opportunism (in the following analysis, it is referred to as a "packaging-
orientation"). This has to be taken into account, especially in the creation
of an appropriate political offering. Therefore, a more general and balanced marketing-orientation (sometimes called "customer-led" marketing) (Piercy 1994) is the guiding principle of political-product policy and
of the organisation in general.

This leads directly to another fundamental concept of political marketing: any marketing approach has several dimensions. Obviously, there is
political marketing as an orientation, a perspective or a philosophy, if
one wishes to use such heroic terms (Dreher 1994). However, this conceptual view is only one facet of (political) marketing. (Political) marketing also comprises an instrumental (or better: technological) element
(O'Shaughnessy 1990a). This is concerned with the "knowing how" to
implement the marketing concept (J. O'Shaughnessy 1995).

Another fundamental aspect of political marketing which determines
the substance of all political marketing activities is its characteristic as
service marketing: the political exchange offer is essentially a service, be
it in a party–voter exchange or other political exchanges such as interest
group–activist, candidate–donor, government–citizens, and so forth
(Harrop 1990; Newman 1994a; O'Shaughnessy 1988). This fact has implications for the whole concept of political marketing and surfaces in
many publications on the topic (e.g. Bauer et al. 1995).[10] Services marketing is characterised by different exchange properties—problems of in-
tangibility, heterogeneity, production/consumption simultaneity and

perishability (Zeithaml and Bitner 1996). It therefore has different demands on the decision-making behaviour of the service recipients, as has been shown in a study by Gabbott and Hogg (1994) and dicussed later in this chapter. However, it can also be argued that in fact *all* marketing is service marketing (Foxall 1985a).

To sum up: this chapter defines political marketing with a special emphasis on its relationship-building qualities. Underlying the relationship approach, the essential normative foundations of the concept of political marketing are, following the principles of a theoretical and holistic understanding of the explanandum,

- its exchange character in a competitive market;
- its enlarged concept of a marketing-orientation;
- its multi-level character of being a philosophy and a technology;
- its service character.

Bearing in mind these conceptual foundations (see Fig. 5.3), each of which is looked at further in the following sections, the content of political marketing can be outlined in a discussion of: first, the macro-

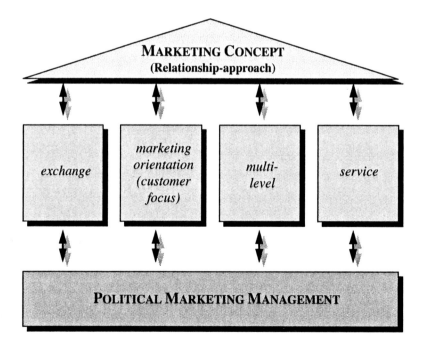

Figure 5.3. Characteristics of political marketing.

elements and, second, the microelements as well as auxiliary functions of political marketing.

Macroelements of Political Marketing

The macroelements of political marketing are those framing (in the sense of restricting) the political marketing management. All political marketing activities take place inside this realm, which sets the scope for further analysis on a micro level. At the macro level of political marketing, three spheres can be distinguished. First, there are the participants in the exchange process—that is, the actors or players. Their characteristics need to be described. However, these actors engage in an exchange, which, second, adds a dynamic dimension. The exchange of political marketing is crucial but also difficult to get to grips with. Third, these two elements have to be brought into context with each other, meaning the establishment of the political "market" and its competition, respectively.

In this section, emphasis is placed especially on political marketing aspects with relevance to the explanandum of this study—that is, the decision-making behaviour of voters and, subsequently, the marketing activities of parties/candidates that are targeted at influencing this behaviour.

Static Exchange: The Players

The players in the political market are more plentiful than normally expected from a glance at the relevant literature. Political parties and candidates as well as voters are constantly focused upon. However, other crucial and interesting players are neglected. Studies on governments (Newman 1995a, 1995b), interest-groups (Maloney 1996), party members (Granik 1997) or political activists (Stirling 1996) are rare. Thus, this aspect of variety of actors in the political market is underresearched, as are the implications of the constituent exchange structures.

Electoral Players. The classical players (primary actors) are, of course, either the parties (in a party-oriented party system like most European democracies) or the political contestants—that is, candidates (in a candidate-oriented party system like that of the United States, where the affiliation of candidates to parties is nominal) (Meny 1993; Ware 1996; see also the articles in Lijphart 1992). Their exchange opponents are the electorate—that is, all eligible voters on federal, state, or communal level.[11] However, even if one is only concerned with this limited exchange during political elections, it becomes evident that there are more actors involved than are visible at first glance. This is in line with the "procedural model" of political decision-making, which superseded mere aggregate models of voting (Hansson 1992). Sweeney (1995) analysed the differences between "primary" and "secondary" audiences for the American political market. If one calls the party/candidate–voter exchange the primary exchange (Henneberg 1996d), there are at least three further exchanges going on that are related to this primary exchange, in the sense that they facilitate and supplement it (see Fig. 5.4). This changes the "electoral exchange" into a four-player market. First, the media (here, in their "aggregate" form) act as an intermediary between the party/candidate and the electorate but have, in addition, a direct effect on the electorate as well as on the parties/candidates (secondary exchange) (Franklin 1994; Kavanagh 1995b).[12] They communicate/interpret the behaviour of parties and candidates but also act in their own right (via opinion influence or agenda setting). Second, parties/candidates depend on donations (monetary or in kind) in order to secure survival in the market (Kotler 1982). This resource-generating (quartery) exchange with donors has to be understood as ranging from party-member fees, donations by individuals/companies or fund-raising events to state subsidies (Himes 1995; Stonecash and Keith 1996). To complete the picture there are, third, party members and party activists (i.e. people who are not members but nevertheless have an interest in the party/candidate and can substantiate that interest) (Granik 1997; Herrnson 1995; Ware 1992).[13] As discussed in the next subsection, party members are of some importance for the determination of the political exchange offer (tertiary exchange).

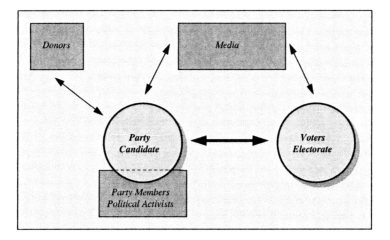

Figure 5.4. Exchange processes in the electoral market.

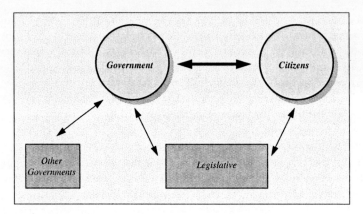

Figure 5.5.   Exchange processes in the governmental market.

Governmental Players.   Besides the electoral market, one can identify at least two more exchange spheres with other players. In the governmental market, the government (also a primary actor) is in primary exchange with the citizens of the relevant country. Further exchanges are with other players such as the legislative power or other governments (see Fig. 5.5).

Political Activism Players.   Another political market with distinct players is that of political activism (Richardson 1995), sometimes called the "alternative political sphere" (see Fig. 5.6). Here, the primary exchange is concerned with the interactions of political-interest groups (these primary actors could be informal initiatives, environmental organisations, political-action committees or other lobbying bodies, etc.) and political activists—that is, citizens with behavioural intentions to back the cause of the interest group (Schmitt-Beck 1996). Furthermore, the resource generation is of pivotal importance for these groups as well, and therefore the actor group of donors is also existent in the market for political activism. Last, interest groups engage in exchange with primary actors of other political markets, governments or parties/candidates.[14] These markets are put into a context and the competitive mechanisms analysed in a later subsection.

Dynamic Exchange: The Processes

For a better understanding of the markets, it is evident that the underlying exchange processes must be analysed briefly. As above, the electoral market—and here especially the primary exchanges—are pivotal to this study and deserve a more detailed understanding.

Exchange in the Electoral Market.   The exchange relationships in the political market are, in general, extremely complex and difficult to get to grips with (Hasitschka 1995). Therefore, many writers on political marketing do not clarify their understanding of what the part of the transactions in the electoral market is. Thurber is essentially right when he states: "Campaigns are competitions over ideas" (1995, p. 3).

This product is therefore essentially an offer of political leadership and representation, a promise to implement policies (once elected) according to certain "principles" (Farrell and Wortmann 1987; Harrop 1990; Newman 1996). To put it more cheekily: "Politicians . . . sell hope" (O'Shaughnessy 1990a, p. 199). However, besides the more manifest aspects of policies, the political offer also has transcendental elements that are embraced in the political values, and a social connectedness of "believers" in these values (Hudelson 1987; O'Shaughnessy 1988; Schedler 1994). Therefore, there are "expressive" elements to it, according to a study by Brennan and Lomasky (1993). In its entirety, the political offer is therefore similar to a so-called systems-exchange in marketing (Bauer et al. 1995).

The electorate has many different ways to "respond" with a reciprocal offer. The most obvious is voting behaviour (i.e. electoral support at one specific point in time), but other possibilities are more permanent—

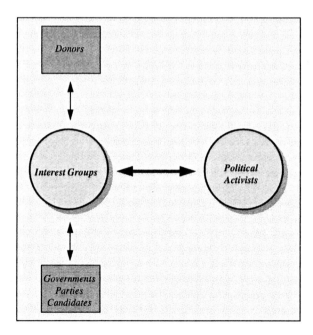

Figure 5.6.   Exchange processes in the political activism market.

value or attitude changes regarding political issues, involvement in the political discourse, positive word-of-mouth or, in a material sense, donations and party-political activities (Farrell and Wortmann 1987; Hasitschka 1995). Furthermore, voters also exchange general information—for example, about attitudes, needs. Such information is sometimes exchanged directly with political parties/candidates or via the media. The media are therefore important information-transaction and -exchange channels (Schedler 1994).

Party members/activists demand a specific political product (as described above) or some party-specific bonuses (positions, power, etc.) while reciprocating through membership, active endorsement and so forth. Therefore, intra-party exchange is about collective and selective incentives for the members/activists, while in return the leaders get participation, but especially a mandate of "freedom of action" (Panebianco 1988).

Donors can have the same (direct) interest in the party/candidate's political offer, or they in general back democratic institutions (like business organisations, which sometimes donate to parties opposing each other) and have therefore only an indirect interest. Their exchange offer is essentially monetary.

Exchange in the Governmental Market. The deliverables of governments are their promised policies but also other (improvised) decisions and their implementation. These are exchanged with the electorate for continuous confidence by the voters (according to Newman 1996, this is represented in the public opinion) and positive attitudes that in the long run allow the government to continue over the initial election period.

Exchange in the Political-Activism Market. Interest-groups offer representation (aggregation of opinion, channelling and lobbying of a specific demand) outside the electoral sphere but with impact on societal decisions. Their activists demand this representation for active backing (be it material or immaterial). Furthermore, donors are needed for additional monetary resources. Because many single-issue groups are financed by their members (who should normally also be activists), who pay a membership fee while remaining passive (meaning the lobbying is done by "professionals"—e.g. Greenpeace), the actor groups "activists" and "donors" can overlap considerably in this market.

Competition in the Political Market

The whole "political market" can now be put together—that is, the isolated market segments can be brought into context and their interactions can be highlighted. Furthermore, this allows for a clarification of the main "clearing mechanisms" in the political-network system. In effect, this means putting together the political subsystems and integrating them into a supra-system of political activity in order to gain an overview of the relevance of the analysed exchange (the party/candidate–voter exchange) from a holistic perspective.

The Supra-Market of Politics.   Integrating all three subsystems of political activities means also introducing a new subdivision between spheres in the political market. The three generic subsystems of electoral, governmental and political-activism markets do not exhibit the same quality of politics. Following an idea put forward by Inglehart (1979), who divided the political sphere via an establishment/anti-establishment cleavage (supplementing Lipset and Rokkan 1966), two possible submarkets can be distinguished (see Fig. 5.7): the electoral and governmental markets have been fused to what can be called "high politics" (following a phrase used in Stirling 1996). "High politics", or the "establishment" in Inglehart's terms, is characterised by a formalised political and democratic competition. It is this market that normally comes to mind first when politics is concerned, and it was until recently the only developed and organised market for exchange in political systems (Birch 1995). Hence, its naming as "high".[15] However, it can be argued that developments over recent years compel the acknowledgement of another aspect of politics, which has now formed a well-organised sphere with a distinct scope. This market of "low politics" comprises the exchange of political activism and has to be seen as in direct competition for resources with the "high-politics" market, exemplified in Schedler's analysis of the "anti-political triangle" (1996). Although without formalised "legitimisation" in Western democracy, it is nevertheless an important trading place for political ideas, resources and interests (Birch 1995; Richardson 1995; Schmitt-Beck 1990) and can also directly influence key players of "high politics", be it directly—for example, candidates or parties—or indirectly—for example, via the media or donors (exogenous intermediaries that stand outside the political sphere in their own subsystems but interact heavily with it) (Schmitt-Beck 1994). As analyses by Stirling (1996) showed, there is evidence for substantial distinctions between these two political spheres (e.g. in their dynamics, their competitive differentiation, their exit/entry-barriers and the allegiance-switching costs). However, it is noteworthy that there are now tendencies that in the future might weaken these differentiations between the two political submarkets. The most prominent of these tendencies is the formation of "anti-political-establishment parties" (an oxymoron by Schedler 1996, p. 291)—that is, a transfer of the logic and politics of "low politics" into the market of "high politics". Altogether, it becomes clear now that the political market is indeed one characterised

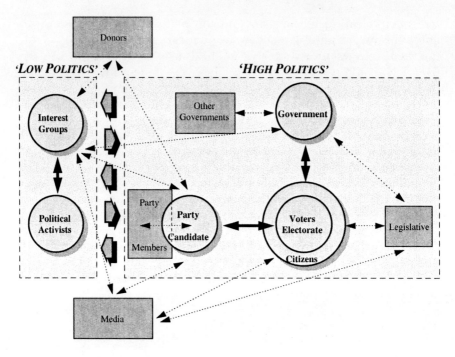

Figure 5.7. The "supra-market" of politics.

by "complex exchanges", to use Bagozzi's (1975) terminology of types of exchange interactions.

From the structure of Figure 5.7, it becomes subsequently clear that an isolated analysis of the main exchange process of the electoral market would mean an oversimplification that does not allow for the systemic view needed for discussions of the managerial implications. Such a holistic understanding shows the contextual boundedness of exchange (Senge 1993).

Clearing Mechanisms. The existence of clearing mechanisms is one of the preconditions for a market analogy between commercial and political transactions. Although this isomorphism is not essential for a marketing discussion (because such a discussion would be guided by exchange structures and not by market structures), some brief statements may assist a better understanding of the political market (Wangen 1983). One major contribution to this is a study by Newman in which he states: "public opinion, the currency in politics" (1996, p. 2). It is certainly true that organisational behaviour, if guided by a marketing concept of pure voter-orientation, would follow such a clearing mechanism. However, with a more "advanced" understanding of political marketing, organisations in the political market may go back to what political economists since Downs (1957) have postulated. This implies an orientation and clearing mechanism guided by the vote/office-seeking goal in the electoral market, exemplified by vote-maximisation attempts (Bartle 1995; Farrell and Wortmann 1987; Wangen 1983). Wortmann, in an elaborate discussion of the problem, derives the main clearing mechanism as defined by the power-seeking objective of the main electoral players, parties and candidates (Wortmann 1989).[16] Power-seeking can be satisfied via different mechanisms: in "high politics", via electoral seats (government position)[17], in "low politics", via general influence. However, some more cynical voices would say that the real clearing mechanism is the "invisible hand" of political consultants—"hired guns" who steer campaigning according to their perceptions (O'Shaughnessy 1990a).

Microelements of Political Marketing

Based upon the framework knowledge gained above regarding the macroelements of political marketing, the theory building will continue with an analysis of functions, instruments and strategies of political marketing—that is, the heart of a managerial analysis of a political organisation's activities in the market. In this section the transformation from the *theory of political marketing* to the *theory of political marketing management* becomes manifest. The concerned organisations could be parties/candidates, governments or interest groups—that is, each of the three primary actors of the three political submarkets identified above.

Functional Analysis of Political Marketing Management

> "when we come to marketing functions, it is [. . .] clear that every organization performs marketing-like activities whether or not they are recognized as such."
>
> Kotler and Levy (1969, p. 11)

A functional analysis of political marketing management is linked to the caveats in the research on the topic in general. So far, there exist no studies about the underlying functions of organisations in the political market from a managerial point of view. Political marketing management theory has not yet scrutinised the underlying problem of utilising these functions for an instrumental and strategic analysis. Instrumental analyses of political marketing use mainly the "4P" concept of McCarthy (1960), either in its pure form (e.g. Farrell and Wortmann 1987; Wring

1996b) or in a derived form (Newman 1994a). However, this classificational scheme can be criticised as providing merely educational value, not representing state-of-the-art marketing theory, and not taking into account the peculiarities of the political market. Furthermore, in an evaluation of the 4P concept, van Waterschoot and van den Bulte (1992) use Hunt's (1991a) criteria for assessing classificational schemes. They conclude that it is flawed by, first, unclear characterisation of the properties on which the scheme is based; second, the fact that the categories are not mutually exclusive; and third, the problematic catch-all category of sales promotion as part of communication/promotion (van Waterschoot and van den Bulte 1992). Thus, without a functional analysis, it can be argued that political marketing instruments are "in the air"—that is, without a sound foundation of their purpose within the organisation. This might explain the caveats of instrumental analyses prevalent in the literature (Henneberg 1995b, 1996d; Wortmann 1989).

Functional analysis in marketing theory is a very old research object (Fulbrook 1940; Sheth et al. 1988), although it has to be stated that it has lost momentum recently (Henneberg 1995b). By analysing marketing functions one subscribes to the view that functions are conditions of marketing entities (organisations), while instruments are means for the fulfilment of these functions. Functions can also be characterised as outputs of organisational behaviour. They "can be accomplished through a variety of specific activities or tools. . . . Any specific marketing activity or tool can serve several functions simultaneously. " (van Watershoot and van den Bulte 1992, p. 87). This quotation clarifies that marketing instruments are the means for satisfying functional prerequisites. In addition, it makes clear that marketing instruments or instrument groups (also called "policies"[18]) are not exclusively focused on the fulfilment of one function. Knowledge of the underlying functions are, therefore, a prerequisite for organisational survival and success because the usage of marketing instruments (their selections, usage intensity and coordination) must be founded on a clear idea of the necessary outcomes that these instruments ought to bring about. Instruments fulfil no purpose *sui generis* but they are defined in terms of the functions they serve (Hunt 1991a; Kotler 1972). In the following, "generic" functions of political marketing management are analysed—that is, those which are not only primary exchange-facilitating functions but also those that are necessary for the survival of the political organisation in general (i.e. in the case of parties/candidates, also the secondary, etc. exchanges in the electoral market as well as additional exchanges in the supra-market) (Henneberg 1995b). Therefore, the underlying exchange process is the one characterised in Figure 5.4—that is, the electoral market. Altogether eight generic functions of political marketing management can be identified, as outlined below.

Product Function. In order to facilitate the main exchange process between parties and the electorate, the political organisation has to offer something of value—that is, the political. As already clarified, this "product" has, in fact, service character; it is a promise of a certain behavioural activity and outcome. However, this product function is restricted in marketing terms by the fact that political marketing management cannot follow the concept of a strict voter-orientation. A more restricted voter-orientation as part of a political marketing-orientation underlies the development of the organisational offer. The political product in a representative democracy with free mandates (Birch 1995; Schedler 1994; Stoiber 1983) is partly fixed (in the short term) by an underlying ideology of the party/candidate as part of latter's history. This ideology sometimes clashes with voter demands. Nevertheless, a free mandate gives politicians the chance to implement their ideals (e.g. ideologies) (Barry 1991a). This ideology constitutes the marketing-irrelevant part of the political product, and it causes a certain stability in the political market—for example, by minimising "leap-frogging" of parties. From a political marketing point of view, these ideological elements of the organisational offer cannot be ignored, because they determine the credibility of the political service (and also that of the party system itself). Services as future-oriented promises have trust and credibility of the person/organisation promising it as one of the main characteristics of the political product (Bitner 1995; Zeithaml and Bitner 1996). Loss of credibility by changing around the values that a party stands for results in immediate loss of credibility with the voters and subsequently electoral defeat. Therefore, the product function in a marketing sense is only applicable to the marketing-relevant part of the political product which is the flexible and dynamic aspect of politics: issue agenda, candidate personality, the corporate culture of the party and so forth (Worcester 1996).[19] This can be named the "packaged" element of the political product. In recent years the candidate has achieved a prominent position in this triad because of personalisation (and centralisation) tendencies of campaigning, even in party-oriented party systems (Field 1994; Wangen 1983; Worcester 1996). Decisions about the product offer are, therefore, in a strategic sense of this marketing function, always decisions about the position of the product on a continuum between inflexible ideological elements and the packaged aspects of politics (see Fig. 5.8).

For example, the British Labour Party has recently made a move rightwards on the continuum and became more marketing- (and voter-) driven (like most catch-all parties, be they challengers or leaders) and therefore similar to a "packaging" party like Berlusconi's *Forza Italia*—that is, "postmodern populism". Niche parties like the German neo-socialist *Partei des Demokratsichen Sozialismus* are normally less flexible and fundamentally ideology-driven (Axford et al. 1996; Butler and

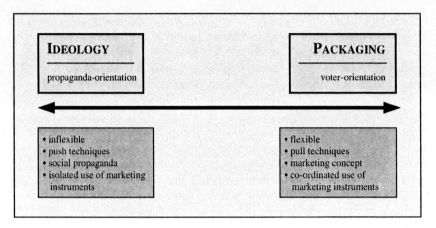

Figure 5.8.   Ideology versus packaging.

Collins 1996; Collins and Butler 1995). The functional decision as to how far the offer should serve ideological or marketing-related aspects has ramifications for the use of instruments and, indeed, for the applicability of the political marketing concept itself. If the party chooses a location near the ideology-orientation end, only isolated marketing instruments can be used and an integrated marketing-orientation is ruled out. A tendency towards the use of social-propaganda methods (the hyper-demic model) is imminent (Baer 1995; O'Shaughnessy 1996b). On the other hand, the use of "packaged" offers is not without risks. O'Shaughnessy (1990a) reminds us that "[r]ealism is essential in the political product . . .; therefore packaging must be disguised as much as possible" (p. 56). Parties and candidates with different "orientations" can exist in the same party system at the same time, according to their strategic understanding of the product function. Altogether, this function is, thus, a political marketing function that has to take into account considerations about strategic aspects as well as genuine political decisions. The political product is not as flexible as its commercial counterpart; therefore, this function has a reduced marketing relevance due to political rigidities.

Distribution Function.   The distribution function is concerned with activities regarding the availability of the exchange offer to the exchange partner. In commercial marketing this includes channel-management strategies (Stern et al. 1996). For a political party/candidate, the picture becomes more complicated. One can define a primary distribution function that is characterised by the ways of implementation of the political service in the sense of governmental policies. However, this is only of minor importance for political marketing in the electoral market. The first aim of the actors is to achieve participation in government (and "change" into the governmental market), not to implement (Downs 1957; Dunleavy 1991). Therefore, a secondary distribution function is of importance for the electoral market—that is, the allocation of the marketing-relevant part of the political offering (the tangible and intangible aspects of the service promise). These elements can be characterised as product surrogates—namely, the candidate and the party image. These surrogates must also be distributed. This can mean "candidate-placing" in a literal sense—for example, by determining the channels of distribution with which the candidate gets in contact with the electorate (or with specific target groups). Meetings, speeches, party conferences and the selection of appropriate media are related to this distribution function (Wortmann 1989). The function will increase in complexity with the arrival of new media—for example, email, web TV and the Internet (Johnson 1997).

Cost Function. The cost function is normally derived from considerations about the price—that is, the direct exchange return that an organisation receives. Recently, this view has been superseded by opportunity- and transaction-cost approaches which are, in fact, more relevant for a discussion of political marketing functions because the primary exchange in the electoral market does not involve any direct monetary exchanges. The cost function has so far been neglected in discussions of political marketing instruments and strategies (exceptions are Schmidtchen 1974 or Wortmann 1989,[20] but the only really relevant study is Wring 1996b).[21] It is, however, a crucial element of an organisation's political marketing management. The political "price" has to be understood in the sense of reducing the electorate's perceived opportunity costs, which can determine inhibition barriers (Downs 1957). These barriers can prevent the implementation of a behavioural intention. Therefore, facilitating the exchange process in terms of costs means for the organisation to minimise the opportunity costs of voters' electoral decision-making process as well as of the electoral act itself. In addition, it also means enhancing the direct benefits from political involvement and the voting process as a symbolic act (Downs 1957; Lane 1993).

Communication Function. Communication serves the function of informing the exchange partner about the offer and its availability, and so forth. In the case of political parties, it is concerned with the manifesto, the agenda and the candidate as well as with images. In addition, it is an aid to the interpretation of the meaning of the exchange process for other exchange partners. This can go as far as creating a communicative image that becomes the primary product benefit for the exchange partner (e.g. the status of a Marlboro-man for smokers or, in the political sphere, the specific rhetoric of *Forza Italia*: see Axford et al. 1996; Rauen 1994).

The communication function is essential for a political organisation/ candidate because it facilitates the voters' decision-making process, feeds necessary information into the political market and brings the political competition and discourse into the electorate's sphere (Popkin 1994). Basic aspects are: name/brand identification, image development, issue/agenda setting and exploitation, and tactical attack/defence (Ansolabehere and Iyengar 1995; Bryant 1995; Roberts and McCombs 1994). The communication function referred to here directly targets the electorate and can therefore be named the primary communication function. Although it can use an intermediary, like the media, via paid advertisements,[22] the message is basically controlled by the political organisation (Bryant 1995; Newman 1993). Primary communication can therefore be via the primary or the secondary exchange channel (Schmitt-Beck and Pfetsch 1994). Through new technologies "the electoral process has changed in this country [USA] from voter participation through political parties to direct contact with the candidates" (Newman 1994a, p. xiv)—that is, primary communication has increased in importance. Because of the service character of the political product and its being a mere "promise", the political communication message can serve as a product surrogate, a cue (Sniderman et al. 1993). However, these two functions (communication and product) should not be confused. They are distinct functions with distinct purposes for the organisation (Wortmann 1989). Nevertheless, their use in the form of communication instruments can be similar, Thus, the distinction is primarily on the functional level and not so much on the instrumental one.

News-Management Function. In addition to the primary communication function, there exists a secondary one that is perhaps of an even greater importance for political marketing (see Fig. 5.9 below). It can be named, with a phrase coined by Franklin (1994), "news-management" (also called "newsmaking": Bryant 1995). While the primary communication message is targeted at the electorate, the secondary one is targeted primarily at the intermediaries, the media that then communicate with the electorate. It is not so much information distribution, more an agenda-setting and information-interpretation effort (Baer 1995; Franklin 1995; Gabor 1995; Schmitt-Beck and Pfetsch 1994). The split of communication into primary and secondary parts has similarities to marketing attempts to get to grips with the diversity of the "communication mix" (van Waterschoot and van den Bulte 1992; van Waterschoot and Voet 1988; Wangen 1983). News-management is of great importance because of the scrutiny that any political activity, statement, decision and so forth is under. Commercial organisations in comparison do not work in the lime-light of media attention all the time. Some political parties speak of a hostile media environment in which they have to live (Bryant

1995) The media communicates political messages/interpretations/ comments concerning the parties and candidates directly to the voters, while getting an inherent credibility bonus (and scope) that parties cannot hope to achieve because they are perceived as biased towards their own interest (Ansolabehere and Iyengar 1995). Therefore, the parties try to influence the influencers (Harrop 1990). The recipients of this news-management of information, interpretations and influencing attempts are journalists and other media opinion leaders (Franklin 1994). This function has gained publicity with the public discussion about "spin-doctoring". This refers to the ability of party press officers (or other "Machiavellian" figures, best typified by Labour's Peter Mandelson) to give political information a spin that is favourable for the concerned party (Vallely 1995).[23] Media reports, by using these interpretations, create political "facts" and opinions founded on this spin (Franklin 1994). The news-management function is more complicated than commercial public relations: it has to be identified as a distinct functional prerequisite for the survival of political parties.[24] However, it is also of great importance to governments and interest groups in other political submarkets (Newman 1995b; Stirling 1996).

Fund-Raising Function. The fund-raising function is incorporated in the price/cost function in the commercial sphere because the exchange offer involves resource generation as a reciprocal measure. However, in the political market of elections, the reciprocal exchange is a non-pecuniary one—that is, no revenue flow exists in relationship to the primary exchange. Therefore, the establishment of a distinct fund-raising function is crucial for the financial base of the political organisation and therefore for the survival of the party in the long run (Himes 1995; Sorauf 1995; Stonecash and Keith 1996).[25] Political candidates/parties normally get their monetary resources through a (quartery) exchange process with donors. These donors can be members of the party (contributing via membership fees or voluntary donations), activists (by providing free services to the party/candidate) or the general public (by donations from individuals or organisations). Today, interactions with these donor groups is the main focus of candidate/party activities during or before electoral campaigns in some party systems, notably the US one (Himes 1995; O'Shaughnessy 1990a) where fund-raising practices are a constant topic of discussion.[26]

Parallel-Campaign Management Function. Coordination is at the heart of the parallel campaign management function. Wortmann describes it as trying "to hide the origin[,] that is the name of the political party from which political activities stem" (1989, p. 306). However, it is sometimes not hiding the origin (as in the case of the Willie Horton advertisement, produced by a non-Republican organisation but evidently coordinated with the Bush campaign) (Jamieson 1992b) but open synergy that is the aim of this function. The function is targeted at organisations whose activities in the political market are similar in their goals and means to those of the party. These organisations can be called the "backing environment". They consist mostly of individuals and organisations that are not players in the electoral market but use the market of political activism ("low politics"; e.g. Greenpeace's backing of Green parties in Europe). The parallel-campaigning function facilitates a synergy optimum between a political party's activity and the "parallel" organisations such as interest groups, social movements, political foundations, think-tanks, but also companies, independent polling institutes and so forth. A prerequisite is an agreement on both sides to argue along the same lines. Such an agreement can be general or concern only some limited issues; in some cases it can also be covert and only implicit. Campaign coordination in the political sphere must be seen as a generic function because of the possible credibility gain by networking with "independent" opinion leaders. Achieving an image of credibility by the use of "objective" communication sources is a crucial element of the promised service in the political competition.

Internal-Cohesion Management Function.   Besides the primary, secondary and quartery exchange processes of the electoral market, there is also an internal (tertiary) exchange relevant to the party itself. The primary exchange process of "party/candidate–electorate/voter" is supplemented by another (group of) player(s) interested in the political product, the service offering. These are the party members but also, to some degree, party activists who are not necessarily members of the party (Duverger 1959). The intra-party negotiations are concerned with the very essence and form of the political offer. The party decision-makers— that is, the party leaders, candidates as well as the outside consultants that are a common characteristic of today's professional parties (Katz and Mair 1995; Newman 1994a; Panebianco 1988)—must therefore accommodate the opinions of their internal clientele as well as market forces and the public opinion (Demsetz 1990). The importance of this functions has been highlighted in a very interesting study by Koelble (1996) that uses the principal-agent theory as a methodological tool for analysing intra-party power distributions. Members and activists normally have a more ideology-oriented understanding of politics which causes a preference for a political product more on the left side of the strategic-product continuum (see Fig. 5.8). Panebianco commented in this context: "One can exercise power over others only by satisfying their needs and expectations; one thereby paradoxically submits oneself to their paneer" (1988, p. 22).

In addition, this function serves a critical role in securing internal stability and therefore the credibility of the party, which is a positive cue for voters in their assessment of the party's/leader's general ability to govern.

This enumeration of managerial marketing functions of political parties/candidates is not exhaustive in the sense that all functional prerequisites of organisational activities have been covered. However, the *generic* functions of political marketing for parties/candidates have been characterised. All exchange relationships, especially those with other actors in the electoral market but also those with the market of "low politics", have been covered by allocating at least one function to them (see Fig. 5.9). It becomes clear that the primary exchange process of the electoral market is naturally the focus of many political marketing management functions of political parties/candidates. Product, cost, distribution and communication functions are mainly facilitators for this relationship. Internal cohesion as well as product function links the party/candidates to the party members. Distribution and news-management functions allow for an interplay with the media, a player that stands outside the political market. The news-management function also influences the connection from the media to the voters/the citizens and

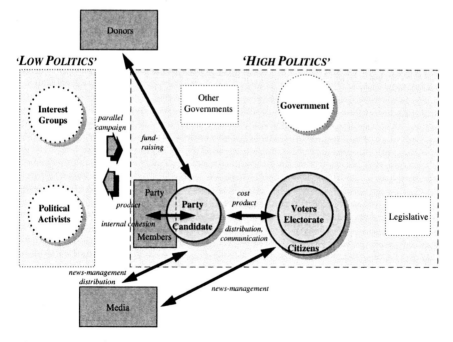

Figure 5.9. Exchange processes and functions for political marketing management of parties/candidates.

therefore has an additional indirect repercussion on the system. Fund-raising functions hold the contact with the other exogenous element of the political market, the donor groups. Last, the market of "high politics", in which parties and candidates operate, and the market of "low politics" are coordinated via the parallel-campaign management function.

Before instruments are categorised within these eight generic functions, the importance of specific functions for different organisational players in the three political markets is highlighted briefly here. Although developed for political parties/candidates, these eight generic functions are not of equal importance in practice for a party's political marketing management. Furthermore, for other actors the importance mix might also be different due to specific managerial necessities of these organisations. Therefore, an overview of the "managerial weighting" for these generic functions completes this subsection (see Fig. 5.10). Notable in a comparison of these "functional mixes" is the fact that in the governmental market much more emphasis is placed on parallel campaign management (i.e. lobbying exchanges, coalition building, etc.) (Franklin 1994; Harris 1994; Harris and Lock 1996) whereas interest groups have a special focus on organisational survival (bearing in mind the extreme amount of churn/fluctuation in membership figures, this seems imminent) (Maloney 1996). Furthermore, the importance of "classical" marketing functions (i.e. product, distribution, cost and communication) is higher in the electoral market than in both the governmental and the political-activism markets. These findings suggest that the political mar-

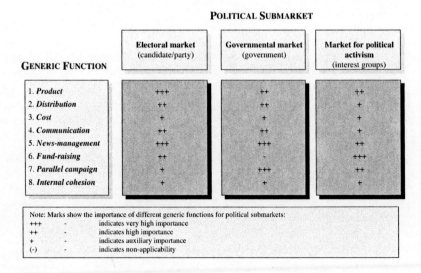

POLITICAL SUBMARKET

GENERIC FUNCTION	Electoral market (candidate/party)	Governmental market (government)	Market for political activism (interest groups)
1. *Product*	+++	++	++
2. *Distribution*	++	++	+
3. *Cost*	+	+	+
4. *Communication*	++	++	+
5. *News-management*	+++	+++	++
6. *Fund-raising*	++	-	+++
7. *Parallel campaign*	+	+++	++
8. *Internal cohesion*	+	+	+

Note: Marks show the importance of different generic functions for political submarkets:
+++   -   indicates very high importance
++   -   indicates high importance
+   -   indicates auxiliary importance
(-)   -   indicates non-applicability

Figure 5.10. Importance of generic functions in different political markets

keting management of parties and candidates is more similar to normal (services) marketing than the management of other political exchange processes.

Instruments of Political Marketing Management

The discussion above regarding functions of political marketing management introduced the idea that in marketing theory the management of an organisation should be seen according to the necessary functions that the organisation ought to cover—that is, the vital ends—and that instruments are merely the corresponding means of doing so (van Waterschoot and van den Bulte 1992). Therefore, political marketing management activities can best be viewed by looking at functions instead of instruments or instrument groups. This perspective is, however, one that has not been widely applied in political marketing. Prevalent are studies concerned with the instrumental use of marketing in the political sphere or studies that utilise political marketing instruments (normally in the form of the 4P concept) as the structural framework for their studies (e.g. Boll and Poguntke 1992; Bowler and Farrell 1992a, 1992b, 1992c; O'Shaughnessy and Wring 1994; Webb 1992). Exemplary of this thinking is the elaborate scheme by Wring (1996b). Because of the large volume of literature on descriptions of instruments in political marketing, this subsection deals with them in a more cursory way.[27]

In the following, instruments are perceived as serving a generic function(s)—that is, contributing to its (their) fulfilment. A second new element to the study of political marketing instruments is the idea of the basic versus complementary nature of instruments, first introduced by van Waterschoot and van den Bulte (1992). This will allow for differentiation according to instrument policy regarding permanent versus short-term and immediate consequences. For political marketing, this helps in understanding the distinction between permanent activities and campaign activities. However, this subsection starts by introducing the main political marketing instruments and discussing some examples (for the electoral market). Initially, the simple 4P scheme of product, place (distribution), promotion (communication) and price (cost) will be used as a guiding framework (Kotler and Armstrong 1996; McCarthy 1960, 1981).

Product Policy. As mentioned earlier, product instruments have to be seen in the context of three product elements. Firstly, product instruments are about images and traits of the candidate—that is, the main "tangible" asset of the service provided/promised by the party (besides the party manifesto, which is more obscure because of its complexity) (Newman 1996). The candidate is the main "product surrogate"—that is, is the *pars pro toto* of the political product. Such candidate traits can be, for example, statesman-like appearance (manifested in the right clothes or intimacy with world leaders) or newcomer/anti-establishment image (exemplified in academic speech, unorthodox political gestures, etc.). Following Kavanagh (1995b): "Achieving a favourable image for the candidate or party is now a key objective of modern campaigning. Parties and candidates will have images freely provided by the mass media and by their political opponents. Hence the incentive to do it for themselves" (p. 13).

Candidate-oriented product instruments are used frequently, both in candidate-centred as well as in party-centred party systems (Wattenberg 1995). One particularly well-researched example is "the marketing of Maggie Thatcher", a politician who would normally be associated more with "principles" than with "packaging" (Scammell 1991, 1994).[28]

Second, party image is another element of product instruments of political marketing management. It is made up of a variety of aspects, all relevant for the credibility of the political organisation as a service pro-vider. These aspects can be related to the party's image of innovativeness or conservativeness, togetherness or volatility, its ability to "listen to the people" in general, or its internal "democracy"—that is, the image of whether the party grass-roots are involved in policy decisions. Instru-ment use can influence the corporate culture (e.g. corporate design, corporate organisation). All these image-related aspects of product in-struments have left some commentators with the conclusion that today in politics "image has supplanted substance" (Franklin 1994, p. 9).

Third, the main "promise" of a party/candidate—its policy inten-tions—are laid out in a kind of manifesto, a long-term, stable policy statement that is, however, normally a very complicated and complex rationale for the party's existence. Specific political "issue-stands" are clarified in the manifesto or can be derived from it. Changes of essential manifesto guidelines appear rarely in the political competition (it is easier in candidate-centred party systems where each candidate is to some extent a new contestant without a political history) and constitute normally a radical product repositioning. Examples of such a radical product policy are the "Clause IV" discussion of the British Labour Party or the "Bad Godesberger Programm" of the German Social Democrat Party (both, incidentally, part of a major repositioning effort of these parties, to "New Labour" and social democracy, respectively). In gen-eral, decisions about emphasis on a specific issue for the political agenda are very important for the instrument use in this regard.

Obviously, all three elements of product instruments are highly inter-related: changes in candidate image have a spin-off effect on the party's image; a product repositioning at the manifesto level must be coordinated with the other elements of this product triangle (Worcester 1996). Therefore, a positioning on the packaging–ideology continuum is always concerned with the effects on all three product instrument groups—that is, candidate-related, party-image related, and manifesto-related product instruments.

Distribution Policy. Distribution instruments constitute the link between the product/service offer and the potential customer/voter. This includes the actual delivery of the political product (or its main derivative, the politician) with the help of campaign meetings, door-to-door canvassing, voter-meetings, and public speeches. However, besides these traditional distribution instruments, "packaged" press conferences, media picture events and "soundbite" opportunities, interviews, and so forth can supplement the easy "distribution" of the candidate (Farrell and Wortmann 1987; O'Shaughnessy and Holbrook 1988; Robinson 1995). Therefore, the physical distribution of the political candidate can be directly (with the electorate) or indirectly (via a targeting of specific media). Here the overlap with communication policy instruments becomes obvious.

Communication Policy. Communication techniques are today the most important political marketing instruments of all political players. This is especially evident for political parties and candidates. The political product—that is, the image elements of it—can be created, influenced or distributed by communication instruments, such as party-political broadcasts, political ads and posters, leaflets, mailings[29] and corporate culture/identity signals (Ansolabehere and Iyengar 1995; Bryant 1995; Farrell and Wortmann 1987; Franklin 1994; Rothschild 1978). In addition, new technology can be used for phone-in/dial-in chat shows, live video discussions, talk radio and so forth. Even "non-political" events can be used, as shown by Bill Clinton's playing the saxophone on chat shows during his first campaign (Johnson 1997; Newman 1993, 1994a, 1995b). At first glance, issue stands and ideology do not seem to fit under these images as the core of communication instruments. However, these also need to be marketed by communication means because they have to be made comprehensible for the electorate in the sense that the underlying rationale (and the unique features of differentiation) must be visible and easy to grasp. In addition, political communication instruments can influence the agenda of the political discourse by bringing up specific themes and repeating them constantly (Gabor 1995). This can be of great importance, as was seen in the 1992 Clinton campaign with the new issue of health care reform (Thurber 1995). In this context, the instruments of attack and negative advertising have to be mentioned without any intention to engage in a discussion about them (Banker 1992; Franklin 1994; Jamieson 1992b; Kaid and Holtz-Bacha 1995b; O'Shaughnessy 1989/90; Scammell no date).

While most of the communication instruments already mentioned are used normally in a very untargeted way (i.e. based on mass-media usage), there are other communication instruments that are personal-based and micro-targeted. These are normally associated with fulfilling news-management functions. These communication instruments are concerned with planting information, interpretations and opinions with crucial "information leaders" via sophisticated methods of personal communication by persuasive experts. Their main thrust is agenda setting, control over politicians' media appearances and influencing the content/style of these appearances via putting constant pressure on the media (Franklin 1994; Scammell 1995).[30] These "micro-marketing" approaches of communication are also used for fund-raising functions with the help of database-marketing (O'Shaughnessy 1987; O'Shaughnessy and Holbrook 1988; O'Shaughnessy and Wring 1994).

Cost-Management Policy.   Instrument usage in this political marketing domain is rare and neglected. However, many cost-management instruments work together with communication instruments. Their main function—that of reducing the information-processing costs of the individual voter by using easy-to-understand argumentations and cues (specific catch-phrases) that trigger specific concepts for retrieving information—is linked to information management.[31] However, in addition to these instrument groups there are those that in general enhance and increase the involvement level of the electorate concerning political issues but also politics in general. Only if voters, party members, activists and so forth perceive a benefit from involvement in the political discourse or in political actions, and if acting in the political sphere (be it voting, political activism or any other political activity) is not costly (in terms of opportunity costs), will there be an individual incentive for the citizen to open up to the political sphere—that is, getting involved psychologically. Such an involvement also constitutes a better basis for the functioning of other political marketing instruments, in the sense that it makes the individual voter receptive to these stimuli. Successful cost-management can be seen as a filter variable that decides the success of other political marketing management variables. Typical cost-management instruments in this regard are concerned with the physical voting act—for example, transport services to the polling station (where allowed), "educational" information about the voting process, enhancing the "hedonistic" elements of voting (e.g. citizen's duty) and so forth. This has become more and more important with the acknowledgement that elections are determined not only by voter preferences but also by turnout (Baer 1995). In addition, lowering the threshold of political activity in general by involving people in community work or communal discussions, fostering their engagement in political actions via appropriately organised events, will help not only the political organisation but has been credited by some writers with a legitimisation function for the whole democratic system (Bauer et al. 1995; Lane 1993; Nimmo 1970; Stirling 1996)

Instruments and Functions: A Matching Exercise. Political marketing functions and instruments are corresponding, but, as mentioned earlier, they are not in a one-to-one fit of one instrument serving one (and only one) function, as has been traditionally assumed (McCarthy 1960; van Waterschoot and van den Bulte 1992). With the more diverse functional requirements of political marketing management, laid down in the eight generic functions, a precise match must be achieved with the instruments available. Therefore, an instrument mix for each function is deemed appropriate. The importance of the four instrument groups in relation to the eight generic functions in the electoral market can be summarised as in Figure 5.11. While the functions are the independent variables, the instrument groups of political marketing are the dependent variables. Hence, the relationship is only unidirectional from functions to instruments, not *vice versa*. Figure 5.11 shows clearly the importance that

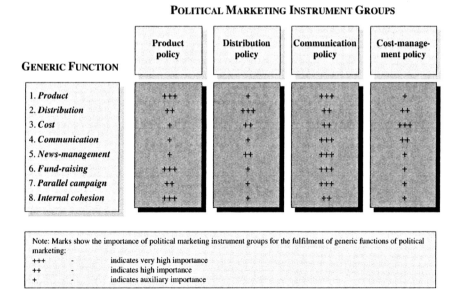

POLITICAL MARKETING INSTRUMENT GROUPS

GENERIC FUNCTION	Product policy	Distribution policy	Communication policy	Cost-management policy
1. *Product*	+++	+	+++	+
2. *Distribution*	++	+++	++	++
3. *Cost*	+	++	++	+++
4. *Communication*	+	+	+++	++
5. *News-management*	+	++	+++	+
6. *Fund-raising*	+++	+	+++	+
7. *Parallel campaign*	++	+	+++	+
8. *Internal cohesion*	+++	+	++	+

Note: Marks show the importance of political marketing instrument groups for the fulfilment of generic functions of political marketing:

+++	-	indicates very high importance
++	-	indicates high importance
+	-	indicates auxiliary importance

Figure 5.11. Matching functions and instruments of political marketing management.

communication instruments have for nearly all functions of political marketing. This backs the emphasis that has so far been given in research to this aspect. However, it also shows that it is vital to see political marketing management holistically as an integrated use of all possible operational aspects in order to meet the functional prerequisites. To give an example: product-related instruments not only have importance for the primary exchange of the product function but also serve the fund-raising and internal-cohesion function prominently. Here, possible clashes between the differing functional demands on operational political marketing management are surfacing. Looking at distribution instruments, their impact lies not only in the area of placing the exchange offer conveniently at the disposal of the prospective exchange partner (distribution function) but also in, for example, managing the cost-management function. Cost-related instruments, on the other hand, also serve the distribution as well as the communication function.

Basic versus Complementary Instruments Usage. The microelements of political marketing management—that is, the functions and instruments—allow for a delineation and clarification of the operational side of the competitive phenomena in the political market. However, these elements have to be brought into context—that is, they have to be understood as an interacting and dynamic entity. Thus, a discussion of the strategic framework of political marketing management must provide a more holistic approach. Before the strategy elements are discussed in the next subsection, an intermediate step between operational and strategic management can be made by distinguishing differing usage categories for political marketing instruments. As mentioned earlier, this is done by taking into consideration the "promotional" character of election campaigning (and other intermediate campaigns) and distinguishing it from the "permanent" aspects of political marketing management, following van Waterschoot and van den Bulte's (1992) approach of separating basic and complementary usage of marketing instruments. The rationale behind this is that there is a basic mix of political marketing instruments, facilitating a constant relationship with the target market players. This basic-instrument usage needs supplementary actions in some circumstances—that is, tactical adaptations of new strategic emphasis for the period of election campaigns (Bowler and Farrell 1992a).[32]

For political parties, most policy issues are determined in the long term (this is more pronounced the more the party follows an ideology-orientation in their product approach); the campaigning phase is normally a high-intensity fine-tuning exercise. However, the used instruments (as well as the underlying functions) of political marketing management are the same, be it for the basic or the complementary instrument mix. The main differences are, however, the intensity, planning detail and re-

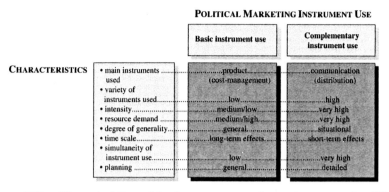

Figure 5.12.   Characteristics of basic versus complementary use of political marketing instruments.

source demand, which are extremely high for the complementary (election) campaign and its situational-orientation, which is based on short-term effectiveness. In all this, campaign political marketing management is exactly what Tocqueville called it 150 years ago: a "national crisis" (1994/1848, p. 135). Regarding the engaged instruments, the election campaign mix uses all possible political marketing instruments simultaneously, compared to a more isolated use of instruments in the permanent and basic political marketing mix. The main political marketing instruments used in the campaign are communication techniques (followed by distribution elements), while the permanent campaign uses more product-related and cost-related instruments (see Fig. 5.12). An integrated picture of constant political marketing activities emerges, with differing intensities according to contextual and situational factors (see Fig. 5.13) (Sweeney 1995).

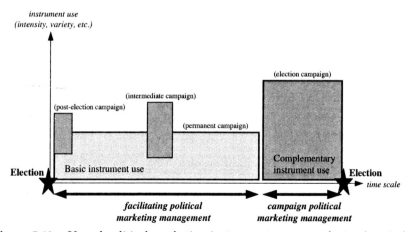

Figure 5.13.   Use of political marketing instruments over an electoral period.

Political Marketing Strategy Elements

> "The competitive nature of both elections and markets means that the strategic problems facing political candidates are essentially the same as those facing product managers."

> Mauser (1983, p. 6)

Strategic elements of political marketing management[33] surfaced earlier in this study as one of the major new characteristics that elevated the mere use of isolated marketing instruments in the political competition to a full-scale political marketing concept. They were also connected to a packaging-orientation of product positioning. This indicates the integrative power of these strategy elements, which pull together all political marketing management elements into a coherent whole with proactive—that is, market-shaping—powers. Political marketing strategy is often equated with facilitating a "rational" electioneering approach (Scammell 1991, 1994). In this subsection, three main aspects of this strategic framework are covered: a starting point is the concept of segmenting the relevant (sub)markets and the targeting of one or several of the identified segments. An appropriate positioning of the political party/candidate with regard to the target segments is the second cornerstone of the political marketing strategy. This is concerned with matching the targeting approach with internal restrictions and capabilities. The transformation of the targeting and positioning elements into an integrated strategy—that is, the coordination between the different operational realms—builds the context for a discussion of the third aspect, the political marketing mix concept.

Political Segmentation and Targeting Strategy. The segmentation approach as a foundation of a political targeting strategy does not fulfil a function *sui generis* but facilitates a targeting strategy—that is, it "reveals [. . .] market-segment opportunities" (Kotler and Armstrong 1996, p. 249).[34] However, it is often defined as a fundamental concept of marketing, although generally perceived as critical in the sense that there is no "best way" to segment the consumption side of the market structure (Loudon and Della Bitta 1993; Saunders 1995; for a comprehensive criticism of the concept see Wensley 1995). Using the classical Kotler definition, segmentation means: "Dividing a market into distinct groups of buyers with different needs, characteristics, or behavior who might require separate products or marketing mixes" (Kotler and Armstrong 1996, p. 235)

In the case of political marketing the electoral market's potential voters are clustered (disaggregated) together in homogenous groups of individuals with the same characteristics. These characteristics could be specific ideologies/issue stands sought by the voters or other "behavioural" traits (e.g. party loyalty of voters) but also geographic differentiations, and differences in demographics, sociographics or psychographics (Collins and Butler 1996; J. O'Shaughnessy 1995; Smith and Saunders 1990; Wangen 1983).[35] One of the main segmentation approaches in politics is that of competitive intensity.[36] Classical strongholds (either one's own or a competitor's) are not targeted specifically, but emphasis is targeted primarily on the constituencies with marginal results in the last elections ("marginal seats")—that is, those that are very contested (e.g. cf. Clinton's segmentation/targeting or that of many UK parties) (Harrop 1990; Newman 1994a, 1996). Multivariate methods of analysis like cluster analysis can help with this, while factor analyses can determine the "demarcation" variables (Worcester 1996). The logic behind this is to apply different political marketing strategies or instruments according to the specific demands and preferences of the identified segments of voters in order to allow for an optimal exchange process (Thurber 1995; Wortmann 1989).[37] It has to be noted that segmentation approaches, also with regard to party strategies, are somewhat conspicuously and latently present in studies of political scientists: "Political science has used a similar term in a more narrow way. Nevertheless, the phenomenon of 'catch all parties' or 'cartel parties' resonates tellingly with marketing understanding of segmentation strategies and tactics" (Collins and Butler 1996, p. 8).

This finding has been backed by a study regarding Kirchheimer's catch-all concept. Segmentation itself allows for a better overview and understanding of the market structure. However, in order to allow for a targeting approach—that is, a decision of what the segments of the markets are that should be targeted (i.e. served) by the political party— one needs to have more qualitative knowledge of the segments. This knowledge is provided by assessing the "profiles" of the market segments (Kotler and Armstrong 1996). This is done, for example, by matching behavioural and attitudinal data ("vote predominantly Social Democrat", "have strong socialist economic views") with the identified segments (of e.g. a psychographic cluster of "underachievers"). This step leads to the transformation of the segmentation approach into a targeting strategy for the political organisation—that is, the party's approach towards groups of the electorate. Before a party can decide about targeting a segment, it must assess its attractiveness—for example, its size, prospective development (e.g. if one wants to target the segment of first-time voters, one must take into account that their percentage of the electorate will decrease in time because the "senior" age groups are increasing in mature democracies)—but also its competitiveness. Competitiveness could mean, for example, that a right-wing, ideology-centred cluster has a good fit with existing niche parties, and therefore it would be a very competitive segment for a left-centre, packaged party to target. Another scenario of competitiveness would be the fact that many single-issue groups have already positioned themselves in the area of environmental anti-establishment issues. Another competitor might find it difficult to convince political activists with its specific offer because it has no "unique selling proposition". The political organisations' objectives and resources are, of course, also important for an assessment of possible target segments. A contradiction of long-standing ideological stances of a party by a chosen target segment would cause credibility losses, as seen above. Here, packaging-oriented parties have more leeway than ideology-oriented ones because their internal capabilities— that is, their potential to meet voter's preferences—are more flexible and their political history is less monolithic and extreme.

In general, a political party can follow several general targeting strategies. In the following, concentrated, undifferentiated and customised political targeting strategies are introduced and discussed in context of the ramifications for a party's competitive position.

Concentrated targeting applies when an organisation's market-coverage is targeted at a large share of one (or a few) subsegments of the electoral market (Dibb et al. 1994; Kotler and Armstrong 1996). In the political competition, this is a strategy that was followed by "mass-integration parties" in an electoral market defined by a clear-cut cleavage line (e.g. the class cleavage) (Kirchheimer 1966; Lipset and Rokkan 1966). Figure 5.14 exemplifies a two-segment market with very homogeneous "left" and "right" subcultures. Normally, two major class-based parties would try to target "their" natural market segment without much hope of appealing to sympathisers of the other segment.

With a more *differentiated* and less easily distinguishable political-preference structure in the market—that is, more voters leaning towards a greater variety of specific positions—a concentrated approach of political marketing targeting loses its appeal. This can be understood as a "remodelling" of the electoral market towards narrower issues of politics (O'Shaughnessy 1987). Such transformations of the market structure has been analysed by Kirchheimer (1966) in order to explain the appearance of what he called the "catch-all party", a *Volkspartei* that essentially follows an undifferentiated targeting approach (see Fig. 5.14) (Wangen 1983). This means a market-coverage that, to a large extent, tries to ignore segment differences and goes after the whole market (or at least a huge part of it) (Kotler and Armstrong 1996). The political offer: "will focus on what is common in the needs of consumers [read: voters] rather than on what is different" (Kotler and Armstrong 1996, p. 250), or, to use Kirchheimer's (1966) words: "National societal goals transcending group interests offer the best sales prospect for a party intent on establishing or enlarging an appeal previously limited to specific sections of the population" (p. 186). In the end, this equates to a "mass standardisa-

concentrated approach (mass-integration party)

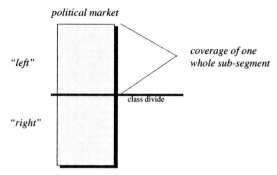

undifferentiated approach (catch-all party)

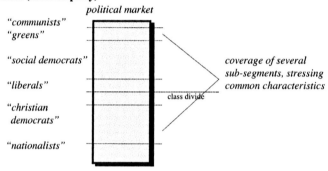

Figure 5.14. Concentrated and undifferentiated targeting approaches of political marketing management.

tion" approach of the political offer. However, even in such a market, a concentrated approach of targeting is possible but restricted to a so-called niche-approach (Collins and Butler 1995; Wangen 1983). The exclusive preference satisfaction of one subsection of the market allows some parties (e.g. "Greens" or right and left fringe parties, but also centralist parties like the German Liberals) to survive in a market of large players (if there is a proportional-representation system). However, leader or challenger positions cannot be achieved with such an approach (Butler and Collins 1996).

Further developments in the market-preference structure in the political sphere can be accommodated by a *differentiated market* coverage. Preference fragmentation has nowadays reached the degree of atomisation—that is, nearly no loyalty structures or high-attachment attitudes of the electorate are visible any more. This phenomenon is known in the political-science literature as the "party-identification decline" and is discussed in the "re-alignment" versus "de-alignment" controversy

(Crewe et al. 1977; Mair 1989, 1993). Reasons for this are social and geographical mobility, increases in educational levels and so forth (Butler and Stokes 1969; Crewe 1974; Crewe et al. 1977; Harrop 1986; Kavanagh 1995b). In such an environment it becomes more difficult to appeal to a sufficient part of the electorate with vague and common-grounded offers, touching basically only on valence issues that stress supra-segmental societal goals.

Such an undifferentiated targeting loses out against niche-market organisations that cater specifically for the benefits of the few and make no attempt to directly gain electoral success in the sense of overall majorities (Collins and Butler 1995).[38] Recent tendencies, especially in most European party systems, show that new niche-party entries into the electoral market indeed take place with increased frequency and cause a more volatile political system (Henneberg 1993).

The old "mass-standardisation" approach of mass-integration and also catch-all parties can be supplanted by a customisation of the political marketing strategy, following a differentiated market-coverage. In its extreme, this means a "micro-marketing" of segment-of-one targets. A differentiated approach involves targeting several distinct target markets not with only one offer and one political marketing strategy (standardisation) but with several separate offers and political marketing strategies/instrument mixes (customisation) for each identified target market (Webster 1994) (see Fig. 5.15). However, achieving this is extremely difficult in political marketing management. Marketing theory lays out ways in commercial marketing that political marketing cannot use—for example, differentiation by new product-line creation (Mercer 1992). Political parties simply cannot do the same. British Labour cannot form a new, additional political-product line with the name "Green Labour" in order to attract the niche-segment of environmentally ori-

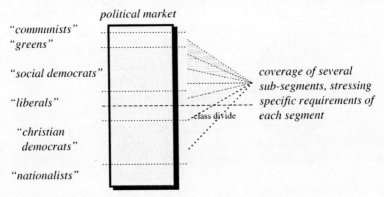

Figure 5.15. Differentiated targeting approaches of political marketing management.

ented voters. Political parties have to live with the fact that they are (perceived as) one organisation, one brand and one image. Therefore, they have to integrate product-development strategies into their existing product offer (Wangen 1983). A political targeting approach can contain several different "political offers" under one "brand framework"—for example, one with emphasis on green topics for environmentally oriented voters, one with emphasis on health care and pensions for elderly voters, one on free-market values for "achievers", and so forth. Each "programme" has a political marketing strategy tailored to suit the segment group it is targeted for. A means of delivering these programmes efficiently is consequent channel segmentation and media selection for the fulfilment of the distribution and communication function (Newman 1994a). The art of a customised targeting is to integrate these differentiated programmes and activities under a party umbrella into a cohesive and relatively consistent whole. This means living with potentially conflicting political offers (e.g. pro-environment versus pro-free-market issue stands and candidates). Such conflicts have to be resolved in a responsible manner according to the party's corporate culture, brand value or "ideology". However, if such an integration is possible, the "customised party" is able to exploit the ever more competitive electoral market, as well as to give the electoral competition stability and long-term credibility. In addition, the customised party regains the ability to proactively shape the electoral market by engaging in "intimate" relationships with their exchange partners, a capability inherent in mass-integration parties (which were themselves an expression of a social subculture) but lost with the adoption of undifferentiated targeting by the catch-all party (Mair 1989). This equates with a concept by Pomper (1992) regarding parties' attempts at regaining an "expressive mode"—that is, an affective relationship with the electorate—which got lost with the introduction of catch-all politics (i.e. an "instrumental mode").

However, targeting, especially in its customised form, is not unequivocally accepted as an optimal political marketing strategy, as the following argument by O'Shaughnessy shows: "Yet targeting contains the danger that, in focusing on particular groups, others will be ignored completely in the political dialogue, for much political material, though actually consumed inadvertently, has the effect of contributing to the citizens' political awareness . . ." (1990a, p. 74).

It will be important to watch how political parties use targeting approaches in practice because of the ethical implications of such a concept. Of interest are the new developments in media selection in the US American presidential election which allow (via cable-TV, talk radio and the flourishing of single-issue and speciality media) a very precise targeting of homogeneous market segments. First indicators of a customisation of the political offer are visible (Johnson 1997; Newman 1994a).

Political Positioning Strategy.   Political positioning strategy helps the political organisation to integrate its approach further. Positioning is concerned with several aspects: the internal capabilities of the party/candidate must be assessed; this must be brought into coordination with the external opportunities of possible target segments; and, eventually, positioning defines exactly where the party/candidate stands in the political competition in relationship to other offers by deciding on the target strategy and subsequently the positioning strategy (Bradshaw 1995; Mauser 1983).[39] This means assessing possible competitive advantages, especially regarding their sustainability (Day 1997a; Kotler and Armstrong 1996).[40] "Positioning is a marketing tool that captures the essence of a candidate's [and party's] vision and structures strategy" (Newman 1994a, p. 86).[41] All three of these aspects are discussed briefly:

Internal-capability assessment is concerned with the assessment of the strengths of the party and the available candidates. This analysis is concerned with personal traits, political assets, historical developments and so forth (Newman 1994a). For example, in order to achieve credibility as a service, the political offer must be aligned with historical characteristics: a traditionally conservative organisation cannot make leeway with Marxist topics, as it would lose its political "roots" and become volatile in the eyes of the voters. However, capability assessment is not restricted to a totally reactive approach; it also includes reasonable changes or the unearthing of unused potential in the sense of the definition of a marketing-orientation. Altogether, this type of analysis also has to be seen in context of other (existing or potential) market offerings and an assessment of the relative position and strength of the candidate/party in the context of other contenders. Mauser (1983) showed how such an approach can be modelled in a similar way to new-product development and testing techniques used in commercial marketing, using multidimensional scaling (MDS) techniques.

External opportunity analysis is based on the findings of, first, the segment assessment and, second, the internal-capability assessment. Finding a match between attractive segments and their political demands, together with possible offers based on the strengths of the party and the candidate, will show scenarios of possible strategy options—that is, competitive advantages. These have to be judged in light of the overall goal of the political organisation—for example, although sometimes the most promising strategy would be one of serving exclusively a very small segment, this is incompatible with the rationale of a people's party which essentially wants to achieve an electoral-majority position.

A *political positioning strategy* is the outcome of the interplay between the internal capability analysis and the external-opportunity analysis. Positioning does not, as seen before, mean a total remodelling of the party/candidate but an optimisation of their market approach (Baer

1995). In general, one can distinguish broadly four different generic positioning strategies, derived from marketing theory. These depend on the goals, capabilities and the existing positioning of the party/candidate. Butler and Collins (1996), in a study on strategic analysis in political markets, show that these "marketing models are robust enough to withstand the distinctive characteristics of noncommercial contexts . . ." (p. 35). They differentiate the strategic positions of

- market leader
- challenger
- follower
- nicher.

Figure 5.16 enumerates the characteristics of these market positions. Typical strategies and targeting approaches are also enumerated. Complications accrue because of the differences of market positions in different electoral systems (Butler and Collins 1996). These differences have not been included in the listing of Figure 5.16, which exemplifies an

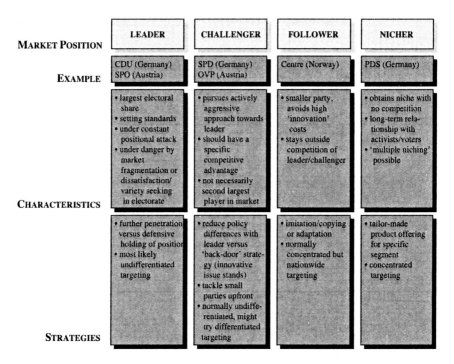

Figure 5.16. Characteristics of four generic market positions in the electoral market.

electoral system of proportional representation. However, it must be said that the system of strategic political positions in the electoral market is not precise. Certain parties—for example, the German Greens—cannot be pigeon-holed in this scheme. Although showing most characteristics of a follower, they are highly "innovative" in their political-product offering. Nevertheless, they are also not a challenger because their more concentrated targeting restricts their electoral scope to that of a small–medium party. Further research specific to the political circumstances is necessary to cover this aspect more convincingly.

Having used segmentation, targeting and positioning approaches, a political organisation has achieved the following elements: it has an overview of the preference structure of the political market, knows about groups of voters with homogeneous characteristics and can assess the general attractiveness of these segments. Furthermore, it has information about its own strength and restriction (as well as that of the other players in the market). Last, the organisation is able to combine all this information into a preferred market position with a specific market-coverage approach.[42]

The political party is now well equipped to implement these strategic aims via the appropriately guided use of political marketing instruments. This aspect of political marketing management comprises the integration of instrument groups with strategic aims as well as functional prerequisites.

Political Strategy Formulation and Implementation—The Political Marketing Mix. In this subsection the elements of the previous subsection meet again: strategic positioning and targeting on the one hand, and political marketing instrument groups on the other. The interface between both is the political marketing mix, which facilitates the formulation and implementation of the strategic issues (Wortmann 1989). The functions of political marketing management constitute the umbrella for this dialectic interplay of strategic and operational level, all in the framework of the concept of political marketing management (see Fig. 5.17) (Henneberg 1996d).

Questions of political instrument mix coordination have been grossly neglected in the literature (e.g. Farrell and Wortmann 1987; Harrop 1990; O'Shaughnessy 1990a; even the excellent study of Newman 1994a does not give them credence) which seems astonishing bearing in mind the "obsession" with the instruments themselves. Wangen (1983, p. 278) explains this as the lacking of understanding of the complexity of strategic political marketing approaches, both in theory and practice. However, when analysed, the marketing mix problem often seems to be misunderstood as representing merely the entirety of political marketing instruments—that is, the "configuration that consists of product, promo-

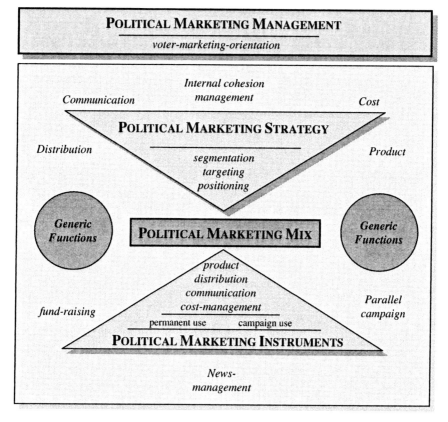

Figure 5.17. Political marketing management—overview.

tion, place and price" (Wring 1996b, p. 9). In fact, the political marketing mix as a part of strategic political marketing is concerned with the selection of appropriate marketing instruments (according to, first, the targeting and positioning strategy and, second, the necessary functional fulfilments). However, along with the mere selection goes the determination of their activity—that is, the intensity level of these instruments as well as the timing problem. Of foremost importance is the coordination of all instrumental activities for the purpose of optimising complementarity and spill-over effects between instruments and instrument groups as well as the forecasting of their interdependency and effectiveness (Kotler and Armstrong 1996; Simon 1992; Wangen 1983). Goal and targeting conflicts as well as instrument overlaps must be resolved, as must problems within instrument groups, when serving several functions (Wortmann 1989).[43] This coordination effort is notoriously difficult in marketing but is a "prerequisite for [. . .] success" (Wortmann 1989, p.

53). Especially in the environment of a "customised party"—that is, one following a differentiated targeting approach—the problems of marketing mix optimisation as well as the variety of possible intervening variables become plentiful. This is further complicated by the existence of two different marketing mixes, determined by the distinction between a basic (permanent) and a complementary (campaign) use of political marketing instruments. While the permanent political marketing mix provides the underlying platform of political marketing management, the campaign mix allows for the party's intense competitive behaviour during election campaign times (Henneberg 1996d).

To complete the tool-kit of political marketing management, some other elements deserve mentioning. Political marketing management's core comprises the strategic and operational translation of the marketing concept. In addition, there exist some auxiliary elements of political marketing that have facilitating potential for the management of polit-ical organisations. Several could be discussed here—for example, political marketing controlling or political marketing organisation and planning (Newman 1994b; Sackman 1992; Wortmann 1989)—all elements of the transformation of political parties to "professional parties" (Katz and Mair 1995; Panebianco 1988). A recent development is the role of the political consultant, a political (marketing) management expert who is essentially an external consultant to the political market (Johnson 1997; Newman 1994a; O'Shaughnessy 1987, 1990b; Peele 1982). However, for this study there is emphasis on another auxiliary element: political marketing research, which is discussed in context in chapter 6. Before that, the circle of argumentation has to be closed.

This chapter started off with some remarks regarding political marketing as a new phenomenon. Part of this was an initial discussion of the development of political marketing—that is, some stage models. The next section reintroduces this thought. However, now having a much better normative understanding of political marketing and its managerial implementation, this discussion of the development of political marketing will be "coming from the end"—that is, from a thorough understanding of the research object. Thus, the next section first argues recursively about the theoretical and conceptual development of political marketing in a marketing theory framework; second, a modified stage model is introduced; and, third, the determinants of changes in political marketing management activities are analysed.

The Development of Political Marketing

The following subsections go back to the level of the *theory of political marketing* by highlighting the genesis of political marketing. Such an analysis must obviously start with a discussion of the conceptual prerequisites of the development of political marketing inasmuch as marketing theory was originally understood exclusively in a commercial context. Therefore, along the way of marketing theory development there must have evolved a "junction" that allowed the conceptual rationale for political marketing to develop.

Political Marketing and Marketing Theory—Developments

Although this is one of the better-documented aspects of political marketing theory (e.g. O'Cass 1996), it is nevertheless important enough to justify a brief recapitulation. The so-called broadening of the marketing concept (Kotler and Levy 1969) introduced a way of thinking that eventually enlarged the scope of marketing from commercial markets of profit organisations with product or service exchanges to those additionally comprising non-profit organisations and their specific exchange relationships (Raffee and Wiedmann 1995). This development was also the theoretical "birthplace" of political marketing. Bagozzi raises this broad approach even to the heights of a new paradigm in Kuhn's sense (Bagozzi 1975). It is noteworthy that this development was partly stimulated and influenced by research on the marketing activities of political parties and candidates in the US political system—namely, the contribution of McGinnis (1969: catch-phrase, Nixon as a "product"). The premise was that every organisation had a product, be it goods, a person, a service or an idea. Social causes, but also religions or ideologies, were now part of marketing-relevant exchange processes because these explananda were acknowledged as falling into the sphere of marketing theory. The theoretical umbrella of non-profit marketing (Hunt 1976) can be divided into two activities, both distinct from commercial marketing: classical non-profit marketing (e.g. marketing of a museum or a university) and social marketing (e.g. marketing of social ideas such as anti-smoking) (Fox and Kotler 1980; Kotler 1979; Kotler and Zaltman 1971).[44] Political marketing falls essentially into the second category.

The concept of widening the scope of marketing was not unanimously regarded as either worthwhile or theoretically justified: several arguments were voiced against the new approach (Arndt 1978; Enis 1973; Luck 1969, 1974). Furthermore, the enlargement of the scope of marketing went through different phases of theoretical development.

Kotler himself enlarged his diffuse concept once again. While originally focusing on non-pecuniary exchanges, he developed a "generic concept" that also included the wider public—that is, indirect exchange partners or stakeholders (Hunt 1976; Kotler 1972). Today, the enlarged concept of marketing, with its introduction of non-profit marketing, is established and is part of the core of marketing. It did not become a "blind alley for the discipline [of marketing]" (Arndt 1978). Nevertheless, caution is needed in the use of marketing and marketing management theories in the area of non-profit marketing. One has to agree with Foxall's argument that these concepts should only be applied in areas where "real" market characteristics and exchange mechanisms are existent. Therefore, the rash incorporation of any activity into the sphere of marketing seems overambitious (Foxall 1984a). However, this problem does not apply to political marketing, as acknowledged by received wisdom and shown in the analysis of macroelements above (Henneberg 1995a).

Political Marketing Management Stages

Phase models of political marketing, developed with an eye to elementary marketing stage models, prove to be unsatisfactory because of their "one-to-one" adaptation. They are normally "comparative static"—that is, they highlight certain points in time of a development without an endogenous understanding of the dynamics in between. However, these dynamics—that is, the reasons and determinants why political marketing management has developed—are of real interest to political scientists as well as marketers. Therefore, this subsection, in conjunction with the next one, tries to outline the stages as well as dynamics of political marketing management. This is done by using the concept of political marketing management philosophies (similar to Wring 1996b) but integrating it with information on strategic and operational elements. Furthermore, all "philosophies" are allowed to coexist in a political system at the same time (indeed, it is assumed that they normally do), determined by the political parties' perceptions of the market structure and its derived political marketing strategy. Underlying this is, again, Kotler and Armstrong's (1996) concept of the gradual development of the complexity of marketing philosophies, developed from the original model (Kotler 1972).[45]

The Political Selling Philosophy. Figure 5.18, shows the characteristics of the political selling philosophy (the "commercial equivalent" has also been juxtaposed in the figure for comparison purposes). Underlying the selling philosophy, as mentioned before, is an "inside-out" perspective. It focuses on existing political programmes and ideologies, uses mainly (social) propaganda and push promotion (isolated-communication approaches), and prefers a concentrated but nationwide targeting approach (O'Shaughnessy 1990a, 1996a, 1996b). The political market (or better: the political party's perception of it) is characterised by a split in clear-cut social subsegments. The main end for the political organisation is electoral power through propaganda and "education". This approach, essentially that of a mass-integration party, is arguably still the underly-

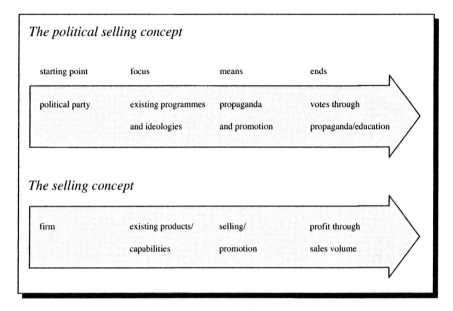

Figure 5.18.   Political selling philosophy.

ing thinking of many political organisations, although the political market has changed considerably. Such a finding is in line with a recent analysis of the adaptation of the "marketing concept" in political parties (O'Cass 1996).

One example of a party following such an approach was British Labour until 1995. Although Neil Kinnock and John Smith led the party into a transition phase, it was still essentially a class-based party of a selling mentality (Bartle 1995; Wring 1995a). A very good summary of this political management philosophy has been given by Kotler himself:

The selling concept [is also] practiced in the non-profit area. A political party, for example, will vigorously sell its candidate to voters as a fantastic person for the job. The candidate works in voting precincts from dawn to dusk—shaking hands, kissing babies, meeting donors, making speeches. Much money is spent on radio and television advertising, posters, and mailings. The candidate's flaws are hidden from the public because the aim is to get the sale, not to worry about consumer satisfaction afterwards. (Kotler and Armstrong 1996, p. 16)

The focus on a fixed ideological and programmatic world view ("how can we sell our ideology to the people") causes parties to neglect voters' wants and alienates them. Ideological rigour is seen to dominate, not the benefits of the electorate. Such a management philosophy of ideology-orientation can cause credibility and legitimacy problems for the whole political party system when it is perpetuated in a changing electoral market, especially when facing shifting value systems and a "consumer ethos" (Bauer et al. 1995; Kirchheimer 1966). One example of a reaction to parties neglecting a necessary adaptation of their political management philosophy is that of the "critical" 1993 Canadian general elections (Clarke and Kornberg 1996).

The Political Marketing Management Philosophy. A concept that allows for a more flexible approach towards the electorate is the political marketing management philosophy (see Fig. 5.19). It is founded on voter-orientation and takes into account the electorate's needs and wants, and it tries to achieve a high level of exchange satisfaction—that is, it is based on responsiveness and reciprocity. This is the opposite of the inward-oriented "ideology-satisfaction" mentality of the political selling concept. In comparison, the political marketing philosophy is not inherently elitist like the political selling philosophy but seems to be better suited to an egalitarian approach and also plebiscitarian and participatory approaches (Abramson et al. 1988; O'Shaughnessy 1990a; Scammell 1995). Integrated marketing approaches—that is, sophisticated and coordinated political marketing strategies (e.g. undifferentiated or differentiated targeting)—are used and a packaging approach of strategic-product positioning is favoured. Tony Blair's "New" Labour Party and most American presidential campaigns fall into this management philosophy. However, especially in the European party systems, it is normally not

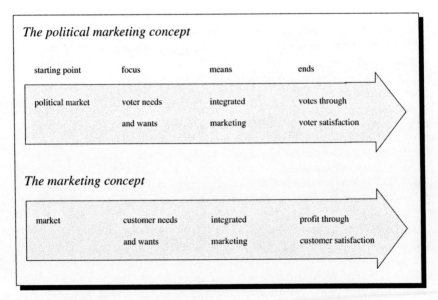

Figure 5.19. Political marketing management philosophy.

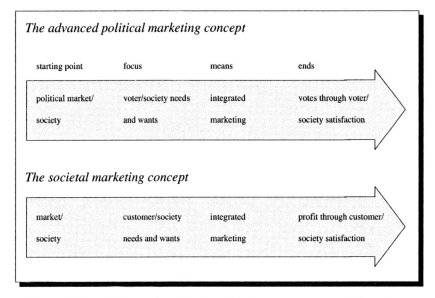

The advanced political marketing concept

starting point	focus	means	ends
political market/ society	voter/society needs and wants	integrated marketing	votes through voter/ society satisfaction

The societal marketing concept

| market/ society | customer/society needs and wants | integrated marketing | profit through customer/ society satisfaction |

Figure 5.20.   Advanced political marketing management philosophy.

widely used and, if at all, normally by the challenger party. However, Blair's significant victory in the 1997 general election makes this concept attractive to other parties and party systems. One first sign of such a development was that of the Norwegian 1997 general elections but also some state elections in Germany.[46]

The Advanced Political Marketing Management Philosophy.   Besides these two relatively opposed political marketing philosophies, one can derive an "advanced" version of the political marketing management philosophy, founded in the conceptual criticism of the fundamentals of marketing. In order to get to grips with the inherently reactive and populistic nature of the classical political marketing concept (its demagogic nature is one of the main targets of critics), Kotler's societal marketing concept can be adapted to the political sphere.

Although customer-orientation is still the core element, society's well-being is also considered (see Fig. 5.20). The (possible) conflict between the wants of the voters and the long-term well-being of society (and the ideological idea of how to bring about such an utopian state) has to be resolved by responsible marketing, inspired by a more general stakeholder approach (Houston 1986). While the political selling concept is too monolithic (elitist), the political marketing philosophy can be too fickle (populistic) (Stoiber 1983). Societal well-being needs a long-term perspective and a general policy framework. Therefore, a restricted political marketing concept seems more appropriate, especially in political markets with more and more "voter sophistication" but also voter disillusionment and competition with the very "opinionated" sphere of "low politics". Not only the wants of the voters but also societal needs are guidelines for the competitive behaviour of parties following this philosophy. The concept is "restricted" insofar as it focuses on more than the immediate target group(s). However, this does not mean a revival of an ideology-orientation, as one might be tempted to believe. If one looks at this philosophy in more detail, it becomes clear that, on the contrary, the societal needs can be incorporated into politics via a general framework concept that is able to learn—that is, the political offer is stable but not monolithic like an ideology, responsive but not educational. Although one may still call these frameworks "ideologies", they have more similarities to corporate cultures of competitive organisations. In this sense, they can be called "image ideologies". Newman (1996) speaks in this context of "ideology as a 'labeling' process" (p. 12). These are behavioural and intellectual guidelines for the party that give the electoral efforts a certain hold by interacting with people's values and preference systems.[47] This new kind of image ideology, though different from ideological concepts of the mass-integration party, reflects its heritage, bringing credibility to the political offer and legitimacy to the political competition. Baer (1995), in an analysis of the US elections, shows that such a rationale underlies the concept of what she calls "strategic candidates" (p. 59). Furthermore, similar ideas surface in political science as well (Budge 1994). An advanced political marketing philosophy is partly the base for Bill Clinton's campaigning activities. However, many aspects of the traditional political marketing philosophy are still visible, especially in his governmental marketing, which is essentially a perpetuation of his campaign marketing strategy (and therefore ineffective in the sense of governing) (Newman 1993, 1995a, 1995b).

It is interesting to note that this restricted concept is in line with the definition of political marketing given above. In particular the societal element, as well as the (long-term) satisfaction of voters, is at the core of both.

Determinants of Political Marketing Management Activities

> "The use of television has probably been the greatest catalyst in changing the marketing/political relationship from implicit to explicit."
>
> Rothschild (1978, p. 58)

It has been said that all three political marketing philosophies can coexist in a party system. In addition, it has been alluded to that parties might change the philosophy of their electoral approach in time. It has been established above that it is important to know about the determinants of these transitions. Received knowledge in political marketing is that changes in the electoral strategy as well as in the overall political marketing philosophy are essentially technology-determined. More often than not, this is enumerated as the dominating, if not the only reason, for political parties to "develop" managerially (Harrop 1990; Wring 1995b; see Newman 1994b, who allows for a more rounded argument). Technology-determination in this context refers to the development of new media technologies, starting with the introduction of mass media like radio and later television (along with the proliferation of advertisements) (O'Shaughnessy 1987) and continuing with the sophistication of these elements—for example, via interactive or cable-TV, but also by the development of new media presentation forms like news conferences or other communication instruments like large-scale direct-mailings (Kavanagh 1995b; Newman 1994a, 1994b). Therefore, political marketing is sometimes also referred to as "electronic electioneering" (Newman 1996, p. 2). Altogether, the sole developer of the understanding of political marketing lies, according to this argument, in communication policies fostered by media-technology developments. Such lines of argumentation can be found among political management practitioners as well as among scholars. Wring (1995b) reports that Nick Grant, the UK Labour Director of Publicity for the 1983 campaign, sees the development of marketing in politics as part of the development of a "science in communication". O'Shaughnessy and Wring (1994) credit the "evolution of mass media-centred electoral races" to "technological advance" via "embrac[ing] the opportunities presented by both television and advertising" (p. 246).

Harrop explicitly concludes that "advances in political marketing respond to developments in the media" (1990, p. 284) and Kavanagh introduces his book on "the new marketing of politics" by stating: "Election campaigning adapts by employing the latest techniques and ideas in effective communications and persuasions" (1995b, p. 8).

This monocausal argument is not conclusive and also contradicts the fact that strategic elements elevate the simplistic use of marketing instruments to a full-scale political marketing concept. Therefore, it is necessary to analyse the determinants within a broader context and use a marketing-related rationale (Mercer 1992). The enumerated aspects of media, its technological development and the subsequently emerging possibilities of new communication instruments are, of course, one of the main aspects of a transformation of political marketing philosophies. However, these are only facilitators—that is, means that enable a reaction to the real drivers of change: first, the underlying electoral market structure and, second, the specific strategic response (Newman 1994a). These determinants have been recognised in a different context—for example, by Farrell and Wortmann (1987):

political marketing can be viewed as part of an overall shift in the electoral process towards a more competitive basis for electoral competition and for electoral choice [read: the structure of the electoral market]. Political marketing represents the evolution of party strategies [read: the strategic response] in a changing electoral process. (p. 314)

A change in the market structure—for example, preferences or characteristic changes of the electorate or new competitors (or new competitive markets like that of "low politics")—is the basic imitator of change (Katz and Mair 1995). To be precise, "objective" changes are not of foremost importance to political parties, they react to subjective—that is, perceived—changes of the market structure. Political parties react to a variety of structural stimuli: the emergence of a new political "ideology" (e.g. green issues), the loosening of party attachment by the voters (e.g. a general party-identification crisis) (Heath and McDonald 1988), or simply by having lost consecutive elections (e.g. Smith's and Blair's attempts to modernise Labour after three lost elections) (O'Shaughnessy and Wring 1994). Strategic development is one way for an organisation to adapt proactively to these market changes (Newman 1994b)—for example, by introducing new targeting strategies, new strategic-product positioning, or a totally new orientation of the whole political party, such as towards advanced marketing philosophies. The deployment of more sophisticated political marketing activities is therefore a sign of markets developing towards more competitiveness and less predictability (Bowler and Farrell 1992a; Farrell and Wortmann 1987). Exactly these strategic adaptations are the essence of what Panebianco (1988), in an analysis of political party's organisational structure, has called "professionalisation" in a so-called "electoral-professional party", brought to an extreme in "cartel parties" (Katz and Mair 1995).[48]

Research on Political Marketing

Having developed political marketing as a concept it is now time to go back to the question of research on political marketing. This chapter has outlined an initial concept of political marketing which serves as a benchmark model for an evaluation of the overall knowledge base, represented by publications (books, articles, theses) in the area of political marketing.[49]

This *tour de force* through an assessment and evaluation of political marketing research is based on a database at the Judge Institute of Management Studies (compiled by the author) containing all available sources on the topic. Although the number of publications between 1980 and 1997 has grown to about 350, the results are still structurally similar to a comparable approach done by Reid (1988) in preparation for his studies on political marketing. The database was assembled using a comprehensive computer-based screening technique of published and unpublished research in the English-speaking world. The criteria for inclusion into the database are divided into hard and soft ones. Hard criteria comprise:

- use and/or naming of the concept "political marketing";
- use of theories, methods and so forth from both areas—political science *and* marketing;
- use of seminal sources of research in political marketing (e.g. Newman 1994a; O'Shaughnessy 1990a).

If two of the three hard criteria are fulfilled, the source is included in the database automatically. If only one (in special cases, none) of the criteria is fulfilled, soft criteria are used in an auxiliary manner. If one or two of these apply, inclusion into the database follows. Soft criteria are:

- the explanandum of the source is important and directly relevant for research in political marketing;
- political marketing is not the main aspect of the source but innovative results/theories are discussed with repercussions for political marketing;
- seminal sources of political marketing refer to this source in relationship to their conceptual analysis of political marketing.

Obviously this procedure is an extremely subjective one. Therefore, the judgement for inclusion was checked by another experienced researcher in the field of political marketing. The overall interrater reliability was 0.92, a very satisfactory figure.

Overview of Research in Political Marketing

The author (Henneberg 1995b) argued that, based on a classificational scheme of political marketing, there are nominally four main areas of research, each subdivided into a normative and a descriptive sphere. Figure 5.21 shows different "research schools of political marketing", using concepts developed by Sheth et al. (1988). All sources have been classified into this scheme.[50] In the *microtheory of political marketing*, the voter-behaviour school is dominant, although there are also some beginnings of an exchange school. In the area of microtheory, a foundation for managerial application is provided by analysing the behaviour of individual parties, voters or other players in the political market. In the normative tradition, the rational/public-choice theory dominates, inspired by approaches of political economy (Brennan and Lomasky 1993).

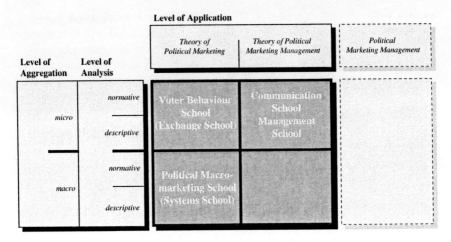

Figure 5.21.   Research schools of political marketing.

In the descriptive area, these approaches are subsumed under the "positive political-economy" umbrella (Alt and Shepsie 1990). However, marketing-related models of party or voter decision-making are very rare. Although many political-science studies of voter behaviour can be subsumed here (Columbia as well as Michigan school and psychological/socio-psychological models), these conventional studies are supplemented by very isolated cases of holistic and political management-related analyses (e.g. Himmelweit et al. 1985; Sniderman et al. 1993; Popkin 1994; especially Newman and Sheth 1987, and Reid 1988). This microtheory level characterises one of the main shortcomings in research on political marketing theory.

The second area of neglected research problems can be found on the macrolevel of the *theory of political marketing* (the same can also be said for the *theory of political marketing management*). In the normative cell, ethical problems of political marketing and aspects touching the theory of democracy are covered (e.g. the ethical repercussions of the use of specific political marketing instruments, or possible problems and developments in the area of the theory of democracy in connection with the use of the marketing concept in the political competition) (e.g. Banker 1992; Denton 1991a, 1991b, 1991c; Fowler 1995; Franklin 1994; Jamieson 1992a; Michalos 1991; O'Shaughnessy 1989/90). This can be subsumed under the heading of political macromarketing (Barry and Jenkins 1977; Meade and Nason 1991). The descriptive macrolevel is of less interest as a focus of research: the characteristics of the political market—its underlying players and processes as well as the competitive interactions as a whole (a political systems school of political marketing)—are the main subject of only some publications; furthermore, definitional attempts and framework theories of political marketing are covered (e.g. Axford and Huggins 1995; Hasitschka 1995; Henneberg 1995a, 1996a; Newman 1994a; O'Shaughnessy and Wring 1994; Wangen 1983; Wortmann 1989).

However, the *theory of political marketing management* is much better covered by research activities. About 70% of all publications can be found here (of which 80% are mainly concerned with micro-topics). Two main schools have "institutionalised" themselves: a communication school and a management school. In the normative cell, all aspects of political marketing management instruments and, less comprehensively, strategies are focused on: political marketing research (e.g. Mauser 1980, 1983; Worcester 1996), political marketing strategies (e.g. Butler and Collins 1996; Newman 1994a; O'Shaughnessy 1990a), political marketing instruments (e.g. O'Shaughnessy and Peele 1985). Even more frequent are, however, descriptive studies concerning election campaigns, with a bias towards communication and news-management aspects (e.g. Arnold 1995; Boll and Poguntke 1992; Bowler and Farrell 1992a, 1992b; Farrell and Wortmann 1987; Harrop 1990; Kaid and Holtz-Bacha 1995b; Kavanagh 1995b; Newman 1993, 1995b; Scammell 1995). The strict "segregation" between political scientists in the descriptive sphere and marketers in the normative one has been mentioned earlier.

Evaluation of Research in Political Marketing

A brief evaluation has to follow this enumeration. Specific interest is on gaps in the research web, especially those that endanger the development of political marketing into a theoretically sound and methodologically rigorous discipline. As seen in the subsection above, although the area of political marketing management has been covered relatively comprehensively, other areas have not been tackled with the same vigour. Nevertheless, even in managerial research on political marketing there are structural deficiencies—for example, the conceptual/terminological problems between marketers and other involved researchers, the suboptimal coverage of strategic aspects, the bias towards communication instruments/functions (Bowler and Farrell 1992a; Butler and Collins 1996; Harris 1996; Henneberg 1995b, 1996a, 1996c). Improvements in these areas are, however, not imminent if the theoretical foundation is neglected, as has been done so far. This is a strong argument for a conceptual foundation of managerial analysis of political marketing (be it descriptive or prescriptive) in a theoretical and definitional framework (as has been provided for this study by this chapter). Two prominent research areas need improvement on the level of the *theory of political marketing:* the mentioned theoretical framework, and the understanding of the main exchange partners—for example, in the electoral market, the electorate. Only if knowledge about the motivations, determinants and processes of voters' rationalisation (or "ir-rationalisation") are available is it possible to develop, analyse or criticise political marketing management.

NOTES

1. Unfortunately, Wortmann's (1989) important study did not follow his own rationale but instead steered clear of "set[ting] up a *useful overall framework*" (p. 10), thus merely descriptively analysing the campaign behaviour of German parties.

2. One example of a "misuse" of marketing concepts in this regard is Franklin (1995, p. 2). In this study he assumes that political marketing activities are a subgroup of communication activities.

3. This is especially important if, as Karvonen (1991) argues, campaign analyses have so far focused more on the American model.

4. For a good discussion of the problem inherent in the comparison of American and European political management activities in the context of differing party systems, see Kavanagh (1995b, chapter 10).

5. The term "analytical definition" refers to its strong linkage with the marketing *concept* itself, in contrast to some definitions of (political) marketing that are built on a mere understanding of what is called by Houston "weak implementation. ... The marketing concept does not consist of advertising, selling and promotion" (1986, p. 86). These "definitions" are in fact not definitions in the narrow sense of the word but descriptions of the necessary behavioural conditions for a fulfilment of the demands of the marketing concept.

6. The best elucidation of transaction/exchange relationships is still that found in Aldersen (1957).

7. It is interesting to note that there is a qualitative difference in the treatment of the attitudes of the target actors (voters/consumers) in political science and marketing. While marketing is concerned with needs and wants of individuals (or small purchasing groups like families) or at least of homogeneous groups, these preference structures surface in political science mostly in their aggregate form of *the* "public opinion", a much more diverse and unfocused concept. This distinction between micro- and macro-perspective seems to be exemplifying genuine differences between these two mother-disciplines of political marketing, which will become important later in the study as well (Scarbrough 1991).

8. For a more detailed discussion of other aspects of criticism of the customer-orientation concept see Dickinson et al. (1986) or Houston (1986).

9. These three behavioural aspects have to be seen in context of two guiding decision criteria—that is, long-term focus and profitability (Narver and Slater 1990).

10. It is noteworthy that marketers as well as political scientists agree in general about this characteristic, even though the very often heard polemic (e.g. by Lord Young, see Franklin 1994, p. 4) that political marketing means treating politics like "washing powder" or "cornflakes" (to mention only two of the most

popular comparisons) would contradict this rationale. The analogy with, for example, a "hair-cut", would show better insight on the side of the critics.

11. In the United States, the "electorate" can be very limited locally—for example, at elections for district sheriff (Johnson 1997).

12. In political science these relationships are still hotly debated, especially regarding who has "highjacked" whom (Franklin 1994, p. 10). However, Franklin also shows very convincingly that the two factions of parties/government and media are, in fact, not totally divided camps but highly interactive.

13. The number of activists in a political system is often underestimated, perhaps because political parties are not good at using this latent potential (Kavanagh 1995b).

14. This analysis overlaps with Newman's (1994a) discussion of "power brokers" in the political sphere. However, his categories of consultants and pollsters have been excluded because they are seen as professional "appendices" of the political organisation/candidate in question (Panebianco 1988).

15. "High" and "low" are obviously neutral connotations in this context.

16. Note that this is opposed to the political-science assumption of political-goal-orientation motivated by the introduction of an idea/ideology while vote-seeking is only and (intermediate) mean. More research on an integrated approach towards goal functions in the political sphere seems necessary (Schmidtchen 1974).

17. It is noteworthy that some parties gain government positions without unambiguous electoral support but due to their power position in the political system (e.g. in a two-and-a-half-party system). One example is the German FDP, where there exists constant coalition-building (Wortmann 1989).

18. This technical term originates from marketing theory and must not be mistaken for political "policies".

19. This study does not follow Wortmann's (1989) limited use of the product function by eliminating candidate-related aspects from product considerations.

20. Wortmann (1989) mixes electoral and governmental political market exchanges in a circular understanding of exchanges in order to allow for the development of a cost element, based on an "imputed balance" in the transaction system (pp. 49–51).

21. Even Newman (1994a), in the most comprehensive analysis of political marketing management to date, substitutes pricing elements by "polling", yet concedes that "the point could be stretched and an argument made that there is a price that comes with voting for one candidate over another" (p. 105). There are other attempts to get to grips with "pricing" in political marketing that do not convince (e.g. Farrell and Wortmann 1987).

22. However, there are also direct ways of communication—for example, via "town-hall" style meetings, canvassing, rallies, mailings, or telephone solicitation.

23. However, this element of news-management is normally overrated in its importance, or, simply put: "Losers spin; winners grin" (Anonymous 1996, p. 79).

24. Besides its communicative element, there is a very tangible aspect to news-management. To quote Anonymous (1996) again: "But the real campaign was what happened *between* those events now. It was about whatever J.S. [synonym for Bill Clinton] chose to say in response to the fusillade from the sullen throng

that began to follow us around; it was about the logistics of ferrying these people—who had suddenly materialized from nowhere, gulls following a garbage barge—from place to place, and providing the facilities, multi-boxes and risers and all the rest, so that they could hound us and pound *us* . . ." (p. 105, emphasis in original).

25. Exceptions from this rule do exist in some countries where the electoral result is the benchmark for state subsidies to political parties/candidates—for example, see the practice of "*Wahlkampfkostenzuschuss*" in Germany (Boll and Poguntke 1992; Sontheimer 1993). However, these subsidies have to be complemented by other sources of party income; they are not sufficient in the long run (Bowler and Farrell 1992b).

26. "We flew a Gulfstream. . . . The plane had been made available by a prominent music-industry homosexual several weeks earlier, when our prospects seemed more plausible. (The 'rental' rate was give-away cheap, the policy implication troubling.)" (Anonymous 1996, p. 145).

27. It must be noted that there are also dissenting arguments that state "that most of the marketing instruments can only be used in terms of planning. The only operational instrument is the communication policy" (Wortmann 1989, p. 298). However, from the context it seems as if Wortmann wants to have this "normative" conclusion understood as a "descriptive" summary of findings regarding the use of political marketing instruments by German political parties.

28. However, Scammell argues convincingly that "Thatcherism was not so much ideology but more a style of leadership and a set of values" (1994, p. 25). This statement corresponds with the concept of an "image ideology" as part of an advanced political marketing concept (discussed below under "Product Policy").

29. These mailings need not necessarily be letters. American elections have seen videotape mailing of ads which in fact have never been broadcast on television but were only used through this highly targeted method (Kaid and Holtz-Bacha 1995a).

30. Thatcher did this by constantly denouncing even sympathetic media like the BBC (Scammell 1991).

31. "Stanton's case against Harris, succinct and deadly as it seemed in real life, was too long, too complicated to communicate in a two-minute spot on the evening news . . ." (Anonymous 1996, p. 178).

32. However, promotional activities can also be used for the management of, for example, the launch of a new "policy offensive" or the introduction of a new party leader. This is called an intermediate campaign.

33. Note that "strategy" in this study is understood as facilitating a matching exercise between (internal) capabilities and (external) opportunities, in accordance with marketing strategy literature (Bourgeois 1996). A different approach towards political marketing strategy, based on a redefinition of operational aspects, can be found in Newman (1994a, chapter 6).

34. Although one can only agree with Collins and Butler (1996) that segmentation in itself is no strategy but only a means for analysis, this study does not follow their argument that the segmentation–targeting–positioning approach for political parties does precede the real strategic consideration (e.g. product differentiation). Legal and technological constraints (Collins and Butler do not elaborate further on this) cannot be used in order to argue that the inflexibility in the

political market does not allow political parties to use full-scale positioning strategies.

35. Typically a multidimensional approach is chosen (Kotler and Armstrong 1996). However, political managers must decide whether they want to use a *post hoc* or an *a priori* segmentation—that is, whether the clustering variables are given (typically used by political scientists: e.g. Wring 1996b or Bradshaw 1995) or will evolve during the segmentation research (Collins and Butler 1996; Smith and Saunders 1990).

36. The approach of competitive intensity is an *a priori* one.

37. Curious in this contest is the assessment of targeting by some political scientists: Harrop, for example, argues in favour of targeting as an effective method of political marketing managers because, if a specific marketing strategy works with the target voters, it also works in general for other groups of the electorate (e.g. Harrop 1990, p. 233, or Kavanagh 1995b, p. 21)! This rationale is diametrically opposed to the logic of targeting and resembles more an argument in favour of the use of focus groups.

38. Although Kirchheimer himself did not see the vulnerability of the catch-all party in such a changing electoral market, other political scientists stress this point (Mair 1989; Smith 1989). In marketing terms, this resembles partly a SWOT analysis (Mercer 1992).

39. In marketing terms, this resembles partly a SWOT analysis (Mercer 1992).

40. Of course, this position always has to be understood as the "perceived" position—that is, the position as seen by the electorate (or specific segments of it). "Objective" positions—for example, obtained by an analysis of manifesto positions (as practised by political scientists)—have no value in this context.

41. Newman's (1994a) approach towards political positioning strategy is slightly different. However, it exemplifies all aspects that are covered in this study.

42. Of course, all these instruments of strategic analysis can also be used by the researcher in order to get to grips with occurrence in the political market. The author would go further and argue that it is indeed a prerequisite to have knowledge about these elements in order to be in a position to assess competitive political behaviour today.

43. It must always be kept in mind that mix management is an extremely complicated process, which, as marketing theory teaches us, is necessarily a compromise: positive instrument interactions have to be weighted with negative ones (Nieschlag et al. 1994).

44. This distinction is only one possible classification. In fact, there exists some uncertainty about the content of the concept of non-profit marketing. Luck (1974) speaks in this context of a "semantic jungle" and an intolerable "anarchy in the terminology" (p. 72).

45. Earlier concepts mentioned in Kotler (1972), like the production or the product concept era, have been neglected in the following analysis.

46. For example, in September 1997 the Hamburgian SPD used an imitation of Blair's concept of a "packaged" social democratic party (sometimes even by literally taking over catch-phrases). This election was notable for the rejection of this concept by the voters.

47. Although this concept seems to be a very modern one, it essentially ap-

pears already in Schumpeter's discussion of the topic: "Denn alle Parteien werden sich natuerlich jederzeit mit einem Vorrat von Prinzipien oder Rettungsplanken vergehen, und diese Prinzipien oder Planken koennen ebenso charakteristisch fuer die Partei, die sie annimmt, und ebenso wichtig fuer ihren Erfolg sein, wie die Warenzeichen der Artikel, die ein Warenhaus verkauft, fuer diese charakteristisch und fuer seinen Erfolg wichtig sind" (1993/1950, p. 449).

48. The concept of the "cartel party" does not fit very well into a political marketing analysis. It is a hybrid of extreme political marketing orientation, professionalisation of politics, a merging of state and party interests, individualisation of competition, and so forth (Katz and Mair 1995, especially table on p. 18). Although very illuminating, the concept needs further clarification (Koole 1996).

49. This subsection is based on work done for special literature at the University of Mannheim as well as on a paper given at the EPOP conference 1995 (Henneberg 1995b).

50. This "clustering" was complicated by the fact that some sources touch upon several aspects/levels of the classification scheme. Normally the dominant argument was used for categorisation purposes. However, again there is a large amount of subjectivity existent in this procedure, checked again by a second researcher (interrater reliability 0.9) (Henneberg 1995b).

REFERENCES

Abramson, J. B., Arterton, F. C., and Orren, G. R. (1988), *The Electronic Commonwealth*, New York, Basic Books.

Aldersen, W. (1957), *Marketing Behavior and Executive Action*, Homewood, Irwin.

Alt, J. E., and Shepsie, K. A. (eds.) (1990), *Perspectives on Positive Political Economy*, Cambridge, Cambridge University Press.

Andreason, A. R. (1993), "A social marketing research agenda for consumer behavior researchers", *Advances in Consumer Research*, vol. 20, 1–5.

Anonymous (1996), *Primary Colors*, London, Chatto & Windus.

Ansolabehere, S., and Iyengar, S. (1995), "Winning through advertising: It's all in the context", in J. A. Thurber and C. J. Nelson (eds.), *Campaigns and Elections American Style*, Boulder, Westview, pp. 101–111.

Arndt, J. (1978), "How broad should the marketing concept be?", *Journal of Marketing* vol. 42, 101–103.

Arnold, S. D. (1995), "Political marketing in the European Parliamentary Elections: The Liberal Democrat campaign in Humberside. A case study", in S. C. Henneberg and N. O'Shaughnessy (eds.), *Political Marketing—Evolving Science or Maturing Art? Conference Proceedings*, Judge Institute of Management Studies, Cambridge University.

Axford, B., and Huggins, R. (1995), "Political marketing and the aestheticization of political identities: Modernist politics and postmodern trends in the UK, Italy and the USA", in S. C. Henneberg and N. O'Shaughnessy (eds.), *Political Marketing—Evolving Science or Maturing Art? Conference Proceedings*, Judge Institute of Management Studies, Cambridge University.

Axford, B., Huggins, R., and Massa, A. (1996), "Is Forza Italia a party-political trope? Postmodern populism and the reconfiguration of Italian politics", in S. C. Henneberg, N. O'Shaughnessy and S. Eghbalian (eds.), *Political*

Marketing. Conference Proceedings, Judge Institute of Management Studies, Cambridge, Cambridge University.

Baer, D. (1995), "Contemporary strategy and agenda setting", in J. A. Thurber and C. J. Nelson (eds.), *Campaigns and Elections American Style*, Boulder, Westview, pp. 47–61.

Bagozzi, R. P. (1974), "Marketing as an organized behavioral system of exchange", *Journal of Marketing*, vol. 38, 77–81.

Bagozzi, R. P. (1975), "Marketing as exchange", *Journal of Marketing*, vol. 39, 32–39.

Bagozzi, R. P. (1978), "Marketing as exchange: A theory of transactions in the marketplace", *American Behavioral Scientist*, vol. 21, 535–556.

Bagozzi, R. P. (1995), "Reflections on relationship marketing in consumer markets", *Journal of the Academy of Marketing Science*, vol. 23, 272–277.

Banker, S. (1992), "The ethics of political marketing practices: The rhetorical perspective", *Journal of Business Ethics*, vol. 11, 843–848.

Barry, B. (1991), "Is democracy special?", in *Democracy and Power: Essays in Political Thought*, Oxford, Clarendon, pp. 24–60.

Barry, B., and Jenkins, R. L. (1977), "Macromarketing", *Journal of Marketing*, vol. 38, 73–76.

Bartle, J. (1995), *Market Analogies, the Marketing of Labour and the Origins of New Labour*, Paper presented at the Elections, Parties and Public Opinion Conference, Guildhall University, London (15–17 September).

Bauer, H. H. (1995), "Ist Marketing (zu etwas) gut?", in H. H. Bauer and H. Diller (eds.), *Wege zum Marketing*, Berlin, Duncker & Humblot, pp. 137–160.

Bauer, H. H., Huber, F., and Herrmann, A. (1995), "Politik-Marketing—Inhalt, Instrumente und Institutionen", *Der Markt*, vol. 34, 115–124.

Bauer, H. H., Huber, F., and Herrmann, A. (1996), "Political marketing: An information-economic analysis", *European Journal of Marketing*, vol. 30, no. 10, 159–172.

Berry, L. L. (1995), "Relationship marketing of services—growing interest, emerging perspectives", *Journal of the Academy of Marketing Science*, vol. 23, 236–245.

Birch, A. H. (1995), *The Concepts and Theories of Modern Democracy*, London, Routledge.

Bitner, M. J. (1995), "Building service relationships: It's all about promises", *Journal of the Academy of Marketing Science*, vol. 23, no. 4, 246–252.

Blumenthal, S. (1982), *The Permanent Campaign*, New York, Simon & Schuster.

Boll, B., and Poguntke, T. (1992), "Germany: The 1990 all-German election campaign", in S. Bowler and D. M. Farrell (eds.), *Electoral Strategies and Political Marketing*, New York, St. Martin's Press, 121–143.

Bourgeois, L. J., III (1996), *Strategic Management from Concept to Implementation*, Fort Worth, Dryden.

Bowler, S., and Farrell, D. M. (1992a), "The study of election campaigning", in S. Bowler and D. M. Farrell (eds.), *Electoral Strategies and Political Marketing*, New York, St. Martin's Press, pp. 1–23.

Bowler, S., and Farrell, D. M. (1992b), "Conclusion: The contemporary election campaign.", in S. Bowler and D. M. Farrell (eds.), *Electoral Strategies and Political Marketing*, New York, St. Martin's Press, pp. 223–235.

Bowler, S., and Farrell, D. M. (eds.) (1992c), *Electoral Strategies and Political Marketing*, New York, St. Martin's Press.

Bradshaw, J. (1995), "Who will vote for you and why: Designing strategy and theme", in J. A. Thurber and C. J. Nelson (eds.), *Campaigns and Elections American Style*, Boulder, Westview, pp. 30–46.

Brennan, G., and Lomasky, L. (1993), *Democracy and Decision: The Pure Theory of Electoral Preference*, Cambridge, Cambridge University Press.

Bryant, J. (1995), "Paid media advertising", in J. A. Thurber and C. J. Nelson (eds.), *Campaigns and Elections American Style*, Boulder, Westview, pp. 84–100.

Budge, I. (1994), "A new spatial theory of party competition: Uncertainty, ideology and policy equilibria viewed comparatively and temporally", *British Journal of Political Science*, vol. 24, 443–467.

Butler, D., and Stokes, D. (1969), *Political Change in Britain*, London, Macmillan.

Butler, P., and Collins, N. (1996), "Strategic analysis in political markets", *European Journal of Marketing*, vol. 30, no. 10, 32–44.

Clarke, H. D., and Kornberg, A. (1996), "Partisan dealignment, electoral choice and party-system change in Canada", *Party Politics*, vol. 2, no. 4, 455–478.

Collins, N., and Butler, P. (1995), "Considerations on market analysis for political parties", in S. C. Henneberg and N. O'Shaughnessy (eds.), *Political Marketing—Evolving Science or Maturing Art? Conference Proceedings*, Judge Institute of Management Studies, Cambridge University.

Collins, N., and Butler, P. (1996), "Political marketing: Considerations on research issues", in S. C. Henneberg, N. O'Shaughnessy and S. Eghbalian (eds.), *Proceedings of the Second Conference on Political Marketing*, Judge Institute of Management Studies, Cambridge University.

Crewe, I. (1974), "Do Butler and Stokes really explain political change in Britain?", *European Journal of Political Research*, vol. 2, 47–94.

Crewe, I., Sarlvik, B., and Alt, J. (1977), "Partisan dealignment in Britain 1964–1974", *British Journal of Political Science*, vol. 7, 129–190.

Day, G. S. (1997a), "Assessing competitive arenas: Who are your competitors?", in G. S. Day and D. J. Reibstein (eds.), *Wharton on Dynamic Competitive Strategy*, New York, Wiley, pp. 23–47.

Day, G. S. (1997b), "Maintaining the competitive edge: Creating and sustaining advantages in dynamic competitive environments", in G. S. Day and D. J. Reibstein (eds.), *Wharton on Dynamic Competitive Strategy*, New York, Wiley, pp. 48–75.

Demsetz, H. (1990), "Amenity potential, indivisibilities, and political competition", in J. E. Alt and K. A. Shepsie (eds.), *Perspectives on Positive Political Economy*, Cambridge, Cambridge University Press, pp. 144–160.

Denton, R. E., Jr. (1991a), "Political communication ethics: An oxymoron?", in R. E. Denton Jr. (ed.), *Ethical Dimensions of Political Communication*, New York, Praeger, pp. 1–5.

Denton, R. E., Jr. (1991b), "Primetime politics: The ethics of teledemocracy", in R. E. Denton Jr. (ed.), *Ethical Dimensions of Political Communication*, New York, Praeger, pp. 91–114.

Denton, R. E., Jr. (ed.) (1991c), *Ethical Dimensions of Political Communication*, New York, Praeger.

Dibb, S., Simkin, L., Pride, W. M., and Ferrell, O. C. (1994), *Marketing Concepts and Strategies*, Boston/London, Houghton Mifflin.

Dickinson, R., Herbst, A., and O'Shaughnessy, J. (1986), "Marketing concept and customer orientation", *European Journal of Marketing*, vol. 20, no. 10, 18–23.

Downs, A. (1957), *An Economic Theory of Democracy*, New York, Harper & Row.

Dreher, A. (1994), "Marketing orientation: How to grasp the phenomenon", in M. J. Baker (ed.), *Perspectives on Marketing Management, Vol. 4*, New York, Wiley, pp. 150–170.

Dunleavy, P. (1991), *Democracy, Bureaucracy and Public Choice. Economic Explanations in Political Science*, New York, Harvester/Wheatsheaf.

Duverger, M. (1959), *Political Parties*, 2nd edition, London, Methuen.

Easton, G. (1995), "Comment on Wensley's 'A Critical Review of Marketing: Market Networks and Interfirm Relationships'", *British Journal of Management*, vol. 6 (Special issue, December), S83–S86.

Enis, B. M. (1973), "Deepening the concept of marketing", *Journal of Marketing*, vol. 37, 57–62.

Farrell, D. M., and Wortmann, M. (1987), "Party strategies in the electoral market: Political marketing in West Germany, Britain and Ireland", *European Journal of Political Research*, vol. 15, 297–318.

Field, W. (1994), "On the Americanization of electioneering", *Electoral Studies*, vol. 13, 58–63.

Fowler, L. L. (1995), "Campaign ethics and political trust", in J. A. Thurber and C. J. Nelson (eds.), *Campaigns and Elections American Style*, Boulder, Westview, pp. 200–212.

Fox, K. F. A., and Kotler, P. (1980), "The marketing of social causes: The first 10 years", *Journal of Marketing*, vol. 44, 24–33.

Foxall, G. (1984a), "Marketing's domain", *European Journal of Marketing*, vol. 18, no. 1, 25–40.

Foxall, G. (1984b), "Evidence for attitudinal-behavioural consistency: Implications for consumer research paradigms", *Journal of Economic Psychology*, vol. 5, 71–92.

Foxall, G. (1985), "Marketing *is* service marketing", in G. Foxall (ed.), *Marketing in the Service Industries*, London/Ottawa, Frank Cass, pp. 1–6.

Franklin, B. (1994), *Packaging Politics*, London, Edward Arnold.

Franklin, B. (1995), "Priming the parish pump: Political marketing and news management in local political communications networks", in S. C. Henneberg and N. O'Shaughnessy, *Political Marketing—Evolving Science or Maturing Art? Conference Proceedings*, Judge Institute of Management Studies, University of Cambridge.

Fulbrook, F. S. (1940), "The functional concept in marketing", *Journal of Marketing*, vol. 4, 229–237.

Gabbott, M., and Hogg, C. (1994), "Consumer behaviour and services: A review", *Journal of Marketing Management*, vol. 10, 311–324.

Gabor, L. (1995), *Driving the News or Spinning out of Control: Politicians, the Media and the Battle for the News Agenda*, Paper presented at the PSA Election, Public Opinion and Parties Conference, London.

Granik, S. (1997), *Beyond Belief: The Consumer Behaviour of Political Party Members*, Unpublished MA dissertation, London, University of Westminster.

Greenley, G. (1995), "Invited comment on the market orientation content of 'A Critical Review of Research in Marketing'", *British Journal of Management*, vol. 6 (Special issue, December), S87–S88.

Grönroos, C. (1990), "Relationship approach to marketing in service contexts: The marketing and organizational behaviour interface", *Journal of Business Research*, vol. 20, 3–11.

Grönroos, C. (1995), "Relationship marketing: The strategy continuum", *Journal of the Academy of Marketing Science*, vol. 23, 252–254.

Hamel, G., and Prahalad, G. K. (1996), *Competing for the Future*, Cambridge, MA, Harvard Business School Press.

Hansson, S. O. (1992), "A procedural model of voting", *Theory and Decision*, vol. 32, 117–142.

Harris, P. (1994), *Political Lobbying or Machiavellian Marketing in Britain*, Paper for the British Academy of Management Conference, University of Lancaster, September.

Harris, P. (1996), "Editorial", *European Journal of Marketing*, vol. 30, no. 10, 18–20.

Harris, P., and Lock, A. (1996), "Machiavellian marketing: The development of corporate lobbying in the UK", *Journal of Marketing Management*, vol. 12, no. 4, 313–328.

Harrop, M. (1986), "Voting and the electorate", in H. Drucher et al. (eds.), *Developments in British Politics 2*, Basingstoke, Macmillan, pp. 34–59.

Harrop, M. (1990), "Political marketing", *Parliamentary Affairs*, vol. 43, 277–291.

Hasitschka, W. (1995), "Politik-Marketing", in B. Tietz, R. Kohler and J. Zentes (eds.), *Handwörterbuch des Marketing*, Stuttgart, Schaffer-Poeschl, pp. 2030–2042.

Heath, A. (1976), *Rational Choice & Social Exchange*, Cambridge, Cambridge University Press.

Heath, A., and McDonald, S. K. (1988), "The demise of party identification theory", *Electoral Studies*, vol. 7, no. 2, 95–107.

Henneberg, S. C. (1993), *Electoral Stability of Change?*, Unpublished MA dissertation, Loughborough University of Technology.

Henneberg, S. C. (1995a), "The political 'market'—An analogy as foundation of political marketing?", in S. C. Henneberg and N. O'Shaughnessy, *Political Marketing—Evolving Science or Maturing Art? Conference Proceedings*, Judge Institute of Management Studies, University of Cambridge.

Henneberg, S. C. (1995b), *A Theoretical Approach of Categorising Research in Political Marketing*, Paper presented at the PSA Elections, Public Opinion and Parties Conference, London, 15–17 September.

Henneberg, S. C. (1996a), "Political marketing—Evolving science or maturing art?", *Party Developments*, vol. 2, no. 1.

Henneberg, S. C. (1996b), "Book review: B. Franklin, 'Packaging Politics'", *Party Politics*, vol. 2, no. 2.

Henneberg, S. C. (1996c) "Conference report: Second Conference on Political Marketing", *Journal of Marketing Management*, vol. 12, no. 8, 777–783.

Henneberg, S. C. (1996d), "Generic functions in marketing—A functional and instrumental analysis of political marketing", in S. C. Henneberg, N. O'Shaughnessy and S. Eghbalian (eds.), *Political Marketing. Conference Pro-ceedings*, Judge Institute of Management Studies, Cambridge University.

Henneberg, S. C. (1997), *Relationship Marketing and Loyalty Management—New Developments in Defensive Marketing Strategy*, Paper presented at the Administrative Science Conference, Dhahran.

Herrnson, P. S. (1995), "Field work, political parties, and volunteerism", in J. A. Thurber and C. J. Nelson (eds.), *Campaigns and Elections American Style*, Boulder, Westview, pp. 152–160.

Himes, D. (1995), "Strategy and tactics for campaign fundraising", in J. A. Thurber and C. J. Nelson (eds.), *Campaigns and Elections American Style*, Boulder, Westview, pp. 62–77.

Himmelweit, H., Humphreys, P., and Jaeger, M. (1985), *How Voters Decide*, Milton Keynes, Open University Press.

Homans, G. C. (1961), *Social Behavior*, London, Routledge & Kegan Paul.

Houston, F. S. (1986), "The marketing concept: What it is and what is it not", *Journal of Marketing*, vol. 50, 81–87.

Hudelson, R. (1987), "A note on the empirical adequacy of the expressive theory of voting behaviour", *Economics and Philosophy*, vol. 3, 127–130.

Hunt, S. D. (1976), "The nature and scope of marketing", *Journal of Marketing*, vol. 40, 17–28.

Hunt, S. D. (1991a), *Modern Marketing Theory: Critical Issues in the Philosophy of Marketing Science*, Cincinnati, South-Western Publishing.

Hunt, S. D. (1991b), "Positivism and paradigm dominance in consumer research: Toward critical pluralism and rapprochement", *Journal of Consumer Research*, vol. 18, 32–44.

Hunt, S. D., and Morgan, R. M. (1995), "The comparative advantage theory of competition", *Journal of Marketing*, vol. 59, 1–15.

Inglehart, R. (1979), "Political action: The impact of values, cognitive level and social background", in S. Barnes and M. Kaase (eds.), *Political Action: Mass Participation in Five Western Democracies*, London, Sage.

Jamieson, K. H. (1992a), *Packaging the Presidency*, New York/Oxford, Oxford University Press.

Jamieson, K. H. (1992b), *Dirty Politics*, 2nd edition, New York/Oxford, Oxford University Press.

Jaworski, B. J., and Kohli, A. K. (1993), "Market orientation: Antecedents and consequences", *Journal of Marketing*, vol. 57, 53–70.

Johnson, D. (1997), *Political Communication in the Information Age*, Paper presented at the Seminar on Political Communication in the Information Age, Wissenschaftszentrum Berlin/Bertelsmann Stiftung, February.

Kaid, L. L., and Holtz-Bacha, C. (1995a), "An introduction to parties and candidates on television", in L. L. Kaid and C. Holtz-Bacha (eds.), *Political Advertising in Western Democracies*, Thousand Oaks, Sage, pp. 1–7.

Kaid, L. L., and Holtz-Bacha, C. (1995b), "Political advertising across cultures: Comparing content, styles and effects", in L. L. Kaid and C. Holtz-Bacha (eds.), *Political Advertising in Western Democracies*, Thousand Oaks, Sage, pp. 206–227.

Karvonen, L. (1991), "The study of election campaigns: An introduction", *Scandinavian Political Studies*, vol. 14, no. 3, 195–203.

Katz, R. S., and Mair, P. (1995), "Changing models of party organization and party democracy", *Party Politics*, vol. 1, 5–28.

Kavanagh, D. (1995a), "Speaking truth to power? Pollsters as campaign advisors", in S. C. Henneberg and N. O'Shaughnessy, *Political Marketing— Evolving Science or Maturing Art? Conference Proceedings*, Judge Institute of Management Studies, University of Cambridge.

Kavanagh, D. (1995b), *Election Campaigning: The New Marketing of Politics*. Oxford, Blackwell.

Kirchheimer, O. (1966), "The transformation of the Western European party system", in J. LaPalombara and M. Weiner (eds.), *Political Parties and Political Development*, Princeton, Princeton University Press, pp. 177–200.

Koelble, T. A. (1996), "Economic theories of organization and the politics of institutional design in political parties", *Party Politics*, vol. 2, no. 2, 251–263.

Kohli, A. K., and Jaworski, B. J. (1990), "Market orientation: The construct, research propositions and management implications", *Journal of Marketing*, vol. 54, 1–18.

Koole, R. (1996), "Cadre, catch-all or cartel?", *Party Politics*, vol. 2, no. 4, 507–523.

Kotler, P. (1972), "A generic concept of marketing", *Journal of Marketing*, vol. 36, 46–54.

Kotler, P. (1979), "Strategies for introducing marketing into nonprofit organizations", *Journal of Marketing*, vol. 43, 37–44.

Kotler, P. (1982), *Marketing for Nonprofit Organizations*, Englewood Cliffs, Prentice-Hall.

Kotler, P., and Andreason, A. R. (1991), *Strategic Marketing for Nonprofit Organizations*, Englewood Cliffs, Prentice-Hall.

Kotler, P., and Armstrong, G. (1996), *Principles of Marketing*, Englewood Cliffs, Prentice-Hall.

Kotler, P., and Levy, S. J. (1969), "Broadening the concept of marketing", *Journal of Marketing*, vol. 33, 10–15.

Kotler, P., and Zaltman, C. (1971), "Social marketing: An approach to planned social change", *Journal of Marketing*, vol. 35, 8–12.

Lane, R. (1993), *Voting and Buying: Political Economy on the Small Stage*, Paper presented at the Annual Meeting of the Society for the Advancement of Socio-economics, New York, March.

Lijphart, A. (ed.) (1992), *Parliamentary versus Presidential Government*, Oxford, Oxford University Press.

Lipset, S. M., and Rokkan, S. (1966), "Cleavage structure, party systems, and voter alignments: An introduction", in S. M. Lipset and S. Rokkan (eds.), *Party Systems and Voter Alignment*, New York, Free Press, pp. 1–64.

Lock, A., and Harris, P. (1996), "Political marketing—*Vive la Différence!*", *European Journal of Marketing*, vol. 30, no. 10, 21–31.

Loudon, D. L., and Della Bitta, A. J. (1993), *Consumer Behavior*, New York, McGraw-Hill.

Luck, D. J. (1969), "Broadening the concept of marketing—Too far", *Journal of Marketing*, vol. 33, 53–55.

Luck, D. J. (1974), "Social marketing: Confusion compounded", *Journal of Marketing*, vol. 38, 70–72.

Mair, P. (1989), "Continuity, change and the vulnerability of party", *West European Politics*, vol. 12, 169–187.

Mair, P. (1993), "Myths of electoral change and the survival of traditional parties", *European Journal of Political Research*, vol. 24, 121–133.

Maloney, W. A. (1996), "The contribution of marketing in an explanation of campaigning group membership", in S. C. Henneberg, N. O'Shaughnessy and S. Eghbalian (eds.), *Political Marketing. Conference Proceedings*, Judge Institute of Management Studies, Cambridge University.

Mauser, G. A. (1980), "Positioning political candidates—An application of concept evaluation techniques", *Journal of the Market Research Society*, vol. 22, 181–191.

Mauser, G. A. (1983), *Political Marketing: An Approach to Campaign Strategy*, New York, Praeger.

McCarthy, E. J. (1960), *Basic Marketing*, Homewood, Irwin.

McCarthy, E. J. (1981), *Basic Marketing*, revised edition, Homewood, Irwin.

McGinnis, J. (1969), *The Selling of the President*, New York, Trident.

Meade, W. K., II, and Nason, R. W. (1991), "Toward a unified theory of macromarketing: A systems theoretic approach", *Journal of Macromarketing*, vol. 11, 72–82.

Meny, Y. (1993), *Government and Politics in Western Europe*, Oxford, Oxford University Press.

Mercer, D. (1992), *Marketing*, Oxford, Blackwell.

Michalos, A. C. (1991), "Ethical considerations regarding public opinion polling during election campaigns" *Journal of Business Ethics*, vol. 10, 403–422.

Morgan, R. M., and Hunt, S. D. (1994), "The commitment–trust theory of relationship marketing", *Journal of Marketing*, vol. 58, 20–38.

Narver, J. C., and Slater, S. F. (1990), "The effect of a market orientation on business profitability", *Journal of Marketing*, vol. 54, 20–35.

Newman, B. I. (1993), "The role of marketing in the 1992 US presidential election: How Bill Clinton was transformed from 'Slick Willie' to 'Mr President'", *Werbeforschung & Praxis*, vol. 38, 195–201.

Newman, B. I. (1994a), *The Marketing of the President*, Thousand Oaks, Sage.

Newman, B. I. (1994b), "The forces behind the merging of marketing and politics", *Werbeforschung & Praxis*, vol. 39, 41–46.

Newman, B. I. (1995a), "Political marketing as a governing tool", in S. C. Henneberg and N. O'Shaughnessy, *Political Marketing—Evolving Science or Maturing Art? Conference Proceedings*, Judge Institute of Management Studies, University of Cambridge.

Newman, B. I. (1995b), "Political marketing as a governing tool", *Werbeforschung & Praxis*, no. 5, 163–167.

Newman, B. I. (1996), *The Role of Marketing in American Politics*, Paper presented at the PSA Conference, Glasgow.

Newman, B. I., and Sheth, J. N. (1987), *A Theory of Political Choice Behavior*, New York, Praeger.

Nieschlag, R., Dichtl, E., and Horschgen, H. (1994), *Marketing*, Berlin, Duncker & Humblot.

Nimmo, D. (1970), *The Political Persuaders: The Techniques of Modern Election Campaigns*, Englewood Cliffs, Prentice-Hall.

O'Cass, A. (1996), "Political marketing and the political marketing concept", *European Journal of Marketing*, vol. 30, no. 10, 45–61.

O'Shaughnessy, J. (1995), *Competitive Marketing: A Strategic Approach,* Routledge.

O'Shaughnessy, N. (1987), "America's political market", *European Journal of Marketing,* vol. 21, 60–66.

O'Shaughnessy, N. (1988), "The peevish penmen: Direct mail and US elections", *European Journal of Marketing*, vol. 22, no. 6, 36–44.

O'Shaughnessy, N. (1989/90), "Political marketing: An ethical conundrum?", *Irish Marketing Review*, vol. 4, no. 3, 39–48.

O'Shaughnessy, N. (1990a), *The Phenomenon of Political Marketing*, Basingstoke, Macmillan.

O'Shaughnessy, N. (1990b), "High priesthood, low priestcraft: The role of political consultants", *European Journal of Marketing* vol. 24, no. 2, 7–23.

O'Shaughnessy, N. (1996a), "Social propaganda and social marketing: A critical difference", in S. C. Henneberg, N. O'Shaughnessy and S. Eghbalian (eds.), *Political Marketing. Conference Proceedings*, Judge Institute of Management Studies, Cambridge University.

O'Shaughnessy, N. (1996b), "Social propaganda and social marketing: A critical difference?", *European Journal of Marketing*, vol. 30, no. 10, 62–75.

O'Shaughnessy, N., and Holbrook, M. D. (1988), "What U.S. businesses can learn from political marketing", *Journal of Applied Business Research,* vol. 4, no. 3, 98–109.

O'Shaughnessy, N., and Peele, G. (1985), "Money, mail and markets: Reflections on direct mail in American politics", *Electoral Studies*, vol. 4, 115–124.

O'Shaughnessy, N., and Wring, D. (1994), "Political marketing in Britain", in H. Tam (ed.), *Marketing Competition and the Public Sector,* Harlow, Longman, pp. 246–270.

Panebianco, A. (1988), *Political Parties' Organisation and Power*, Cambridge, Cambridge University Press.

Peele, G. (1982), "Campaign consultants", *Electoral Studies,* vol. 1, 355–362.

Piercy, N. (1994), *Marketing-led Strategic Change*, Oxford, Butterworth-Heinemann.

Pomper, G. M. (1992), "Concepts of political parties", *Journal of Theoretical Politics,* vol. 4, 143–159.

Porter, M. F. (1996), "What is strategy?", *Harvard Business Review* (November/December), 213–223.

Popkin, S. L. (1994), *The Reasoning Voter*, Chicago/London, University of Chicago Press.

Popkin, S. L. (1995), "Strategic perspectives on the 1992 campaign", in J. A. Thurber and C. J. Nelson (eds.), *Campaigns and Elections American Style*, Boulder, Westview, pp. 213–223.

Raffee, H., and Wiedmann, K.-P. (1995), "Nonprofit-marketing", in B. Tietz, R. Kohler and J. Zentes (eds.), *Handworterbuch des Marketing*, Stuttgart, Schaffer-Poeschl, pp. 1930–1942.

Rallings, C. (1995), "From mass propaganda to political marketing: The transformation of Labour Party election campaigning", in *British Elections and Parties Yearbook 1995*, London, Frank Cass.

Rauen, B. (1994), "Berlusconi: Wahlkampf mit den eigenen Medien", *Media Perspektiven*, vol. 7, 349–361.

Reid, D. M. (1988), "Marketing the political product", *European Journal of Marketing*, vol. 22, no. 9, 34–47.

Richardson, J. (1995), "Interest groups: Challenge to political parties", *Western European Politics*, vol. 18, no. 1, 116–139.

Roberts, M., and McCombs, M. (1994), "Agenda setting and political advertising: Origins of the news agenda", *Political Communication*, vol. 11, 249–262.

Robinson, W. (1995), "Organizing the field", in J. A. Thurber and C. J. Nelson (eds.), *Campaigns and Elections American Style*, Boulder, Westview, pp. 138–151.

Rothschild, M. L. (1978), "Political Advertising: A Neglected Policy Issue in Marketing", *Journal of Marketing Research*, vol. 15, 58–71.

Sackman, A. (1992), *The Marketing Organisation Model: Making Sense of Modern Campaigning in Britain*, Paper presented at the PSA Conference, Political Communications in Elections, Queens University Belfast.

Saunders, J. (1995), "Invited comment on the market segmentation content of 'A Critical Review of Research in Marketing'", *British Journal of Management*, vol. 6 (Special issue, December), S89–S9l.

Scammell, M. (1991), *The Impact of Marketing and Public Relations on Modern British Politics: The Conservative Party and Government under Mrs. Thatcher*, Ph.D Thesis, London School of Economics and Political Science, University of London.

Scammell, M. (1994), "The phenomenon of political marketing: The Thatcher contribution", *Contemporary Record*, vol. 8, no. 1, 23–43.

Scammell, M. (1995), *Designer Politics*. Basingstoke, Macmillan.

Scammell, M. (no date), *The Wisdom of the War Room: US campaigning and Americanization*, internal paper, Liverpool University.

Scarbrough, E. (1991), "Micro and macro analysis of elections", *European Journal of Political Research*, vol. 19, 361–374.

Schedler, A. (1994), "Die (eigensinnige), kommunikative Struktur demokratischer Wahien", *Zeitschrift für Politik*, vol. 41, 22–43.

Schedler, A. (1996), "Anti-political-establishments Parties", *Party Politics*, vol. 2, no. 3, 291–312.

Schmidtchen, D. (1974), "Der 'politische' Preis [The 'political' price]", *WiSt*, vol. 12, no. 1, 17–21.

Schmitt-Beck, R. (1990), "Ueber die Bedeutung der Massenmedien fuer soziale Bewegungen [On the importance of mass media for social movements]", *Koelner Zeitschrift fuer Soziologie und Sozialpsychologie*, vol. 42, no. 4, 642–662.

Schmitt-Beck, R. (1994), "Eine 'vierte Gewalt'? Medieneinfluss im Superwahljahr 1994 [A 'fourth power'? The importance of the media in the super election year 1994]", in W. Buerklin and D. Roth (eds.), *Das Superwahljahr*, Koeln, Bund-Verlag, pp. 267–292.

Schmitt-Beck, R. (1996), *Mass Media, the Electorate, and the Bandwagon: A Study of Communication Effects on Vote Choice in Germany*, Internal paper, Mahheim.

Schmitt-Beck, R., and Pfetsch, B. (1994), "Politische Akteure und die Medien der Massenkommunikation: Zur Generierung von Oeffentlichkeit in Wahlkaempfen [Political actors and the media of mass communication: On the generation of publicity in election campaigns]", *Koelner Zeitschift fuer Soziologie und Sozialpsychologie* [Opladen] (Special issue: *Oeffentlichkeit: Oeffentliche Meinung soziale Bewegungen*, ed. F. Neidhardt), no. 34, 106–138.

Senge, P. M. (1993), *The Fifth Discipline*, London, Century.

Shama, A. (1973), "Applications of the marketing concept to candidate marketing", in *4th Conference of the Association of Consumer Research, Proceedings*, pp. 793–801.

Shama, A. (1976), "The marketing of political candidates", *Journal of the Academy of Marketing Science*, vol. 4, no. 4, 764–777.

Sheth, J. N., Gardner, D. M., and Garrett, D. E. (1988), *Marketing Theory: Evolution and Evaluation*, New York, Wiley.

Simon, H. (1992), "Marketing-Mix-Interaktion: Theorie, empirische Befunde, strategische Implikationen [Marketing mix interaction: Theory, empirical findings, strategic implications]", *Zeitschrift fur betriebswirtschaftliche Forschung*, vol. 44, 87–110.

Smith, G. (1989), "'Core persistency' change and the 'People's Party'", *Western European Politics*, vol. 12, 157–168.

Smith, G., and Saunders, J. (1990), "The application of marketing in British politics", *Journal of Marketing Management*, vol. 5, 295–306.

Sniderman, P. M., Brody, R. A., and Tetlock, P. E. (1993), *Reasoning and Choice: Explorations in Political Psychology*, Cambridge, Cambridge University Press.

Sorauf, F. J. (1995), "Competition, contributions, and money in 1992", in J. A. Thurber and C. J. Nelson (eds.), *Campaigns and Elections American Style*, Boulder, Westview, pp. 78–83.

Sontheimer, K. (1993), *Grundzüge des politischen Systems der neuen Bundesrepublik Deutschland* [Essentials of the new political system of the Federal Republic of Germany], Munich, Piper.

Stern, L. W., El-Ansary, A. I., and Goughlan, A. T. (1996), *Marketing Channels*, Englewood Cliffs, Prentice-Hall.

Stirling, A. (1996), *Private Interest and Public Virtues in the 1990s? An Analysis of the Changing Marketplace for Political Activism in the UK*, M.Phil. dissertation, University of Cambridge.

Stoiber, E. (1983), "Marketing und Politik", *Marketing ZFP*, vol. 5, no. 2, 98–102.

Stonecash, J. M., and Keith, S. E. (1996), "Maintaining a political party: Providing and withdrawing party campaign funds", *Party Politics*, vol. 2, no. 3, 313–328.

Sweeney, W. R. (1995), "The principles of planning", in J. A. Thurber and C. J. Nelson (eds.), *Campaigns and Elections American Style*, Boulder, Westview, pp. 14–29.

Thurber, J. A. (1995), "The transformation of American campaigns", in J. A. Thurber and C. J. Nelson (eds.), *Campaigns and Elections American Style*, Boulder, Westview, pp. 1–13.

Thurber, J. A., and Nelson, C. J. (eds.) (1995), *Campaigns and Elections American Style*, Boulder, Westview.

Tocqueville, A. de (1994/1848), *Democracy in America*, London, Fontana.

Vallely, P. (1995), "Politicians rely on them, tycoons swear by them, even the Queen has one: The unstoppable use of the spin doctors", *The Independent*, section 2, Friday, 15 September, pp. 2–3.

van Waterschoot, W., and van den Bulte, C. (1992), "The 4P classification of the marketing mix revisited", *Journal of Marketing*, vol. 56, 83–93.

van Waterschoot, W., and Voet, R. (1988), "Naar een meer generiecke indeling van de marketing mix [On a more generic understanding of the marketing mix]", *Bedrijfskunde*, vol. 60, no. 4, pp. 350–358.

Wangen, E. (1983), *Polit-Marketing*, Opladen, Westdeutscher Verlag.

Ware, A. (1992), "Activist–leader relations and the structure of political parties: 'Exchange' models and vote seeking behaviour in parties", *British Journal of Political Science*, vol. 22, 71–92.

Ware, A. (1996), *Political Parties and Party Systems*, Oxford, Oxford University Press.

Wattenberg, M. P. (1995), "Why Clinton won and Dukakis lost: An analysis of the candidate-centered nature of American party politics", *Party Politics*, vol. 1, 245–260

Webb, P. (1992), "Britain: The 1987 campaign", in S. Bowler and D. M. Farrell (eds.), *Electoral Strategies and Political Marketing*, New York, St. Martin's Press, pp. 43–62.

Webster, F. E., Jr. (1994), *Market-Driven Management*, New York, Wiley.

Wensley, R. (1995), "A critical review of research in marketing", *British Journal of Management*, vol. 6 (Special issue, December), S63–S82.

White, J. (1986), "The domain of marketing—Marketing and non-marketing exchanges", in *Quarterly Review of Marketing*, vol. 11, no. 2, 1–6.

Worcester, B. (1996), "Political marketing: The application of market research instruments for political marketing", in S. C. Henneberg, N. O'Shaughnessy and S. Eghbalian (eds.), *Political Marketing. Conference Proceedings*, Judge Institute of Management Studies, Cambridge University.

Wortmann, M. (1989), *Political Marketing—A Modern Party Strategy*, Ph.D. thesis, European University Institute, Florence.

Wring, D. (1995a), "Political marketing and intra-party power: Perspectives on Labour, 'Old' and 'New'", in S. C. Henneberg and N. O'Shaughnessy, *Political Marketing—Evolving Science or Maturing Art? Conference Proceedings*, Judge Institute of Management Studies, University of Cambridge.

Wring, D. (1995b), *Political Marketing and Organisational Development: The Case of the Labour Party in Britain*, Research Papers in Management Studies, University of Cambridge.

Wring, D. (1995c), *Political Marketing and Power in the Labour Party*, Paper presented at the PSA Election, Public Opinion and Party Conference, London.

Wring, D. (1996a), "Political marketing and party development in Britain: A 'Secret' History", *European Journal of Marketing*, vol. 30, no. 10/11, 100–111.

Wring, D. (1996b), "The political marketing mix: A framework for election campaign analysis", in S. C. Henneberg, N. O'Shaugnessy and S. Eghbalian (eds.), *Political Marketing. Conference Proceedings*, Judge Institute of Management Studies, Cambridge University.

Zeithaml, D., and Bitner, M. J. (1996), *Services Marketing.* New York, McGraw-Hill.

6

Conceptualising Political Marketing: A Framework for Election-Campaign Analysis

Dominic Wring

In their seminal article, Kotler and Levy (1969) argued that elections should be one of the new arenas of marketing interest: "Political contests remind us that candidates are marketed as well as soap." However, the earliest recorded use of the term "political marketing" did not appear in a formal management study but in the pioneering work of political scientist Stanley Kelley which charted the emergence of the professional campaign industry in the United States. Commenting on the activities of the first election consultancies, Kelley wrote: "The team relies heavily but not entirely upon their own intuitive feel for providing political marketing conditions. They pride themselves on having 'good average minds' that help them to see things as the average man sees them" (Kelley 1956, p. 53).

In spite of the opposition from marketing purists, those in sympathy with the "broadening" thesis began to attempt to clarify, refine and establish the subfield of political marketing. By the mid-1970s, American scholars such as Avraham Shama (1974, 1976) and the prolific Philip Kotler (1975) were to the fore in developing theoretical foundations for the subject. Similarly, experts in Europe began to consider the political dimension to marketing, positing the view that an exchange relationship existed between democratic elites and their voters (O'Leary and Iredale 1976). By the mid-1980s, a steady stream of research discussing the emergence of the phenomenon helped confirm its importance (Mauser 1983; Newman and Sheth 1985). Writing in 1988, David Reid concluded that: "In western terms, although seldom recognised by politicians, the problem of getting elected is essentially a marketing one. Political parties must determine the scope and the most effective way of communicating its benefits to a target audience" (Reid 1988, p. 34).

MARKETING AND POLITICAL MARKETING

Seymour Fine identifies the 1985 decision of the American Marketing Association (AMA) to redefine its central concern as a milestone in the integration of social (and political) issues into mainstream marketing thinking. New phraseology added the crucial word "ideas" to the list of legitimate product concerns: "Marketing is the process of planning and executing the conception, pricing, promotion and distribution of ideas, goods and services to create exchanges that satisfy individual and organizational objectives" (cited in Fine 1992, p. 1).

Since its revision, the American definition has continued to enjoy wide currency in the literature in spite of various complex arguments over what the precise nature of the subject is, is not and ought to be (Hooley et al. 1990; Hunt 1976; Whyte 1988). The British equivalent of the AMA statement, as agreed by the Chartered Institute of Marketing (CIM), places similar emphasis on the notion that organisational success is an integral part of strategic concerns: firms do not seek to satisfy consumers out of altruism but from a desire to realise their own profit-making goals. To the CIM, marketing is "the management process responsible for identifying, anticipating and satisfying customer requirements profitably" (cited in Whyte 1988). The British and American definitions are useful in that they counteract the crude and oversimplistic belief that marketing is simply about firms giving their customers what they want. Such a cliché may convey clarity but it obscures more complex truth. And because some in political science (not to mention other disciplines) may have misunderstood marketing in this way, it helps explain why relatively few in the field have sought to use it as a tool of electoral analysis.

Marketing, then, is a process in which the notion of "consumer focus" plays a major strategic role but not to the exclusion of organisational needs. Compared with oversimplistic customer-centred understandings of the subject, this theoretical interpretation fits more easily with the world of *realpolitik*. In analysing the electoral market, Adrian Sackman emphasises this point, arguing that: "Marketing is thus built upon a paradox; it starts with the customer, is directed at the customer, but is fundamentally concerned with the satisfaction of the producer's own interests" (Sackman 1992, p. 6). Such sentiments resemble J. K. Galbraith's stricture that marketing and advertising are activities governed and to some extent created by producer groups (Galbraith 1969). In political science, this view is reflected in theoretical considerations of competition that attempt to marry the need of the organisation (i.e. the party) to win support with its desire to maintain some degree of programmatic consistency between elections.

Due to the peculiar nature of the environment in which they operate and despite the existence of "voter sovereignty", parties rather than firms are perhaps more adequately equipped to influence the deliberations of their market. Thus, for Schattschneider (1960) elections are based around the organising principle that: "Democracy is a competitive political system in which competing leaders and organizations define the alternatives of public policy in such a way that the public can participate in the decision-making process" (p. 141). This "realist" concept of democracy underpins Andrew Gamble's isolation of the key variables in the electoral marketplace:

The actual workings of the mass democracy has divided the political market into two camps. There are those that compete for office and those that vote. Like the producers and consumers in economic markets it is a mistake to believe that these two functions are of equal importance. One is active, creative and continuous; the other is passive, receptive and intermittent. (Gamble 1974, p. 6)

It should be noted that while the statements of Schattschneider and Gamble place emphasis on a party's ability to shape voter preferences, neither commentator would deny the fundamental role that the electorate play in determining outcomes within a competitive political market situation. Consequently, by emphasising the fact that it is both an organisational as well as consumer-focused exercise, it is possible to understand the usefulness of marketing analysis to political scientists.

POLITICAL MARKETING: A DEFINITION

Making reference to the management literature outlined in the previous section, it is possible to conceive of political marketing as: the party's or candidate's use of opinion research and environmental analysis to produce and promote a competitive offering which will help realise organisational aims and satisfy groups of electors in exchange for their votes.

At the root of this definition is a framework developed by Philip Niffenegger (1989). Designed with reference to the classic 4P marketing model popularised by McCarthy (1960), Niffenegger's formulation highlights the roles played by environmental analysis, strategic tools like market research and, ultimately, the "mix" of variables (product, promotion, place and price) in the design of political campaigns. The desirability of applying this "mix" model to non-profit not to mention commercial marketing has been challenged by some who consider the "Ps" approach outdated and inherently flawed (Blois 1987). Similarly, recognising the implicit difficulties in analysing the" chimerical nature of elections", O'Shaughnessy cautions against the application of overly rigid marketing frameworks to politics (O'Shaughnessy 1990, p. 4). Nevertheless, in spite of these objections, the Niffenegger framework has been adopted by Butler and Collins (1993), and other derivations of the mix model can be found in the work of Farrell (1986), Farrell and Wortmann (1987) and Newman (1994).

THE POLITICAL MARKETING PROCESS

The political marketing process as outlined in Figure 6.1 consists of four parts: the party (or candidate) organisation, the environment that conditions its development, the strategic mix it deploys, and, ultimately, the market in which it must operate.

The Political Market

Adopting the maxim of Schumpeter (1943) that democracy is primarily concerned with parties' "competitive struggle for [the] people's vote", Gamble contends that: "The main components of the modern political market are three; the existence of a mass electorate; competition between two or more parties for the votes of this electorate; and a set of rules governing this competition" (Gamble 1974, p. 6).

Within the political market, the key relationship is based around a concept central to marketing theory—namely, that of exchange between buyer and seller. Thus, citizens give their votes to politicians who, when elected, purport to govern in the public interest (Lane 1993; Scott 1970). In a modem democracy, the right to vote, commonly associated with the age of majority, allows for a mass electorate that can typically number well into the millions.

Commercial markets tend to resemble the competitive structure found in an electoral system run on the grounds of proportionality as opposed to "first past the post". This is not to argue that market criteria cannot be applied to a political situation such as that in Britain where purely majoritarian rules of voting operate. Indeed, the need for the parties to maintain vote share as well as court new groups of "swing" voters is as relevant to participants in this system as it is to those operating under conditions of proportional representation.

Analysing the Environment

On reflection, it may appear that business organisations have a considerable advantage over politicians in respect of the amount of resources they are able to invest in analysing their environment. However, such a

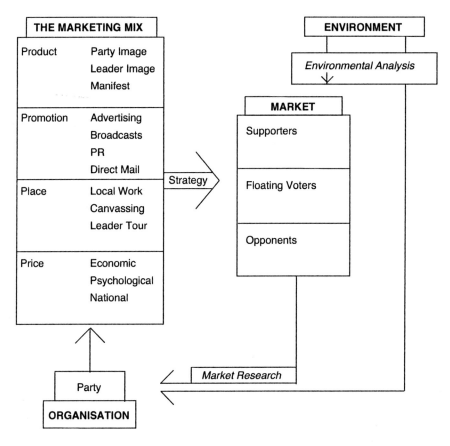

Figure 6.1. The political marketing process (adapted from Niffenegger 1990).

perception of the marketing process perhaps discounts the immense amount of pertinent information which candidates and party professionals can draw upon in planning their campaigns. Broadsheet newspapers, specialist magazines and academic briefs offer a plethora of reports, analysis and opinion-research material on which political strategists can base their decisions and better understand the economic, media and other factors shaping electors' concerns.

In contrast to the environment, which constitutes the "givens", Hunt (1976) identifies what he calls "controllable factors"—namely, the collection of strategic decisions that an organisation can implement as part of its marketing programme. Together these variables are commonly known as the "mix", a configuration that consists of the 4Ps: product, promotion, place and price.

Product

The product is central to a marketing mix. In electoral terms, the product—a "mix" of variables in its own right—combines three key aspects: "party image", "leader image" and "manifesto" (i.e. policy commitments). This configuration has been popularised by several analysts, including Bob Worcester, head of the MORI polling organisation (Farrell and Wortmann 1987; Shaw 1994; Worcester 1987, 1991). Using survey data, Worcester points out the extent to which each element of the product influences opinion among different groups of voters. Thus, where one segment might be susceptible to primarily issue-based appeals, others will display a preoccupation with the dimensions of leader or party image. Consequently, Worcester represents the preoccupations of different electors in a series of triangular diagrams, the length of whose sides can be equated with the emphasis that voters give to each of the product concerns (Worcester 1987).

The notion that politicians are increasingly using appeals based on the promotion of image at the expense of issues has become a common feature of journalists' election coverage. However, such a view can no longer be regarded as a cliché and commands significant academic support (Biocca 1991; Franklin 1994). As Terence Qualter has concluded: "The marketing of politics means, of course, the reduction of politics to marketable images" (Qualter 1985, p. 138).

While the notion of party image is built around factors such as the organisation's record in office, recent history and unity of purpose (Harrop 1990), the substance underpinning the concept is more likely contained within the policy platform on which an election manifesto is based. In the last twenty years, psephological research has begun to place greater emphasis on the rational-choice notion of the elector as a consumer evaluating the issues and voting for the party most in tune with individual policy preferences (Harrop 1986; Himmelweit et al. 1985). However, the overall picture is not simply one of a shift from party image to issue-based explanations of voter choice, because the situation has been complicated by another factor—that of leader image—which forms the third constituent in the political product mix.

Once a largely ignored factor in electoral research, the growing and potential future importance of leader image has been recognised in several studies into the increasing presidentialisation of British politics (Crewe and King 1994; Foley 1993; Mughan 1993). Media coverage of current affairs has helped extenuate this trend; as Philip Kotler comments: "Voters rarely know or meet the candidates; they only have mediated images of them. They vote on the basis of their images" (Kotler 1982).

Promotion

Promotion, in its various forms, is the most obvious part of a political marketing campaign. Misinformed commentators sometimes inflate the importance of advertising, the most recognisable communications tool, to the extent that it is held to represent the entire marketing process (see, for instance, Tyler 1987). Such a mistake fails to appreciate the complexities of a complete strategy, not to mention other parts of the promotional mix. Given the centrality of advertising within the modern marketing industry, it is perhaps not surprising that its public profile is considerably higher than that of its "stablemates", in the fields of direct mail and public relations. Nevertheless, with the advent of modernised forms of the latter in the shape of "junk mail" and "spin doctors", these parts of the promotional mix are beginning to gain increasing public prominence and particularly in the electoral arena.

The promotional mix can be divided into two principal parts, commonly referred to as "paid" and "free" media. The term "paid" media covers all forms of advertising, be it poster, print or broadcast. It should be noted that, though the primetime television and radio advertising slots for Party Election Broadcasts (PEBs) in Britain are free, those parties that qualify for them are technically in receipt of a state subsidy in kind (Scammell and Semetko 1995). Hence, PEBs can be placed in the same category as other forms of political advertising. Paid media also covers the burgeoning sector of telephone and direct-mail marketing, an increasingly common feature of contemporary election campaigning. Party colours, designs, slogan copy and symbols provide an additional dimension to the overall communications mix.

"Free" media refers to the publicity that parties receive but do not buy. In contrast to purchased advertising campaigns, organisations have less control over their product's exposure in the mass media. Consequently, political strategists—not to mention the voting public—tend to view this kind of coverage as being of greater importance. Electoral organisations are becoming increasingly reliant on the techniques of news management. In recent years, the American term "spin doctor" has entered the political lexicon in recognition of the increasing role that press, publicity and broadcasting officers can and do play in the British electoral and parliamentary process (Jones 1995). This aspect of campaigning provides perhaps one of the most striking contrasts between commercial and electoral marketing strategies: unlike their political counterparts, communications staff working for even the most senior corporate executives are unlikely to be deluged on a daily basis by some of the most experienced journalists eager for information and answers to highly sensitive questions.

Free media strategies are not solely concerned with defensive news-management activities. More common to commerce and increasingly a part of the political process, public relations is a tool designed to attract favourable media attention for the organisation concerned. It is now almost obligatory for senior British politicians to participate in "photo-opportunities", news conferences and other scenarios designed to enhance the status of themselves and their message (Cockerell 1989; Franklin 1994). This is particularly true of the period in the run-up to an election.

Place

At the heart of a placement or distribution strategy is a network of regional suppliers. In politics, the equivalent form of organisation is the party at grassroots' level. Parties in Britain organise their membership and machinery on a regional and local basis. The executives of these bureaucracies help coordinate and supply volunteer labour and strategic inputs during election campaigns. In addition, this network also liaises with the national apparatus in order to devise and coordinate regional events and tours by the party leadership. It should be noted that, precisely because it is a political marketing "mix", some of the activities that may constitute part of one variable can be found in another. In this way, the methods of the distribution policy closely mirror those of a promotional strategy in that both are reliant on tools such as direct mail despite having different aims (Farrell 1986).

Local electioneering commonly takes the form of traditional activities such as canvassing, leafleting and what American strategists call "getting the vote out" on polling day (Denver and Hands 1992; Kavanagh 1970). Contrary to some perceptions, most modern campaign canvassing is now more preoccupied with identifying and contacting potential and confirmed party supporters than it is with persuading them. This may derive from the fact that local activities have had to change due to a decline in the availability of volunteers coupled with the increasing desire of central headquarters to assert a common "brand" awareness in all party electoral communications.

The postwar decline in grassroots' membership perhaps reflects an assumption that localised forms of campaigning are largely ineffectual. Such a view has been widely fostered in the United States, where the use of political consultants has had an unfavourable effect on the strength of precinct organisation (O'Shaughnessy 1990; Ware 1985). However, recent research in Britain has begun to challenge the notion that local campaign work is ineffectual by demonstrating the potential electoral benefits of maintaining a healthy organisation at this level (Seyd and

Whiteley 1992). Furthermore the implementation of new and more affordable forms of campaign technology may even increase the value of electoral initiatives at constituency level (Farrell and Wortmann 1987). Existing evidence suggests that computers, telephone canvass banks and direct-mail initiatives became the norm in British by-elections before later establishing themselves as standard general-election practice in most key marginal seats (Swaddle 1988).

Price

Pricing, the fourth part of a conventional marketing mix, enables a commercial firm to develop a strategy that will help maintain competitiveness and profitability in the marketplace. Some electoral commentators have discounted the pricing element in the belief that it adds little to the analysis of campaign planning and implementation (Farrell 1986; Farrell and Wortmann 1987). Wangen takes the variable to mean the way an organisation raises campaign finance and attracts members (Wangen 1983).

In contrast, the theoretical basis of this chapter is built on a conception of the political marketing process defined by Philip Niffenegger (1989) and which includes all the central tenets of conventional theory (see Fig. 6.1). Niffenegger justifies the relevance of the pricing mix by outlining its constituent parts. These elements, relating to environmental phenomena as interpreted by the electorate, comprise voter feelings of national, economic and psychological hope or insecurity. This notion of the political "price" reflects Reid's observation that a vote is a "psychological purchase" (Reid 1988). The parallels between electoral and consumer behaviour have been more comprehensively analysed by Lane (1993).

There are always problems inherent in designing campaigns according to market research findings. These pitfalls are augmented when candidates seek to capitalise on the reported anxieties or aspirations of a given electoral group. One public sign of the importance attached to this kind of strategy is the growth in "negative campaigning". This type of electioneering, most commonly associated with American politics, involves attempts by party or candidates' organisations to frighten voters with robust and often startling denunciations of opponents. The frequency with which many leading national candidates in the United States have used this type of campaign has offended even the late David Ogilvy, a staunch defender and senior member of the marketing industry: "There is one category of advertising which is totally uncontrolled and flagrantly dishonest: the television commercials for candidates in Presidential elections" (Ogilvy 1983, p. 209).

Negative "appeals" usually focus on only one aspect of the pricing mix at a time. Depending on the audience being targeted, common economic themes include an opponent's intention either to raise tax and spending or else make sweeping budget cuts. In times of international insecurity or domestic uncertainty, politicians—particularly incumbents—often stress their rivals' apparent lack of diplomacy or administrative competence. Such appeals are often couched in images that stress the need to counter what is posed as a threat to the "national interest" from "undesirable elements", be they at home or abroad. Perhaps the least tangential element of the pricing mix relates to the psychological cost implicit in voting. A popular feature in negative campaigns, such strategies tap into often deep-seated and unspoken prejudices about a given politician's lack of ability, judgement and trustworthiness. As O'Keefe notes: "in no other campaign situation are target audiences required to take into account not only ideas, issues, and policies, but also such human traits as honesty, professional expertise, and managerial style" (O'Keefe 1989, p. 261). Famous victims of this type of attack advertising have included American presidential and vice-presidential hopefuls such as Barry Goldwater, Spiro Agnew, Michael Dukakis and Bill Clinton (Jamieson 1992).

"Pricing" policy need not necessarily form a wholly negative part of the political marketing mix. It is possible to conceive of a campaign strategy that promotes the idea of a domestic "feel-good factor" or boasts a perceived increase in the country's international standing in order to make political capital and win votes. Similarly, incumbent politicians often allude to psychological notions of "a nation at ease with itself" in their attempt to secure re-election. Despite the fact that pricing is the least tangible aspect of a marketing strategy, it is nevertheless a useful concept which complements the other variables. Precisely because it is a "mix", pricing can be seen to interlock and overlap with the other strategic tools, particularly those concerned with communications and product management. Marketing can be analysed in its constituent parts but should ultimately be seen in its totality.

Strategic Considerations:
Market Research, Segmentation and Positioning

Market research plays an important role in modern electoral politics. Since its first recorded use by an American candidate in the 1930s, private polling has mushroomed in terms of both its expense and its importance (Hodder-Williams 1970; Kavanagh 1992; Teer and Spence 1973). The rise of opinion research offers party leaderships potential enlightenment but also a challenge. Political élites who were once able to rely on channels of mass communication to influence a captive public are now faced with commissioning often unedifying polling findings in order to help sharpen strategy and sustain their electoral good fortune (Wring 1996). In the past, opinion research has commonly taken the form of quantitative-based surveys of key demographic groups. More recently, politicians have begun to employ consultants who specialise in the "psychographic" forms of private polling designed to explore voters' more deep-seated values and attitudes (Kleinman 1987; Worcester 1991). Increasingly, campaign-research studies are beginning to combine traditional quantitative research with focus groups and other types of qualitative methods.

Feedback in the form of opinion research is an important component in the design of an effective marketing mix. It also forms an integral part of the wider strategic process, helping to segment and target the market. Market segmentation takes place when an organisation uses research to divide available customers into categories according to their likely need or ability to purchase the firm's offering. Having identified key consumer segments, a marketing programme can then be targeted at defending or expanding current market share. Given their similar strategic aims, political strategists have also drawn on segmentation and targeting tools. Marketing analysis has pointed to the possible benefits to be derived from dividing voters according to demographic, psychographic or geographic criteria (Smith and Saunders 1990; Yorke and Meehan 1986). From the perspective of political science this trend has been exacerbated by psephological studies stressing the importance of parties' need to target the masses of uncommitted or "floating" voters in their bids to secure electoral victory (Miller et al. 1990).

In implementing marketing strategy, organisations use research to help them best position their offering in the market. The concept of positioning has a central place in political marketing analysis. Downs' classic study of party competition was based on a market model in which rival organisations maximised electoral support by moving themselves towards the electoral centre ground (Downs 1957). This model has since become a popular analytical starting point for many strategists. More recently, other theorists have developed alternative concepts of positioning that emphasise the value of continuity in the electoral offering and the importance of leading as well as following opinion. In their work, Smith and Saunders (1990) point to the potential political problems caused by "the flight to the centre" whereby parties fail to differentiate the brand values of their "product" through use of its Unique Selling Point (USP) or other positioning tools (Fletcher 1984).

In a marketing analysis of an American senatorial race, Schoenwald (1987) demonstrates the centrality of positioning theory to candidate-image management. Similarly, in his groundbreaking work on political marketing, Gary Mauser places the concept at the core of his research (Mauser 1983). Developing a multidimensional scale, Mauser demonstrates how a candidate can use cluster analysis and other statistical methods to isolate those issues and attributes that unite partisans with potential voters in a common resolve. The logical consequence of this argument is that the adoption of marketing strategies does not necessarily mean the dilution of party ideology (see also O'Cass 1996), a view most amply demonstrated by the electoral success of the Thatcher and Reagan administrations.

CONCLUSIONS

This chapter has been concerned with demonstrating the usefulness of marketing analysis in the study of political campaigning and has shown how the writings of democratic theorists might be reconciled with those of management scholars. A framework based on the basic 4P marketing model has been used in order to identify and explore the various elements that constitute an election campaign. Such an approach is arguably useful in analysing the increasingly marketing-driven politics evident in many of the major Western democracies.

REFERENCES

Biocca, F. (ed.) (1991), *Television and Political Advertising: Vol. 1, Psychological Processes,* New York, Lawrence Erlbaum.
Blois, K. J. (1987), "Marketing for non-profit organizations", in M. J. Baker (ed.), *The Marketing Book,* London, Heinemann.
Butler, P., and Collins, N. (1993), "Campaigns, candidates and marketing in Ireland", *Politics,* vol. 13, no. 1.
Cockerell, M. (1989), *Live from No. 10,* London, Faber and Faber.
Crewe, I., and King, A. (1994), "Did Major win? Did Kinnock lose? Leadership effects in the 1992 British General Election", in A. Heath et al. (eds.), *Labour's Last Chance?* London, Dartmouth.
Denver, D., and Hands, G. (1992), "Constituency campaigning", *Parliamentary Affairs,* 45, 528–544.
Downs, A. (1957), *An Economic Theory of Democracy,* New York, Harper & Row.
Farrell, D. (1986), "The strategy to market Fine Gael in 1981", *Irish Political Studies,* vol. 1, 1–14.
Farrell, D. M., and Wortmann, M. (1987), "Party strategies in the electoral market: Political marketing in West Germany, Britain and Ireland", *European Journal of Political Research,* vol. 15.
Fine, S. (ed.) (1992), *Marketing the Public Sector: Promoting the Causes of Public and Non-Profit Agencies,* New Brunswick, Transaction.
Fletcher, W. (1984), *Commercial Breaks: Insights into Advertising and Marketing,* London, Advertising Press.

Foley, M. (1993), *The Rise of the British Presidency*, Manchester, Manchester University Press.

Franklin, B. (1994), *Packaging Politics: Political Communications in Britain's Media Democracy*, London, Edward Arnold.

Galbraith, J. K. (1969), *The Affluent Society*, Harmondsworth, Penguin.

Gamble, A. (1974), *The Conservative Nation*, London, Routledge & Kegan Paul.

Harrop, M. (1986), "Voting and the electorate", in H. Drucker et al. (eds.), *Developments in British Politics 2*, Basingstoke, Macmillan.

Harrop, M. (1990), "Political marketing", *Parliamentary Affairs*, vol. 43, 277–291.

Himmelweit, H., Humphreys, P., and Jaeger, M. (1985), *How Voters Decide*, Milton Keynes, Open University Press.

Hodder-Williams, R. (1970), *Public Opinion Polls and British Politics*, London, Routledge & Kegan Paul.

Hooley, G., Lynch, J., and Shepherd, J. (1990), "The marketing concept: Putting theory into practice", *European Journal of Marketing*, vol. 24, 8–23.

Hunt, S. D. (1976), "The nature and scope of marketing", *Journal of Marketing*, vol. 40, 17–28.

Jamieson, K. H. (1992), *Dirty Politics: Deception, Distraction, and Democracy*, New York, Oxford University Press.

Jones, N. (1995), *Soundbites and Spin Doctors: How Politicians Manipulate the Media and Vice Versa*, London, Cassell.

Kavanagh, D. (1970), *Constituency Electioneering in Britain*, London, Longman.

Kavanagh, D. (1992), "Private opinion polls and campaign strategy", *Parliamentary Affairs*, vol. 45, 518–527.

Kelley, S. (1956), *Professional Public Relations and Political Power*, Baltimore, Johns Hopkins Press.

Kleinman, P. (1987), "The research market: Did psychographics win the general election?", *Admap* (September), 16–18.

Kotler, P. (1975), "Overview of political candidate marketing", *Advances in Consumer Research*, vol. 2, 761–769.

Kotler, P. (1982), "Voter marketing: attracting votes", in *Marketing for Non-profit Organizations*, Englewood Cliffs, Prentice-Hall.

Kotler, P., and Levy, S. J. (1969), "Broadening the concept of marketing", *Journal of Marketing*, vol. 33, 10–15.

Lane, R. (1993), *Voting and Buying: Political Economy on the Small Stage*, Paper presented at the Annual Meeting of the Society for the Advancement of Socioeconomics, New York School for Social Research, New York, March.

Mauser, G. A. (1983), *Political Marketing: An Approach to Campaign Strategy*, New York, Praeger.

McCarthy, E. J. (1960), *Basic Marketing: A Managerial Approach*, Homewood, Irwin.

Miller, W. L., et al. (1990), *How Voters Change: The 1987 British Election Campaign in Perspective*, Oxford, Clarendon.

Mughan, A. (1993), "Party leaders and presidentialism in the 1992 election", in D. Denver et al. (eds.), *British Elections and Parties Yearbook 1993*, London, Harvester Wheatsheaf.

Newman, B. I. (1994), *The Marketing of the President*, London, Sage.

Newman, B. I., and Sheth, J. (eds.) (1985), *Political Marketing: Readings and Annotated Bibliography*, Chicago, American Marketing Association.

Niffenegger, P. (1989), "Strategies for success from the political marketers", *Journal of Consumer Marketing*, vol. 6, 45–51.

O'Cass, A. (1996), "Political marketing and the political marketing concept", *European Journal of Marketing*, vol. 30, no. 10, 45–61.

Ogilvy, D. (1983), *Ogilvy on Advertising*, London, Pan.

O'Keefe, G. J. (1989), "Political campaigns: Strategies and tactics", in C. T. Salmon (ed.), *Information Campaigns*, Newbury Park, Sage.

O'Leary, R., and Iredale, I. (1976), "The marketing concept: Quo vadis?", *European Journal of Marketing*, vol. 10, 146–157.

O'Shaughnessy, N. J. (1990), *The Phenomenon of Political Marketing*, Basingstoke, Macmillan.

Qualter, T. (1985), *Opinion Control in the Democracies*, Basingstoke, Macmillan.

Reid, D. M. (1988), "Marketing the political product", *European Journal of Marketing*, vol. 22, no. 9, 34–47.

Sackman, A. (1992), *The Marketing Organisation Model: Making Sense of Modern Campaigning in Britain*, Paper presented at the UK Political Studies Association Annual Conference, Belfast, April.

Scammell, M., and Semetko, H. (1995), "Political advertising in television: The British experience", in L. L. Kaid and C. Holtz-Bacha (eds.), *Political Advertising in Western Democracies*, London, Sage.

Schattschneider, W. (1960), *The Semi-Sovereign People*, New York, Holt Rinehart.

Schoenwald, M. (1987), "Marketing a political candidate", *Journal of Consumer Marketing*, vol. 4, 57–63.

Schumpeter, J. (1943), *Capitalism, Socialism and Democracy*, London, Unwin.

Scott, A. M. (1970), *Competition in American Politics*, New York, Holt, Rinehart & Winston.

Seyd, P., and Whiteley, P. (1992), *Labour's Grassroots: The Politics of Party Membership*, Oxford, Clarendon.

Shama, A. (1974). "Political marketing: A study of voter decision-making process and candidate marketing strategy", in *Annual Proceedings of the American Marketing Association*, New York, American Marketing Association.

Shama, A. (1976), "The marketing of political candidates", *Journal of the Academy of Marketing Sciences*, vol. 4, no. 4, 764–777.

Shaw, E. (1994), *The Labour Party since 1979: Crisis and Transformation*, London, Routledge.

Smith, G., and Saunders, J. (1990), "The application of marketing to British politics", *Journal of Marketing Management*, vol. 5, 295–306.

Swaddle, K. (1988), "Hi-tech elections: Technology and the development of electioneering since 1945", *Contemporary Record* (Spring), 32–35.

Teer, F., and Spence, J. D. (1973), *Political Opinion Polls*, London, Hutchinson.

Tyler, R. (1987), *Campaign! The Selling of a Prime Minister*, London, Grafton.

Wangen, E. (1983), *Polit-Marketing: Das Marketing-Management der Politschein Parteien*, Opladen, Westdeutscher Verlag.

Ware, A. (1985), *The Breakdown of Democratic Party Organization, 1940–80*, Oxford, Clarendon Press.

Whyte, J. (1988), "Organization, person and idea marketing exchanges", in M. Thomas and N. Waite (eds.), *The Marketing Digest*, London, Heinemann.

Worcester, R. (1987), "The triangular equation behind the Tory victory", *The Times*, 13 June.

Worcester, R. (1991), *British Public Opinion*, Oxford, Blackwell.

Wring, D. (1996), "From mass propaganda to political marketing: The transformation of Labour Party election campaigning", in D. Broughton et al. (eds.), *British Parties and Elections Yearbook 1995*, London, Frank Cass.

Yorke, D. A., and Meehan, N. (1986), "Acorn in the political marketplace", *European Journal of Marketing*, vol. 20, 63–76.

7

Political Marketing and the Aestheticisation of Politics: Modern Politics and Postmodern Trends

Barrie Axford and Richard Huggins

For some time now, it has been fashionable, if not actually prescient, to claim that politics in the West is being transformed (Giddens, 1994; Krieger, 1999; Mulgan, 1994). The roots of this putative change are held to be both structural and motivational. Globalisation, the withering of class, the framing qualities of "new" media and media culture (Axford and Huggins, 2000a; Castells, 1996), and, of course, the faltering of the universalist project in an age where difference rules, are among the usual suspects. For students of politics and for style gurus, there are a number of identifiable symptoms of change, often glossed as signs of crisis, that suggest that politics is not what it was. These symptoms include the "hollowing out" of public life, the "death" of civility and the elision of public and private spheres of life. Each of these symptoms has a mordant quality, but they are also a tad elusive. More tangible signifiers of crisis are perceived in the fall in membership of many political parties and in trades union membership, far greater volatility in election turnout figures, a reluctance to join civic associations, and higher levels of distrust in conventional politics and politicians (Norris, 1999). While these trends can be read in different ways, for many observers they depict a political landscape that is depleted in terms of social and cultural capital and less amenable to the aggregation and brokerage of a wide range of interests and identities (Putnam 1996).

At the same time, there is a growing intensity of group activity, with selective mobilisation over numerous single issues such as transport, environmental damage, gender equality, the rights of indigenous peoples, gun-law reform and animal rights. Such interventions stretch the definition of political participation and thus increase the sites at which politics is conducted and the number of players engaged, but they leave many observers and some practitioners unsettled for precisely these reasons. The more liminal feel of the times also extends to the conduct of governance, exemplified in the heavily marketed leadership styles of Bill Clinton, Silvio Berlusconi and the paradigm case of Tony Blair and the "New" Labour Party in the United Kingdom.

More than any other recent leader, Tony Blair has provoked a good deal of comment as the exemplar of the postmodern politician. The transformation of the Labour Party into *new* Labour, which is leader dominated, image sensitive and media savvy, epitomises the coming of age of an aesthetic, self-referential and market-oriented style of politics. But New Labour is only the prime example of a more general trend in party development towards "media parties", which are characterised by greater leader autonomy and also by forms of electronic populism that facilitate discursive links between party leaders and both general and targeted publics (Axford and Huggins 2000b; von Beyme 1996). The trend towards what is sometimes labelled "anti-partyism", or "anti-party politics" is treated with a good deal of circumspection by apologists for a more traditional style of brokerage politics, and this response is typical of the nostalgic temper that often informs much discourse about what we will call "modernist" politics (Axford and Huggins 1997; Bardi 1996; Owen and Dennis 1996; Webb 1996)

Media parties—or, as they are sometimes called, professional-framework parties—are now taken as key signifiers of a postmodern turn in the politics of many Western democracies. In this transformation, nowhere complete, new communications technologies and media industries are important factors in fashioning the changing character of politics. Marketing in general and advertising in particular are quintessentially postmodern culture industries (Brown 1993; Firat et al. 1995; Kellner, 1995) and are features of what are now thoroughly mediatised cultures. The massive impact of information technologies upon economic development has been apparent since the 1970s and now pervades much cultural production as well (Fiske 1993, 1995; Lash and Urry 1994; Skovmand and Schroder 1992; Thompson 1995). Like employment, entertainment and sex, politics nowadays is conducted within the "space of media" (Castells 1996).

MODERNITY AND POSTMODERNITY

The terms "postmodern", "postmodernity" and "postmodernism" are deeply contested. Without getting too mired in the debates, we can distinguish three main ways in which the concept "postmodern" is used (Axford 1995; Parker 1993). The first usage is as a philosophical critique of foundationalist ideas about the philosophy of knowledge, especially as this forms part of the Enlightenment project. The second is as an aesthetic strategy, which, among other things, looks to relativise scientific discourse and to privilege the affective and existential qualities of life. The third, also germane to the argument of this chapter, is as denoting an epochal cultural shift seen in many features of the external world. Thus, what is generally (if somewhat contentiously) called postmodernism offers a means of describing and understanding the changing contexts of politics.

The burden of these changes is better grasped if we contrast them with what we described earlier as "modernist" politics. Modernity refers to those intellectual, social, political and economic developments most readily associated with the European Enlightenment: commercial and industrial capitalism, the emergence of scientific rationalism, and the paradigm political form of the modern territorial state. The modern world was ordered through reason, and human beings (the modern subject or self) were defined as rational actors in it. This was a world of universal truths, meta-narratives of progress, secularisation and technology, in which the rational subject was both centred *and* at the centre of all things.

In this world, politics was about the representation of fixed identities, primarily through mass political parties, territorial and (sometimes) functional representation, and rule-driven forms of governance within bounded states and societies. Particular claims (e.g. those based on ethnicity, class, religion or region) were legitimated through their willingness to accede to the ambient rules of the game and through their commitment to a regulated pluralism in the guise of the theory and practice of democratic elitism. Political change occurred mainly through incremental shifts in the enfranchisement of different sections of the population, through the impact of various social factors on political allegiance, and from the dislocating effects of periodic critical elections. In certain circumstances, change was born of major social and economic shifts and, on key occasions, was revolutionary rather than incremental.

The seeming fixedness of this style of politics is now being eroded. In the last few decades, and particularly since the collapse of communism in Central and Eastern Europe, there has been a growing conviction that modern politics, like history, is being superseded. Typically this conviction partakes of musings over decline of the territorial state, the redundancy of the usual Left versus Right framework of politics and the appearance of a tranche of "anti-political" phenomena, including forms of "techno-populism". Among those not alarmed by change there is still an urgent sense that politics is in the throes of re-invention (Bardi 1996; Beck 1999; Giddens 1994, 1998; Krieger 1999; Miliband 1994; Mulgan

1994; Owen and Dennis 1996; Phillips 1994; Webb 1996). For Geoff Mulgan, the ultimate point of collapse has now been reached and, as a consequence, the world of modern politics has "the feel of something archaic: a set of rituals, a container of tensions, a symbolic link with the past rather than a dynamic force in the present" (1994, pp. 8–9). Most commentators are agreed that in the period of transformation from industrial to post-industrial societies, the main casualties are the social structures of production and the class politics and meaning systems to which these gave rise. Anthony Giddens (1994) talks of a period of "manufactured uncertainty" and systemic risk, where modern politics is being displaced by a politics that is much less centred—a politics of life-styles, of consumption rather than production, and, critically, a politics of shifting identities.

We believe that these sorts of changes, while still inchoate, are usefully labelled postmodern, since their credo is the antithesis of the universal-ism, rationalism and wholeness of modern politics. The icons of modern politics—indeed, of modern life—are being attenuated by a number of developments:

1. The emergence of a "new" politics of identity in which a growing number of claims are thematised, whether from individuals, groups and move-ments previously on the fringes of usual politics, or else from complete outsiders.

2. The greater mutability of established social and political institutions (such as social class and the nation-state) and a decline in the power of established normative and cultural scripts to anchor identities, phenomena caused in part by:
   a. the stretching of social and economic relations across time and space through the processes of globalisation;
   b. the aestheticisation of everyday life (including working life) and politics under the impact of media cultures.

As a result rationalism, foundationalism, universalism and "whole-ness" are replaced—or at least challenged—by fragmentation, differ-ence, disintegration, post-foundationalism and de-centredness. Where the modern world celebrated the possibilities for the discovery of the "real", postmodern consciousness acknowledges no single reality, or, more accurately, suggests that there are infinite realities (often compet-ing and contradictory) depending on where we stand and from where we speak. Such claims are contestable, but they depict a political realm that is undeniably more mutable than it was. In the rest of the chapter, we examine aspects of identity politics under postmodern conditions and discuss the qualities of a postmodern politics thoroughly impreg-nated by political marketing and framed by media.

IDENTITY, MODERNITY AND POSTMODERNITY

Hall (1992) usefully distinguishes three very different conceptions of identity. First, there is the Enlightenment subject, in which the individual is whole, centred, fixed, conscious and rational. Second is the sociological subject, in which identity is formed by the interaction between the essence of the individual and the society and culture that he or she inhabits. Both of these conceptions traffic identity formation under modernist conditions, where standard modern signifiers like occupation, race and nation function as total contexts for identity construction. Under postmodern conditions, identities are malleable and contexts much less assured. The complexity of social relations and behaviour—and in particular the influence on these of consumer ideologies and marketed images of both morally and aesthetically pleasing lifestyles—destabilises the process of identity formation and the idea of fixed identity itself. So Hall's third category is the postmodern subject, for whom identity is a construct or an affectation, to be put on or changed to suit fashion and circumstance. For the postmodern subject, contexts (and their identity-generating power) are as transient or as fixed as he or she chooses. There are no privileged contexts, and thus the "narrative of the self" is little more than a convenient storyline (or storylines) that we construct out of the richness and the confusion of our daily lives (Hall 1992).

Crucially, who we are becomes now more and more a matter of choice, rather than the outcome of either history or social location. As the deference shown towards modernist "narratives" like social class recedes, anything becomes credible as a peg on which to hang an identity. Body politics, the politics of genderquake and, most pervasive of all, "lifestyle" politics are now part of a headier and more fragmented political discourse. Appeals to the lowest common denominator in a brokered politics also give way to single-issue movements and to messages tailored to niche or targeted audiences.

POSTMODERN POLITICS?

The developments outlined above seem to have significant implications for the organisation and conduct of politics, primarily because they signal the implosion of politics and culture. In the modern period, power and politics were tied through economics. In postmodernity the role of cultural production in the construction of the social and the political is central. Michael Ryan has it thus:

Rather than being expressive of representations of a substance taken to be prior, cultural signs become instead active agents in themselves, creating and evoking new substances, new social forms, new ways of acting and thinking,

new attitudes, reshuffling the cards of "fate" and "nature" and social "reality".
(1988, p. 563)

The upshot is the creation of new arenas for political conflict and communication. Images of animal-rights protesters at British docks, or of opponents of the WTO in Seattle forming alliances across social and national boundaries, populate our political landscapes with increasing regularity. They are the most visible symptoms of the fragmentation of what Bertens has called the "macropolitics" (1995) of modernity, by the "micropolitics" of identity, culture and consumption. Of course, they do not entirely displace modern forms, but the ease with which such counter-cultural or non-mainstream political phenomena can become visible in today's networked societies (Castells 1996; Thompson 1995) means that it is increasingly difficult to treat them as just peripheral or risible.

The reliance of many such causes and social movements on what Vattimo calls "the giddy proliferation of communications" (1992) underscores the importance of the new information and communications order in this changed political milieu. However, most commentators who acknowledge this fact are still ambivalent about it. Jean Baudrillard's view of a postmodern world, developed in *Symbolic Exchange and Death* (1976) and *Simulations* (1983), remains the seminal vision of a postmodern dystopia. He argues that we are witnessing the emergence of a new stage of history and of a new type of society or realm of experience, due to the proliferation of media and to the lifestyle-defining power of communications networks. Baudrillard's "society", if such is the appropriate term, is characterised above all by the centrality of the sign, rather than the spoken or the written word, and this characteristic is, he argues, bringing about significant changes in representation and in the demeanour of political actors. These changes are part of a shift from a modern political economy based on the production of things, to a new sort of cultural economy—postmodernity—based on a radical semiurgy and the production and proliferation of signs (Lash and Urry 1994). Signs are not simply representations of a given reality, but are themselves reality.

All of which leads to an aestheticisation of everyday life in which experience is saturated by a constant and rapid flow of signs. Desire is constantly recharged or reworked through the medium of advertising, forms of consumerism celebrated in media performances and through the whole "postmodern carnival" of images now available via the information and entertainment media. The ubiquity of such images and their enfolding in many lifestyles—for example, by way of aspiration marketing—has dissolved the distinction between "reality" and "image", leading, as Baudrillard puts it, to an "implosion" of the two and thus to a state of "hyper-reality". In hyper-reality, images as representations of reality are not distinguishable from, and may indeed subsume, quotidian reality. So today's reality is *hyper-reality*, a condition that is only a simulacrum of modernist narratives in politics, economics and culture.

In hyper-reality, major reference points implode, dissolving the cardinal modernist tenet of separate subject and object and producing a conflation of discourse and figure. It is worth reiterating the point that the aestheticisation of everyday life is possible only because of the declining significance of social structures and their partial displacement by the structures of information and communication. Media and culture industries assume great power in the constitution of identities at a time when many of the old rules are in retreat, providing new signifiers for audiences still in need of reference points. We continue to be uneasy about this sort of notion, in part because of the relativising or "niche-ing" of identities that is entailed, and in part because "real" identities seem certain to be swallowed in the flux of postmodern cultural dilation and excess, or "lost in an aestheticisation of life that reduces big issues to language games and morality to entertainment values" (Axford 1995, p. 204).

Much of this worry centres on the power of images as "circulating fictions" and thus on the influence of those culture industries that disseminate such "fictions". Many theories of the postmodern privilege media cultures as sites for the implosion of identity and the fragmentation of the subject (Kellner 1995), sites where the individual may either become overwhelmed by the flow and intensity of images or, at best, achieve a sort of unsettled reflexivity. Images are not signifiers in the conventional sense of the term; indeed, in this fluid cultural economy there cease to be any firm reference points at all, only what Kellner calls a "fun house of mirrors", and a growing liminality. Into the liminal space once called society spill the increasingly sophisticated arts of the creative director and a plethora of media-produced images. Viewer-consumers accustomed to "zap" between channels and cultural fare in their search for new experiences and stimuli are either rendered victims of the media commodification of culture or (and this is a crucial difference) act out their parts as savvy members of diverse audiences (Boggs 1997). In either case, there is little resemblance to the modernist conception of the individual as citizen.

Now there is little doubt that advertising is a powerful medium for the communication of cultural messages, and one infused with a high aesthetic content. It is also promiscuous in its appropriation of cultural messages, forms and genres, ranging from rock music and football anthems to shock-inducing pictures of famine. Advertising strives to capture the aspirations of any desired "lifestyle" and either endorse or challenge the existing world view of particular target or "niche" groups. For example, as a paradigm for "youth" culture, the series of Tango ads (a non-alcoholic soft drink available in the UK) broadcast in the mid-

1990s, and in a mock political format during the UK general election in 1997, are marvels of image compression. They contained at least three elements of youth culture—the stylised laddishness of the soccer commentator and terrace culture, the surreal imagery induced by mild hallucinogens and, above all, the sense that experience can be captured and replayed endlessly. Most UK political advertising is still in the aesthetic Dark Ages set against this standard, although the Mitterand campaign's collage of "Frenchness" comes to mind as a piece of pyrotechnic and image-saturated postmodernism. In the 1987 "Kinnock" election broadcast, the nostalgic feel is both pre-modern and postmodern, with a stress on traditional values and personality. The overall format is irredeemably kitsch. During the 1997 general election, New Labour made use of "fly on-the-wall" documentary techniques to personalise the appeal of Tony Blair, and it raided Capra's sentimental and moralistic vehicle for Jimmy Stewart in *It's a Wonderful Life*, complete with angel. In Italy, Berlusconi was said to be contemplating a full-blown "videocracy" to fashion a plebiscitary democracy using satellite and cable TV, and cutting out the press and conventional parties as intermediaries between governors and governed. Before his fall from grace, he had already sanctioned the making of a number of "news/documentary ads" devoted to both explaining and promoting his government, in areas like pension reform and taxation.

"METACOVERAGE"

The importance of the electronic media, entertainment values and marketing techniques in political communications has led some to argue that this is an era of "metacoverage" (Gitlin 1991), where the relationships between politicians and activists and the various media are symbiotic rather than just adversarial or instrumental. Alistair Campbell, Press Secretary to Tony Blair, captures the flavour of the relationship when he says that while the media are obsessed with spin-doctors and often rail against them, they are still "addicted to our medicine" (Campbell 2000). In the same vein, the phenomenon of "permanent" campaigning is witness not only to the ease with which political messages can be delivered to mass or selected audiences, but to the fact that promotion is endemic in media cultures. Because all politics now occurs in the space of media, many kinds of political occasion achieve validity only as media events. Metacoverage also refers to the way in which politics and political messages are carried outside the conventional news and current affairs formats.

John Fiske makes a useful contribution to this debate. Commenting on the mixing of reality and fiction in an episode of the soap opera *Murphy Brown* during the 1992 US presidential elections, he notes that politicians and newsreaders were aware that the line between fiction and reality had disappeared in this campaign. In TV land, the "fictional" Murphy Brown watches the news report of the "real" Dan Quayle criticising her status as a single parent. Later the same day, "real" television news carries pictures of Dan Quayle surrounded by single mothers watching Murphy Brown watching Dan Quayle. The real news report ends with the information that Quayle has sent the fictional child a toy and thus consciously implicated himself in the fictional storyline. Characters in the show are also pictured reading both real and fictional newspaper reports of the incident during the programme itself (Fiske, 1995). This conflation of "real" and "fictional" politics is now a routine formula in entertainment products and can be seen in the motion picture *Dave* (about a hitherto feckless presidential look-a-like), in the drama documentary *Jack Tanner*, and in Old Labour leader Neil Kinnock's appearance in the British television satire *Drop the Dead Donkey*. In these prime examples of Baudrillardian "hyper-reality", it is very hard to say where reality ends and fiction begins, or vice-versa. On a more pragmatic note, it is also quite hard to discern who is using whom and for what purpose, for if Baudrillard is right, we live everywhere "in a state of aesthetic hallucination of reality" (1983, p. 151).

Even if he is halfway correct, the individual may be in danger of losing any sense of certainty as well as the ability to distinguish between real and representational forms. However, the conflation of image and reality need not be discommoding. Because postmodernism rejects the position that we can experience reality directly—that is, without mediation— direct experience of the real cannot serve as a touchstone by which to measure the truth or accuracy of representation (Fiske 1995). There is also the feeling that some moral and cultural arbiters of taste and political discourses may be protesting a bit too much. As Fiske notes: "The structural difference, for instance between information and entertainment television (roughly, between fact and fiction), is a residue of modernity that contains the hierarchical evaluation that the former is superior to the latter" (1995, p. 63).

While it is commonplace to make this distinction, the fact is that election campaigns in the United States are now carried out more and more through the "entertainment" genres of television and radio, especially talk shows, talk radio, popular-music channels like MTV and forms of "drop-in" TV (Boggs 1997; Moog 1997). These outlets may not be conventional channels for political marketing, but they just may be sites at which new forms of public talk are taking place. Clearly, there is much more to be said on this topic, but it is commonplace that entertainment media and values are being used routinely to package politicians as cultural products—in media cultures, how could it be otherwise? The question is, does all this mean that democracy is going to hell in a handcart? Arguably, the groups that deplore these developments are those who have most to lose by them—including "the old white men of journalism", as Fiske describes them. Their function as mediators, gate-keepers, or legislators, in Bauman's sense, is challenged by the recognition that politics is no longer located where it "should" be and, as a result, is being subjected to the kind of "dumbing down" that is now staple fare on "low-brow" television. But, as Fiske also notes, "lower-brow television is low only because its taste patterns appeal to disempowered and subordinated social formations (particularly by gender, class, and age), and so dissolves the structured relationship between politics and serious, informational media encouraging more social formations to participate in the political process" (1995, p. 63).

POLITICAL MARKETING

Political marketing now occupies a central position in the political landscape, but much of the academic study of the genre deals largely with the conduct of election campaigns and tends to neglect the wider aspects of political communications (Newman 1999; Norris 1999) . In much of the literature, political marketing is approached in one of two ways. First, there are accounts of heavily marketed campaigns. This style of analysis involves recording the strategies of marketers and image-makers, cataloguing the techniques they employ and attempting to assess both the short- and long-term effects of marketing. Since Richard Nixon's "Sweaty Lip" and running "Lazy Shave" (Bruce 1992) in the 1960 US presidential campaign, and the Saatchi & Saatchi inspired "Labour Isn't Working" campaign for the Conservatives in 1979, the power of images has been acknowledged, but we remain ambivalent about the processes and techniques of an increasingly marketed politics. These techniques include brand-management, negative and positive advertising, the sound-bite, the ad-bite, photo-opportunities and press conferences, and the overarching tactics of news-agenda management and framing (Axford et al. 1992; Bowler and Donovan 1998; Diamond and Bates 1984; Jamieson 1992a; Franklin 1994; Norris et al. 1999; O'Shaughnessy 1990; Wernick 1991).

The second approach is that which either emanates from or draws heavily upon the discipline of marketing itself. This approach is almost entirely prescriptive or hortatory, in the manner of a professional critique of campaigns. It deals with how politics *should* be marketed and how that process can be made more efficient (Butler and Collins 1994; Reid 1988; Smith and Saunders 1990). The key problem of getting elected is seen primarily as one of effective marketing (Butler and Collins 1994, 1999; Reid 1988). Media and marketing specialists tend to conceptualise the process as a kind of professional game, a predilection exemplified by texts that equate the selling of politics with the selling of all other products. Brendan Bruce's *Images of Power* (1992) falls into this category and provides clear testimony to the centrality of the media and image professional in politics. At the same time, Bruce does not endorse a hypodermic view of the relationship between product and consumer, or between politician and voter. In the same positive vein, Martin Harrop argues that because politics is a service, it can be legitimately marketed. He concludes that political marketing has improved the extent, quality and efficiency of communication between voters and parties (Harrop 1990).

Placing the media professional at the centre of the political process brings with it a number of complications (Wernick 1991). For one thing, there is the fear that parties may contend for votes in the way film studios or TV channels tout for audiences, and that marketing can be employed to sell politics like any other commodity. As a consequence, the art of promotion is placed at the centre of the political process, and, because television is a medium that trades on personality, individual politicians are transformed into product presenters who "have come to serve as key media signifiers for the parties, ideological positions and social forces which they represent" (Wernick 1991, p. 139). In other words, politics—"real" politics—have been suborned by marketing.

Of course, none of this happens by default, through some kind of technological determinism, it is all highly self-conscious on the part of both politicians and the various media who cover them. Kiku Adatto's comparison of the 1968 and 1988 US presidential elections examines the emergence of what she calls "Sound Bite Democracy" and the "Warhol-isation" of political reporting (Adatto 1990). But in the same reports, journalists routinely offer conscious and often critical deconstructions of the campaigns they cover as well as providing unvarnished reportage. Media events, where campaign managers try to convey non-rhetorical, visually powerful, symbolic political messages to selected groups of voters, are often high-risk occasions. The infamous Dukakis tank ride and Bush's Labour Day appearance at Disneyland in 1988, and, in the case of the UK general elections, the Labour Party's Sheffield Rally or John Major's apparent improvisation in using a "soapbox" to address a crowd in Luton during the 1992 campaign, are all clear examples of managed events that went wrong or that succeeded for unplanned reasons. If the campaign has become one of image-management, stunts, visuals and media events, these are not always successful and may indeed themselves become the raw materials of scurrilous attacks by opponents and commentators and ridicule from the audience. In the early stages of the 1992 campaign in the United Kingdom, BSkyB turned straight news coverage into an art form and a critical comment when they assembled a series of photo-opportunity shots and showed them as a pastiche to the theme of *Would I Lie To You* performed by the Eurythmics. This is mediatised politics of a highly self-referential kind.

ALL CHANGE?

To reiterate: our position is that it is appropriate to locate the phenomenon of political marketing and the mediatisation of politics and culture as part of an epistemic change, or transformation, that is conveniently (if still contentiously) understood as the shift from a modern *order* to a postmodern *disorder*. These changes are most apparent in the "post-historical" core of the global system, in such countries as the United Kingdom, Italy and the United States. However, they are by no means confined to these regions and need to be seen as a reworking of politics and political communications in line with the emergence of what John Thompson calls "mediatised" cultures (1990). They are also part and parcel of the deconstruction of modernist grand narratives like the nation-state and national economies, and of modern solidaries like social class, along with the politics reliant on them (Giddens 1994; Jacques 1993; Krieger 1999).

The point is that it is easy to mistake many of these developments as no more than an intensification or incremental reworking of modernist political genres under the impact of new technology. Indeed, much of the discussion of the effects of the electronic media on the conduct of political campaigning is exercised entirely by the extent to which *usual* politics is suborned by the cynical use of media and technology by politicians, or by sheer bad faith and inefficiency on the part of media professionals. This is particularly true of much of the treatment of "image-dominated" elections, where Reagan, Bush and Clinton in the United States and Berlusconi in Italy were all taken to task for the unseemliness of their media-led campaigns as much as for the platforms on which they stood (Axford and Huggins 1996). In the United Kingdom, the former leader of the Labour Party, Neil Kinnock, was also castigated for the presidential style of his campaigns in 1987 and, perhaps with greater justification, in 1992. During the 1997 UK general election campaign, the American journalist Joe Klein referred disparagingly to the "magisterial vacuity" of Tony Blair's media-wise campaign style. Outside the fevered atmosphere of the election campaign, complaints about the Blair government still emphasise its obsession with image and product rebranding. Of course, we should not be unmoved by the trend towards wholesale image-management or towards the systematic marketing of candidates and political parties, but we must take care not to dismiss such developments as aberrant features of a public sphere that can be rescued simply by breathing life into the tired narratives of usual politics or by getting broadcasters and print journalists to shape up.

In a well-known critique of the excesses of media-dominated campaign strategy in the United States, Kathleen Hall Jamieson (1992a) has written about the power of television (and political advertising) to "reconfigure reality". Viewers are seen as mesmerised by the televised treatment of elections as horse-races and by the visceral appeal of powerful imagery and half-truths, often conveyed to them by broadcasters seemingly content to offer "ad-bites" and "ad-stories" as news, without any sort of contextualising of the story and the storyline. While her diagnosis leaves little room for optimism, Jamieson's remedy is to demand more argument, more engagement with issues and more accountability from candidates and their advisers, as well as from the nominal guardians of the public interest in the print and broadcast media. But leaving aside her particular gloss on this media-saturated politics, in one key respect her jeremiad misses the point, which is that such developments are no longer aberrations but are features in the new contours of American political culture, as well as British and Italian. These changes are hardly amenable to remedial action seeking to refurbish a particular form of publicness that is irrecoverable in this kind of cultural milieu, if it ever existed in anything like a pristine condition.

In a sense, this is what is missed by polemics decrying the growth of the "politics of anti-partyism". For example, in a critique of what they call "techno-populism", Lipow and Seyd (1996) try to marry proper normative concerns about the future of democracy in a mediatised and party-less politics with the message that "hard" evidence suggests that there is still life in the old dogs of brokerage politics and democratic elitism. No doubt their thesis has some mileage, despite the fact that it is tempting to agree with Monty Python that what we have been talking about is *something completely different*. But in the short term at least, a growing number of postmodern characters must continue to perform in resolutely modernist plays (Rosenau and Bredemeier 1992). The by now hackneyed dichotomy between the demands of "Doctor Spin" on the one hand, versus the allegedly substantive realities of policies and issues on the other, will continue to fuel debate in the world of meta-politics, ironically due to the very machinations of media people and marketing professionals, anxious to have their own gloss on events taken as authentic. None of this should come as any surprise, because if usual politics is dying, it is experiencing a creeping death.

And yet, as Martin Jacques says (1993), it is clear that the formal boundaries of politics are dissolving as part of a "meltdown" of the nation-state and the crisis of modernity. The political world of parties and the state is being invaded by a growing range of groups, movements and institutions from civil society, and in Britain, as elsewhere, the core of contemporary politics is undergoing change (Krieger 1999). Jacques talks of the "pick and choose" hypermarket society, where from food to holidays, from sport to fabrics, from sexual identity to clothes, and tellingly, from print titles to cable and video channels and Internet commerce, we can choose like never before. It does not commit too many hostages to fortune to suggest that the political realm cannot remain immune from these trends, despite Lipow and Seyd's cautionary data on the extent and impact of "new" forms of politics. Moreover, arguments about the decay of conventional politics and the emergence of a postmodern genre are not likely to be settled simply by reference to figures on party membership, or on the turnover in membership of single-issue interest groups. Rather, it is the qualitative changes taking place in the demeanour and functions of political parties (Katz and Mair 1994; von Beyme 1996) and in the allegiance of members and supporters that are the critical, but less visible, signs of the onset of a postmodern politics.

More visible changes include the rise of the "professional" party, or "media" party, which is leader orientated, a party that is responsive to changes of opinion in niche electoral "markets", rather than the opinions of members, and is completely practised in the arts of self-presentation in both the public and commercial media. Six years after its dramatic intervention in Italian politics, it is just possible that Berlusconi's *Forza Italia* remains the first wave of a postmodern political future, but the British Labour Party too has been remade in the image of its leader, Tony Blair, and shows many of the features of the professional-framework party. Bruce Newman (1999) draws attention to the phenomenon of "electronic marketing" in recent American presidential races, suggesting that party politics has taken a back seat to a market-driven politics, where polls not ideology dictate the construction of a campaign agenda and also the policy agenda of an administration once in office. To reiterate, what is also remarkable about this new style of politics is its highly self-referential nature. The self-images of the party and leader are fed by responses to cues that they have already tried to implant in the consciousness of this or that public, through various marketing strategies. As we have noted, this world is never hermetically sealed, nor completely self-referential. Positive image-management begets negative advertising from opponents, and unintended consequences test the cool of the best-planned marketing strategy. Even so, the "success" of a party or a leader is measured increasingly by the appropriateness and impact of their own campaign style and their ability to ride out the knocking copy from rivals.

Writing of the wider European context, Klaus von Beyme suggests that during the shift to a postmodern form of party politics, the links between parties and members have become much looser than in the heyday of mass parties. Party leaders and government ministers increasingly try to establish links between electors, or targeted groups of electors and themselves, without resort to the inconvenience of party organisation and party ideology (1996, p. 146; Axford and Huggins 2000b). At the same time, voters—and, arguably, members too—adopt more instrumental or less committed attitudes to party allegiances. The cynicism of "Generation X", the blunt rationality of "Essex Man", the numbers of uncommitted voters waiting to be convinced right up to polling day, serve to make political parties convenient shelters for the ideologically footloose or uncommitted, rather than permanent homes. This putative motivational shift is not just the result of the translation of more fluid lifestyle preferences into the political arena; it is also related to a growing frustration with usual politics and usual politicians. There are different (and not always compatible) manifestations of this unease. Concerns with the democratic deficit in territorially organised polities, the inadequacy of systems of accountability, accusations of endemic sleaze and so on, all point to an actual crisis of motivation and identity for some voters and a putative legitimation crisis of systemic proportions too.

These are pertinent observations, but not at all at odds with our argument that postmodern politics subsists in the wrack of modernist forms. Even so, this fact must not be allowed to obscure the transformative potential of recent developments. For example, Silvio Berlusconi's short-lived freedom coalition in Italy in the Spring of 1994 is noteworthy because it was an "authentically" televisual administration (*Guardian Weekend*, 3 December 1994) based on a "party", *Forza Italia*, that was still little more than an advertising and marketing vehicle—a political trope (Axford and Huggins 1996). Suppress any *frisson* of distaste, or the knee-jerk response that it could never happen in countries like Britain because of the (steadily weakening) restrictions on trans-media monopolies, and consider the implication of Berlusconi's victory.

In many ways, the success of *Forza Italia* epitomises the cultural changes gathering pace throughout the 1980s, being a distillation of the television and communications revolution served up in a digestible political and populist form. This judgement is valid, despite *Forza Italia*'s failure to recapture control of the Italian government in the general election of April 1996. Indeed its longer-term significance may be precisely that it exemplifies a kind of postmodern populism (Axford and Huggins 1996; Piccione 1996). There are a number of clues to its potential as a transformative force. Some relate to Berlusconi himself, but others to the significance of *Forza Italia*'s brand of televisualist politics. First, at least part of Berlusconi's appeal to the Italian electorate in 1994 was based on the fact that he was not an established politician and hence, at the time, was unsullied by the accusations being levelled at *Tangentopoli* [Bribesville]. Second and closely related is the sense that postmodern populism surfaces as an expression of growing frustration with conventional politics and politicians. In 1994, Italian politics was ripe for the intrusion of just such a transformative force. Third is the background of Berlusconi himself. As a political Johnny-come-lately, he carried clout with the Italian electorate because he was a media mogul and a success- ful businessman, one attuned to the demands of managerialist rather than outworn ideological politics. Fourth is the sense that a political phenomenon like *Forza Italia* exemplifies the postmodern aestheticisa- tion of everyday life to which we referred earlier in the chapter. Its function in this respect may be to operate as a populist vehicle for the spread of cultural capital to particular sections of society in a political style that makes sense to them. Young people and those groups at ease with image-saturated messages of the culture industries saw in *Forza Italia*'s brand of televisualist politics a sort of hermeneutic or "life-good", closer to their own experience than the outputs of other, more conven- tional political parties. Fifth, *Forza Italia*'s campaigns placed the art of promotion (Wernick 1991) at the centre of the political process. Politics was subsumed (some would say suborned) by advertising. As a result, Berlusconi was offered and received as a "personality" or a "product presenter". In common with similar leader-dominated campaigns, like that of Tony Blair in Britain in 1997, what the movement stood for is reported through the prism of the leader and his personal attributes (Axford 1992).

Italy aside, these developments produce a campaign politics that is highly self-conscious, intensely reflexive and introverted, with the cam- paign itself constituting almost a virtual environment or context created out of the uneasy symbiosis between the protagonists, pollsters, those charged with the business of positive and negative image management, and, of course, the electronic media. Finally, postmodern populism of the sort exemplified by *Forza Italia* and New Labour also transforms the very idea of publicness. Berlusconi made much of the idea of a "videocracy" to replace the dishevelled concept of "partitocracy", while Blair's con- cern to fashion a "new kind of politics" has little room for the traditional functions of political parties. Yet the notion of rule through the media sets alarm bells ringing because of the prospects for undermining a largely electronic public sphere by having an advertising free-for-all over the outcome of electronic plebiscites.

The possible loss of referential identities in a marketed, electronic politics is a source of concern to some commentators on the Italian scene but also more generally. Creating reflexive individuals in a highly medi- atised politics is one thing; producing atomised, rootless selves quite another. For Berlusconi, and also for other media-savvy politicians with a populist bent, the temptation is to emphasise that their use of "instant communication" to target audiences is meant to restore referential iden- tities in a world dominated by intermediary organisations, government and (in the case of Italy) corrupt bureaucracy. The use of electronic communication is offered consciously as a means of by-passing the usual channels of mediation between leaders and led. Wired leaders, runs the message, can cut through the alienated and alienating forms of interest representation to express the needs and desires they and their supporters experience in everyday life. This is the putative up-side of Lipow and Seyd's "techno-populism"—but does it, can it, play?

The impact of media populism of a more down-home and, for some, less savoury variety can be seen in the combustible antics of the "shock jocks" of American talk-radio: Bill Cunningham, Rush Limbaugh and Howard Stern. Their particular brand of populism played no small part in the routing of the Democrats in the 1994 mid-term elections. Depending on where you stand, the shows are either providers of an electronic soapbox in a period when fewer people read newspapers and election discourse is reduced to a series of largely negative television ads, or further evidence of the corruption of the public sphere (Adatto 1990; Boggs and Dirmann 1999) and further evidence of the "dumbing down" of American culture. Nor are the big players themselves immune from indulging in a little commercial populism. In the extended campaign before the 1992 presidential elections, Bill Clinton staged his "Comeback kid" act through such "new media": CNN, talk shows, local stations and, of course, MTV—on which the future president once confided, in that mock intimate or revelatory style now obligatory for candidates hoping to qualify as "real" people, that he preferred Y-fronts to boxer shorts. From Bill Clinton's soft focus rerun of his Arkansas-Kennedy boyhood and the docu-soap authenticity of Tony Blair's Islington lifestyle, to the crassness of "Chicken George" and "Butt-Man", visual images are enfolded into and flow through postmodern campaigns (Axford et al. 1992).

These developments are part of a growing challenge to conventional, party-mediated politics. This conclusion is hardly contestable; nor is the extent to which the new media have become the touchstone—although Jaques (1993) says the mirror or the interlocutor—for a new kind of politics, which is detached from the social structures and holistic ideologies and from traditions. In short, politics and the presentation of politics has taken a marked cultural turn (Street 1997), where culture must be understood as a transitory aesthetic experience, a postmodern "carnival", rather than as the expression of social divisions and traditional "habits of the heart" (Bellah et al. 1985). Certainly these developments represent substantial challenges to the grand narratives of left versus right and to the identities that were constructed around them. Newer modalities, reflecting the "plasticity of cultural expression" (Krieger 1999, p. 119), now populate the political landscape.

These modalities reflect the changes to which postmodernists refer and signal the emergence of a more fluid politics of identity in reaction to the coded genres of modern politics, *whose forms are still in place, if not intact*. Instead, narrative politics is being traduced by the dominance of images, and stability of identity by confusion or multiplicity of identities, as the availability of newer and more exotic codes expands, and the domain of ontological security and certainty contracts (Lash and Urry 1994).

It will be apparent that we do not share the pessimism that often attends discussion of the postmodern. Much of the debate about the media and politics carries a heavy burden of nostalgia for the (mythologised) political world we have lost or are in danger of losing, as well as a *frisson* of elite distaste for the excesses of tabloid campaigning and low-brow populism. In this respect, such interpretations as Katherine Hall Jamieson's (1992a, 1992b) lament for the future of American electoral politics, to which we referred earlier, are neglectful of the active construction of reality by individuals, of the interpretative powers of viewers, and of the extent to which changes in politics and political communications are embedded in wider social and, more significantly, cultural currents and not simply imposed on a supine public.

We could do well to note these considerations. If politics and political identities were ever "whole" in the sense conveyed by modernist intellectuals, the "new times" in which we live have undone (or are undoing) modernist political narratives and allegiances, although this remains a live issue among practitioners and observers (Lipow and Seyd 1996). The politics of "personhood" (O'Sullivan 1993), individuality and difference are reshaping the traditional boundaries of the political and deconstructing some of the cardinal features of modern politics—including the nation-state, social class, maybe even forms of "mass" political participation. In the sense conveyed earlier in this chapter, these developments and others may be producing a politics in which identity is becoming a matter of cultural manufacture, of choice or invention (at least if one is not in Rwanda or Kosovo). At such a pass, a person is "whole" only in the reflective awareness of the possibility of any number of "selves", none of which is any more "real" than any other. Politicians reinvent themselves prior to successive elections—why not voters? We continue to be uneasy about this notion, but questions about authenticity, or breast-beating over the destruction of a *particular* form of publicness, are increasingly redundant in this kind of cultural milieu. While we agonise over the passing of "real" political debate, we also rehearse the aestheticisation of political life and the conflation of image and reality in the treatment of routine and dramatic events. The point is that this sort of thing is not, or need not be, a distortion of the political or democratic process, a misuse of the public sphere or a weak simulacrum of the same. To treat all these changes solely in these terms does no service to a critical social science of the democratic process.

REFERENCES

Adatto, K. (1990), "Sound bite democracy", *Network Evening News*, Presidential Campaign Coverage, 1968 and 1988.

Axford, B. (1992), "Leaders, elections and television", *Politics Review*, vol. 1, no 3, 17–20.

Axford, B. (1995), *The Global System*, Cambridge, Polity.

Axford, B., and Huggins, R. (1996), "So you think you've been 'Tango'd'?—Volatile identities and flat politics", in B. Axford and G. Browning (eds.), *Modernity–Postmodernity: From the Personal to the Global*, Oxford, Oxford Brookes University, pp. 169–196.

Axford, B., and Huggins, R. (1997), "Anti-politics or the triumph of postmodern populism in *Promotional Cultures?*", *Javnost: The Public*, vol. 4, no. 3, 5–27.

Axford, B., and Huggins, R. (2000a), "Public opinion and postmodern populism: A crisis of democracy or the transformation of democratic governance?", in S. Splichal (ed.), *Vox Populi—Vox Dei?*, Denver, Hampton Press.

Axford, B., and Huggins, R. (eds.) (2000b), *The New Media and Politics*, London, Sage.

Axford, B., et al. (1992), "Image management, stunts and dirty tricks: The marketing of political brands in television campaigns", *Media, Culture and Society*, vol. 14, no. 4, 637–651.

Bardi, L. (1996), "Anti-party sentiment and party system change in Italy", *European Journal of Political Research*, vol. 29, 345–363.

Baudrillard, J. (1976), *Symbolic Exchange and Death*, London, Sage.

Baudrillard, J. (1983), *Simulations*, New York, Semiotext (e).

Beck, U. (1999), *Global Risk Society*, Cambridge, Polity.

Bellah, R., et al. (1985), *Habits of the Heart*, Berkeley, University of California Press.

Bertens, H. (1995), *The Idea of the Postmodern*, London, Routledge.

Boggs, K. (1997), "The great retreat: Decline of the publice sphere in late twentieth century America", *Theory and Society*, vol. 26, no. 2, 141–180.

Boggs, C., and Dirmann, T. (1999), "The myth of electronic populism: Talk radio and the decline of the public sphere", *Democracy and Nature*, vol. 5, no. 1, 65–94.

Bowler, S., and Donovan, T. (1998), *Demanding Choices: Opinion, Voting and Direct Democracy*, Ann Arbor, University of Michigan Press.

Brown, S. (1993), "Postmodern marketing", *European Journal of Marketing*, vol. 27, no. 4, 19–34

Bruce, B. (1992), *Images of Power: How the Image Makers Shape Our Leaders*, London, Kogan Page.

Butler, P., and Collins, N. (1994), "Political marketing: Structure and process", *European Journal of Marketing*, vol. 28, no. 1, 19–34.

Butler, P., and Collins, N. (1999), "A conceptual framework for political marketing", in B. I. Newman (ed.), *Handbook of Political Marketing*, Thousand Oaks, Sage.

Campbell, A. (2000), "A man more spinned against than spinning", *The Times*, 30 January, p. 15.

Castells, M. (1996), *The Network Society, Vol. 1*, Oxford, Blackwell.

Diamond, E., and Bates, S. (1984), *The Spot: The Rise of Political Advertising on Television*, Cambridge, MA, MIT Press.

Firat, A., et al. (1995), "Marketing in a postmodern world", *European Journal of Marketing*, vol. 29, no. 1, 40–56.

Fiske, J. (1993), *Power Plays—Power Works*, London, Verso.

Fiske, J. (1995), *Media Matters: Everyday Culture and Political Change*, Minneapolis, Minnesota Press.

Franklin, B. (1994), *Packaging Politics: Political Communications in Britain's Media Democracy*, London, Edward Arnold.

Giddens, A. (1994), *Beyond Left and Right: The Future of Radical Politics*, Cambridge, Polity.

Giddens, A. (1998), *The Third Way*, Cambridge, Polity.

Gitlin, T. (1991), "Bites and blips: Chunk news, savvy talk and the bifurcation of American politics", in P. Dahlgren and C. Sparks (eds.), *Communication and Citizenship: Journalism and the Public Sphere*, London, Routledge, pp. 119–136.

Hall, S. (1992), "The question of cultural identity", in S. Hall, D. Held & A. McGraw (eds.), *Modernity and Its Futures*, Milton Keynes, Open University Press.

Hall, S., Held, D., & McGraw, A. (eds.) (1992), *Modernity and Its Futures*, Cambridge, Polity.

Harrop, M. (1990), "Political marketing", *Parliamentary Affairs*, vol. 43, 277–291.

Jacques, M. (1993), "The end of politics", *Sunday Times*, 18 July.

Jamieson, K. H. (1992a), *Dirty Politics*, New York, Oxford University Press.

Jamieson, K. H. (1992b), *Packaging the Presidency*, 2nd edition, New York, Oxford University Press.

Katz, R., and Mair, P. (1994), *How Parties Organise*, London, Sage.

Kellner, D. (1995), *Media Culture: Cultural Studies, Identity and Politics between the Modern and the Postmodern*, London, Routledge.

Krieger, J. (1999), *British Politics in the Global Age: Can Social Democracy Survive?*, Cambridge, Polity.

Lash, S., and Urry, J. (1994), *Economies of Sign and Space*, London, Sage.

Lipow, A., and Seyd, P. (1996), "The politics of anti-partyism", *Parliamentary Affairs* (March), 271–284.

Miliband, D. (ed.) (1994), *Reinventing the Left*, Cambridge, Polity.

Moog, S. (1997), *Television, Mass Polling, the "New Media" and the Current Mass Media Communications Regime*, Paper presented to the International Conference on Media and Politics, Katholieke Universiteit, Brussels, 27 February to 1 March.

Mulgan, G. (1994), *Politics in an Antipolitical Age*, Cambridge, Polity.

Newman, B. I. (ed.) (1999), *Handbook of Political Marketing*, Thousand Oaks, Sage.

Norris, P. (ed.) (1999), *Critical Citizens: Global Support for Democratic Governance*, Oxford, Oxford University Press.

Norris, P., Curtice, J., Sanders, D., Scammell, M., and Semetko, H. (1999), *On Message: Communicating the Campaign*, London, Sage.

O'Shaughnessy, N. J. (1990), *The Phenomenon of Political Marketing*, Basingstoke, Macmillan.

O'Shaughnessy, N. J. (1993), "Political integration, the limited state, and the philosophy of postmodernism", *Political Studies*, vol. 41, no. 4, 21–42.

O'Sullivan, N. (1993), "Political integration, the limited state, and the philosophy of postmodernism", *Political Studies*, vol. 41, no. 4, 21–42.

Owen, D., and Dennis, J. (1996), "Anti-partyism in the USA and support for Ross Perot", *European Journal of Political Research*, vol. 29, 345–363.

Parker, M. (1993), "Post-modern organizations or post-modern organization theory?", *Organization Studies*, vol. 13, no. 1, 1–17.

Phillips, A. (1994), *Democracy and Difference*, Cambridge, Polity.

Piccione, P. (1996), "Postmodern populism", *Telos*, vol. 103, 45–86.

Putnam, R. (1996), "The strange disappearance of civic America", *American Prospect*, 24.

Reid, D. M. (1988), "Marketing the political product", *European Journal of Marketing*, vol. 22, no. 9, 34–47.

Rosenau, P., and Bredemeier, H. (1992), "Modern and postmodern conceptions of social order", *Social Research*, vol. 60, no. 2, 337–362.

Ryan, M. (1988), "Postmodern politics", *Theory, Culture and Society*, vol. 5, 559–576.

Skovmand, M., and Schroder, K. (1992), *Media Cultures: Reappraising Transnational Media*, London, Routledge.

Smith, G., and Saunders, J. (1990), "The application of marketing to British politics", *Journal of Marketing Management*, vol. 5, no. 3, 295–306.

Street, J. (1997), *Politics and Culture*, Cambridge, Polity.

Thompson, J. (1990), *Ideology and Modern Culture*, Cambridge, Polity.

Thompson, J. (1995), *Media and Modernity: A Social Theory of the Media*, Cambridge, Polity.

Vattimo, G. (1992), *The End of Modernity*, Cambridge, Polity.

von Beyme, K. (1996), "Party leadership and change in party systems: Towards a postmodern party state?", *Government and Opposition*, vol. 3, no. 2, 137–159.

Webb, P. (1996), "Apartisanship and anti-party sentiment in the United Kingdom: Correlates and constraints", *European Journal of Political Research*, vol. 29, 345–363.

Wernick, A. (1991), *Promotional Culture*, London, Sage.

8

The Marketing of Political Marketing

Nicholas J. O'Shaughnessy

HAS POLITICAL MARKETING BEEN OVER-MARKETED?

Perhaps now is the right time to raise the question: has political marketing itself been over-marketed? This may seem a strange question to ask, both since political marketing is very far from being universally accepted among political scientists at the conceptual level, and because of obvious resonances as a normative–rational model of what is occurring in electioneering to-day, particularly in the United States. But its advocates, such as Kotler and Kotler (1999), perhaps too easily perceive the political and commercial contexts as essentially similar. They are not. We are, of course, operating a definition of political marketing that places it in the realm of primarily commercially derived persuasion techniques and concepts, an organising paradigm imported from commerce. This excludes, for example, the chicaneries of spin and the political management of news, as well as the traditional political arts of rhetoric and symbol manipulation (and some of those writing in the area would dispute this). The argument is that media and the press, with their own agendas of information manufacture, are demonstrably of more influence on public opinion than are political advertising and other communication techniques of commercial derivation. Marketing is fundamentally a business discipline whose supreme relevance lies in business: we cannot assume that political contexts are analogous to business to the extent that methods can be simply imported and used with equal effect.

However, the genre "political marketing" functions at two levels, for it is both descriptive and prescriptive. Descriptive, obviously, in that political marketing analyses provide us with a structure of business-derived labels to explain, map, nuance and condense the exchange dynamics of an election campaign, offering the possibility of a fresh, new perspective for interpreting elections. But it is also prescriptive. Implicitly or explicitly, many academics have been saying that this is something that parties and candidates ought to do if they are to fulfil their mission of winning elections. "Political marketing" may now be a recognised discipline, but it is also a recommendation.

It is this prescriptive status that this chapter questions, not in the sense of doubting that the application of political marketing has clear value as an organising concept and as a tool-kit, but rather to claim that this value has significant limits. "Political marketing" is seldom alone a panacea. The claim of this chapter is that political marketing's evangelists arguably ignore the fact that they advocate a volatile weapon that can on occasion do active harm to those who employ it. The foundation, though not the proof, of such a claim is established through the use of two historically significant case studies, the British general election of 1992 and the Canadian general election of 1993. The argument is that the political imperative to "market" is weaker than the business imperative.

VALUES AND ETHOS

There are, in fact, important differences between the political and consumer "product", and these lead to distinct differences in the content and the texture of their marketing. Politics is intimately concerned with affirmation of values. Thus, a political issue is not merely a product to be merchandised, but a vibrant value symbol connecting with an individual's sense of who and what he or she is at the deepest level. In such cases, political views and decisions are part of the social construction, the self-articulation or public persona of the individual, arguably at a more fundamental level than a Hermes scarf or handbag. Governments are more than just big customer-service organisations, and while appeals in consumer marketing are seldom value-free, the function of politics as a major source of value affirmation makes it inherently more complicated than consumer marketing. Voting for a particular party can be, and certainly has been historically, a source of social identity. Indeed, this is why the emotional appeal to values can be more effective politically than almost any other kind of appeal (Etzioni 1984), certainly more so than one that used reason-giving appeals grounded in facts, figures and statistics. The exchange process of business cannot compare with the polemical intensities of politics, arising from its role as theatre—and crucible—of values and value conflicts.

Political partisanship is affirmed by a moral ethos that is different from that of consumer marketing—one that can, of course, be ideological and even cruel. Consumer marketing has nothing like negative advertising, and so-called comparative advertising is a faint echo. Ansolabehere and Iyengar (1995) point out that in 1992, fifty states with 62% of the voting-age population suffered full negative campaigns. Negative advertising is, of course, not confined to the United States: it was a significant presence in both the 1992 and 1997 British general elections. Further consider this evidence: what is called political marketing sometimes goes well beyond the boundaries of distortion to the upper realms of fantastic invention. The phrase "political marketing" is used as a convenient shorthand for a host of loosely related activities and can, in fact, actively mislead. The point is that technological resources are being actively used to edit truth. A 1996 study found that 28% of the 188 commercials scrutinised contained questionable usage of technology: "news conferences that were never held, debates that never took place, use of audio or video to stereotype or ridicule opponents" (*USA Today*, 23 May 1996).

MEDIA, COMPLEXITY AND TURBULENCE

Political marketing, and political communication phenomena, are distinguished from consumer marketing also by the arbitration of an independent communications power centre—the mass or "free" media that they may be able to influence but cannot control, such as purchased political advertising. Yet the availability of such free media is limited in most business situations; indeed, many business schools do not even run courses on public relations. In politics, media are more important. Thus political marketing has to be viewed as a complex two-step communication process that influences the consumer directly, but also indirectly through the medianship of the free media. Free media—as with the ad-watches, which have become an institutionalised feature of the US press—comment on political marketing but in the process relay its imagery: in this dialogue between political marketing and the mainstream media, the advertisements and such become political occurrences themselves. Political marketing texts may thus stand in their own right as autonomous historical events with political consequences of their own, such as the "Daisy" advertisement of 1964 (O'Shaughnessy 1990).

Moreover, to succeed a party must deal with multiple and often conflicting segments within some overall market—that is, with the eclectic population of potential support that can be unified in the perhaps ephemeral coalition of interests that wins elections. The complexity of politics, with its multiplicity of issues to be argued, debated and marketed, might be analogous to the complexities facing a multinational like, say, Proctor and Gamble; however, we would argue that there exist so many different "faces" to a party and government that we cannot control communication as we would in a business, since there are too many facets to political communication and too many autonomous, mediating centres of media power. What is inscribed in a piece of political communication is merely the beginning of a journey that could end anywhere, even having the reverse consequences to those anticipated.

Furthermore, the degree of turbulence in the political environment—especially during elections, which are the primary focus of political marketers—makes the problem of control much greater than in the business environment. In this sense, consumer marketing as an analogy is overly static. A business can control its image in a way that a party cannot: one only has to look at the Conservative administration of John Major in Britain (1992–97) with its circa fifty scandals (of very varying degrees of magnitude) to realise this. Marketing is a normative paradigm, but actual politics contains critical differences of control, pace and intensity. The need for initiative and opportunism is probably greater than in business, even though businessmen write books with titles like "guerrilla marketing" (Levenson 1990) because of this fluidity and unpredictability of the political environment. Thus, as well as a distinctive media set, political communications involves a different dynamic to consumer marketing. The fluidity of political situations is partly because new communications media have made political pace a rapid thing, particularly in the condensed space of an election, so that parties and politicians can post immediate replies on the website when once there would have been a one- or two-day delay for a measured response (Johnson 1997).

SPIN, RHETORIC AND SYMBOLISM

The British (Labour) government has often been cited in debates on the practice, and the ethics, of political marketing. But the phenomena of the Blairite regime also offers us the chance to inject some rigour into the argument. "Political Marketing" can be used too loosely to refer to anything from rhetoric to spin doctoring, or simply to every kind of political communication that has its genesis in public-opinion research. It has become a useful hold-all, a glad-bag of disparate entities that at an earlier phase in history would have been called "populism" or "propaganda", or, when used in the strictly business context, would go under headings like "corporate communications" or public relations.

But what is being done to communicate the policies of the British government actually bears limited resemblance to anything that would be described by the textbooks of consumer marketing, or inscribed in its practice. Labour are specialists, certainly, in the manipulation of free media or "spin", the art of affixing a desirable interpretation on to a still fluid situation, and the rhetorical and symbolic strategies that might further such manipulation. But it is comparatively rare that a business will need the arts of "spin" in communicating with its public. What I think critics really mean by calling this marketing is "political corporatism", with its associated activities of coordinating party spokespersons to be "on message", the clearing of ministerial speeches with communications officers, the issuing of MPs with pagers etc. But, the term "political marketing" is being used as a too convenient hold-all.

Thus it is possible, though unusual, to speak of a "marketing rhetoric", which is simply created and propelled to its chosen target via the purchased media. Political rhetoric, on the other hand, requires the cooperation of the free media for it to be conveyed, and hence part of its aim is to secure the cooperation of free media. New Labour became adept at rhetoric. The word "socialism" was dropped: Labour was "coming home" to be "tough on crime, tough on the causes of crime", with its vision of a "stakeholder society" offering "education, education, education", reminding people (and who could disagree?) that it was "time for a change".

And similarly with symbols. While consumer marketing does, of course, employ symbolism—what, after all, is a brand?—it is possible to argue that symbols are more important in the construction of political meanings. As they are a comparatively low-cost venture, they are attractive to parties and, again, need the cooperation of the free media to be placed in circulation. Thus, a political campaign is constructed through a series of managed symbolic events, which will be a visual parable, eluding critical scrutiny in a way that language cannot.

Symbols are emotionally arousing but cost-free: thus Labour could attack harmless targets (the £60-million royal yacht) and support virtuous ones (a minister for women, but with no salary), conceal its patches of red (out of television-camera-shot on the conference set) and make a general claim to "care" (as with the "caring" taxi driver in one of their 1997 political commercials)—a claim that as a moral property of private individuals can be neither proved nor disproved.

PARTICIPATION

It may be argued that reliance on commercially derived political marketing techniques to win elections helps undermine the role of active participation in politics today, to the long-term detriment of those who employ them. Britain's "New" Labour Party, which created a substantial "credit-card" membership through advertising—their membership telephone number was showcased in all its communications (O'Shaughnessy 1999)—was later to discover the fickleness of its new membership base. Under this argument, the virtues of political marketing for a party could be more short term than long term. Marketing fails to engender the kind of proselytising organisation that Ellul (1965) reckons to be central to the successful working of propaganda. An important part of the theory of persuasion is that we internalise our adherence by working for a cause, therefore engaging in self-persuasion and retrospectively justifying our actions. The lack of active participation in politics today (Richardson 1995) makes for a superficiality of support, quickly lost, and no direct link between governors and governed. An extreme case of this was *Forza Italia*. Political marketing methodologies also tempt us to use communication to fill the space vacated by ideas and ideology (Sherman 1987), as with the Tories in Canada in 1993, but the combination of marketing acumen and intellectual vacuity is one that voters might recognise and resent.

WHAT MARKETERS NEGLECT

We might even ask whether political marketers have actually ignored the most relevant concepts and techniques among those offered by consumer marketing. "Relationship marketing", for example, is a valuable concept: it is not that politicians do not seek to build relationships with party members, or with voters, merely that the concept of relationship marketing and the literature on it would both sensitise political practitioners to the importance of that dimension and provide them with a litany of procedures and ideas for implementing the concept. Again, the writings on brand loyalty (Aaker 1991; Keller 1993) could be of considerable benefit—how brands, essentially a form of condensed meaning, are sustained and how loyalty to them is kept alive. Politicians should realise that their parties—indeed, they themselves—function as brands. And the meaning, coherence and integrity of brands can be undermined, in politics as in business, by abrupt changes in continuity and identity—as British Airways found with its disastrous "tail-fin" experiment. Are political marketers really learning the important lessons from marketing?

Criticisms of political marketing can also be translated from generic criticisms of consumer marketing, as, for example, the allegation that research-led domestic consumer marketing restricts itself to the consumer's view. It is thus importantly limited by the limitations of consumers' imagination and cannot surface their latent, unarticulated wants: that is the function of creativity and not marketing. Politicians, like consumer-market researchers, come up with the same product specifications. Yet some of the most original products, such as the Sony Walkman under the leadership of Akito Mori, were created in defiance of market re-

search. In consumer marketing, research convergence and producer bureaucracy make for a sometimes alarming uniformity in product forms
and functions, the political equivalency is unadventurous leadership
and bland policies. It would be better if marketers spoke about interpreting rather than researching the consumer: the latter is essentially a static
model that is governed by the consumer's self-knowledge and knowledge of what is possible, based on an economist's image of the consumer
as having complete self-knowledge and an established and stable hierarchy of preferences, whereas interpretation involves a deeper and almost
intuitive understanding of their unrecognised or half-articulated desires.

TWO CASE STUDIES: CONTROL AND INTERPRETATION

Two case studies have been chosen to illuminate the potential pitfalls
of political marketing. In the first place, political marketing always
carries a high risk factor, especially if its fabricators wish to achieve
originality. We cannot control the destination of a communication text
but merely initiate that voyage, for what is encoded is not necessarily
what is decoded. Political marketing can make a bad situation worse,
providing much material for a party's enemies, including its enemies in
the media, who can fix a malign interpretation on a text which is quite
different from that which the party intended. The interpretation chosen
by an autonomous agency, the media, is of particular importance, and
this the party cannot control. Yet, paradoxically, it is through the media's
role as self-appointed election referee that much political advertising is
viewed. But when, say, television news shows a slice of a political
advertisement, it is framed by a comment—as, of course, are the multiple
"ad-watches" orchestrated by the American press. It is often the case,
then, that we can speak not of political marketing but of a media-
arbitered image of political marketing. This, of course, is why research
into the public impact of a marketing text is perhaps harder than in the
case of conventional consumer marketing, since we must adjust response figures for the intervening variable of media reaction.

A political marketing text can thus suffer unintentional readings; a
message can give a particular reading, but it can also give off a feeling or
tone that undermines it. Thus, a projection of "slickness" would be
acceptable in a commercial context, but in politics it might suggest
manipulativeness, a lavishly financed campaign, and so forth. And in
the context of another culture, the meaning might be different again—in
Peru, for example, the polished, American-style campaign advertisements made for Vargas Llosa (de Lisle 1990) were interpreted by Peruvi-
ans (most of them poor) as an index of a rich, out-of-touch candidate. A
political context changes the parameters of interpretation of a message: a

"bold" attack message might be seen not as courageous but as desperate, for example. Political advertising may be seen as an index of a party's mind or even a bearing of its naked soul, but in the process it may provide unintentional reinforcement of people's deep or semi-articulated fears about a candidate or party. A political marketing text can thus act as a symbol to trigger inconvenient memories; thus, the rejection of the Canadian Tory advertisement in the case described below occurred partly because it was perceived as symbolic of the uncaring political ethos of the 1980s: the Tories were seen as wishing to confine Canadians to an era and an ethos that they felt they had outgrown.

Canada 1993

The aim of the Canadian Tory advertising in the 1993 election campaign was to stigmatise the leadership qualities of the Liberal candidate, Jean Chretien: a sequence of somewhat ugly photographs depicted him becoming increasing confused, with the comment "I personally would be very embarrassed if [Chretien] were to become the Prime Minister of Canada" (Whyte 1994). One of these images revealed the right side of Chretien's face, his mouth crooked from nerve injury sustained in youth. There seemed ample strategic justification both for the choice of target and the manner of execution. Canadian Tory polls revealed that the largest segment of least committed liberal voters were dubious about his leadership. Focus groups agreed: Chretien was incompetent; it would be embarrassing to have him represent them at international events. Nobody even mentioned the pictures (Whyte 1994).

Yet the electoral consequences of this strategy were devastating (*Globe*, 16 October 1993). Why? Primarily because the media seem to have decided that they would be, affixing an interpretation on the text that said that the advertisement was a grotesque attack on physical disability; thus, to be Tory was to hate people with disabilities. Television reports chose the ugliest parts of the images and the script; pundits denounced. For most voters, their only exposure to the advertisements was through the interpretative framework attached by television. They never did "decide for themselves". Chretien himself was quick to exploit the situation politically and to foster the media's interpretation: "They have a new ad that doesn't talk about their policies or my policies. They try to make fun of the way I look. God gave me a physical defect and I've accepted that since I was a kid" (Whyte 1994). An experiment at Simon Fraser University found people reacted far more negatively to the broadcasts than to the advertisements themselves. The result of the election was the worst ballot-box defeat in history of a ruling party. The Tories were left with just two seats. It had become "politically incorrect to be a Tory" (Whyte 1994).

Britain 1992

Another example of failure in political marketing is the British general election of 1992. In marketing terms, Labour's campaign was a text-book case. The party appeared to win the campaign and yet lose the election. Why? Labour's campaign, superficially flawless, contained several errors, and the ostensibly mediocre Conservative marketing had a number of strengths. In retrospect, Labour's campaign was too sentimental. It did not cohere with known reality: Labour leaders were idealised, the dull footage edited out. It was "too good to be true", maybe raising fears of a hidden agenda—the manipulative intent was visible.

"Jennifer's Ear", an advertisement using the story of a sick child to attack the Conservative government's NHS policy, was shown in the second week of the 1992 general election campaign. Again, the strategy and execution seemed to make eminent sense. The Conservatives were probably at their least believable when they claimed that "the N.H.S is safe in our hands", and it was natural for Labour to seek to exploit their area of perceived greatest vulnerability. A powerful "attack" advertisement at the start of the campaign would put them on the defensive where they had least to defend. Such an advertisement should not be rational but emotional, seeking to achieve the kind of resonance with viewers and media re-duplication that the sinister "Willie Horton" had achieved in the United States. And that resonance would be gained by a human story and not abstract argument. Moreover, if the story was also true, grounded in fact, the power of its symbolism could sustain the entire Labour campaign.

The failure, as with the anti-Chretien advertisement in Canada, lay essentially in the fact that the advertisement further irritated an already suspicious media that was determinedly fault-finding. They criticised "Jennifer" for accuracy, undermining the claim to truthfulness that was central to its power to persuade. Moreover, the charge of "exploitation" of a sick child was what actually resonated with the public, not the attack on the NHS: the child's vulnerability worked against, not for, Labour's advocacy. It all went horribly wrong. Two child actresses portrayed the allegedly true story of two little girls with "glue ear", one immediately treated privately, the other whose treatment was repeatedly delayed on the NHS. But newspapers discovered the identity of the real child and pursued the family: nor was it clear whether the failure to treat was due to lack of resources or incompetence (Harrison 1992). That week, "Jennifer" constituted nearly 20% of stories on both main television news programmes. "Jennifer Bennett and her glue ear received more coverage than housing, transport, pensions, law and order, defence, foreign affairs or Europe—indeed, than several of those put together" (Harrison 1992). Harrison further argues that "before the election the

NHS had seemed Labour's strongest suit. However, the momentum the party had built up by the middle of the campaign was never regained after the Jennifer Bennett affair broke on March 25."

Thus, in 1992 a political campaign that was impressive in orthodox marketing terms failed against one that appeared almost to embrace a species of anti-marketing. The rival, Conservative campaign relied exclusively on appeals to fear about the alleged tax consequences of a Labour victory, and its advertising was crude and simplistic, with imagery of boxers, blacksmiths, chains, bombs, barrage balloons, bristling hedgehogs. In particular, an apparently uncontrived gesture by Tory leader John Major—where he addressed voters in one town by standing on a soapbox—really did appear to achieve that critical resonance with the public. The soapbox was conscripted as his symbol. The Tory effort succeeded despite its mediocrity and strategic incoherence, and Labour's failed in spite of its gloss. Major's soapbox is perhaps a warning that in certain circumstances people rebel against an over-sold product and go for something that signals truthfulness.

These cases suggest that television and the press are still incomparably more powerful agents of political influence than political marketing via the paid or free media. At times, even a free press can conspire to present a powerful "dominant view" against which all other opinion is perceived as deviant. When opinion becomes universal among major press protagonists like this, no amount of savvy political marketing can rectify the situation. In 1992, the Labour Party under Neil Kinnock was leading at the polls. The British press "decided to crucify him". From December 1991 to April 1992, the relatively apolitical readers of the *Sun* newspaper registered an 8.5% swing to the Tories (Mckie 1995). Techniques used by the press to demonise the Labour Party and its leader Neil Kinnock (Seymour-Ure and Scott 1995) included the *Sun*'s eight-page pre-election special, "Nightmare on Kinnock Street", where, for example, readers were warned that loft conversions would need the approval of lesbian and gay groups on left-wing councils: on election day itself, the front page featured Mr Kinnock's head within a light bulb and the headline:"If Kinnock wins to-day, will the last person to leave Britain please turn out the lights" (Harrop and Scammell 1992). Propaganda-like distortions were the order of the day. For example, the *Sun* in the critical "Jennifer's Ear" case presented Jennifer's father as being opposed to Labour's use of the story, whereas the reverse was true. And the *Daily Express* operated as "in effect, a daily propaganda agency for Conservative Central Office" (Harrop and Scammell 1992).

Thus, the press had become direct participants in the creation of propaganda and not mere conduits of it. The demonstrable impact of this kind of news manufacture may seem to put the attempts of parties to "market" themselves in the shade. Under this argument, political marketing may be seen as the poor relative of press activism: this would not negate its importance, merely that its impact must be seen in the context of often more significant drivers of political influence.

CONCLUSION

Case studies, of course, "prove" nothing, they merely establish a foundation for further argument. What this chapter has sought to achieve is a sensitising—for both researchers and students alike—of the acute differences between contexts in which political and business managers operate. They are separate ecologies, and the aim of this chapter has been to challenge notions of political marketing as universal panacea: there is no simple, easy transport from a business context, where social values are one of many considerations, to the political one, where values are the core of the process. Has political marketing been overmarketed? The question cannot be proven and is perhaps trivial. What is ultimately important is perhaps less the establishment of the stature of political marketing along some hierarchy than an understanding of the contexts in which it succeeds and fails, and why.

REFERENCES

Aaker, D. (1991), *Managing Brand Equity*, New York, Free Press.

Ansolabehere, S., and Iyengar, S. (1995), *Going Negative*, New York, Free Press.

de Lisle, L. (1990), *Election in Peru*, MBA thesis, University of Loughborough Business School.

Ellul, J. (1965), *Propaganda*, New York, Alfred A. Knopf.

Etzioni, A. (1984), *New York Times*, 5 October.

Harrison, M. (1992), "Politics on air", in D. Butler and D. Kavanagh, *The British General Election of 1992*, London, Macmillan.

Harrop, M., and Scammell, M. (1992), "A tabloid war", in D. Butler and D. Kavanagh, *The British General Election of 1992*, London, Macmillan, pp. 180–210.

Johnson, D. (1997), *Political Communication in the Information Age*, Paper presented at the Seminar on Political Communication in the Information Age, Wissenschaftszentrum Berlin/Bertelsmann Stiftung, February.

Keller, K. L. (1993), "Conceptualising, measuring and managing customer based brand equity", *Journal of Marketing*, vol. 57.

Kotler, P., and Kotler, N. (1999), "Political marketing: Generating effective candidates, campaigns and causes", in B. Newman (ed.), *Handbook of Political Marketing*, Thousand Oaks, Sage.

Levenson, J. C. (1990), *Guerrilla Marketing Weapons*, Harmondsworth, Middlesex, Plume Books.

Mckie, D. (1995), "'Fact is free but comment is sacred' or, Was it *The Sun* wot won it?", in I. Crewe and B. Gosschalk (eds.), *Political Communication: The General Election Campaign of 1992*, Cambridge, Cambridge University Press.

O'Shaughnessy, N. J. (1990), *The Phenomenon of Political Marketing*, Basingstoke, Macmillan.

O'Shaughnessy, N. J. (1999), "Political marketing and political propaganda", in B. I. Newman (ed.), *Handbook of Political Marketing*, Thousand Oaks, CA, Sage.

Richardson, J. (1995), "Interest groups: Challenges to political parties", *West European Politics*, vol. 18, no. 1 (January), 116–139.

Seymour-Ure, C., and Scott, S. (1995), "Characters and assassinations: Portrayals of John Major and Neil Kinnock in *The Daily Mirror* and *The Sun*", in I. Crewe and B. Gosschalk (eds.), *Political Communication: The General Election Campaign of 1992*, Cambridge, Cambridge University Press.

Sherman, Sir A. (1987), "The ad man cometh", *Guardian*, 6 May.

Whyte, K. (1994), "The face that sank a thousand Tories", *Saturday Night*, February, p. 14.

Bibliography

Alesina, A., and Rosenthal, H. (1995), *Partisan Politics, Divided Government, and the Economy*, Cambridge, Cambridge University Press.

Alt, J. E., and Shepsie, K. A. (eds.) (1990), *Perspectives on Positive Political Economy*, Cambridge, Cambridge University Press.

Anonymous (1993a), "Konsumentenverhalten", in *Vahlens Grolies Wirtschaftslexikon*, Munich, Verlag C. H. Beck/Verlag F. Vablen, pp. 1177–1178.

Anonymous (1993b), "Konsumentenverhaltensmodelle", in *Vahlens Grolies Wirtschaftslexikon*, Munich, Verlag C. H. Beck/Verlag F. Vablen, p. 1178.

Ansolabehere, S., and Iyengar, S. (1995a), *Going Negative: How Political Advertisements Shrink and Polarize the Electorate*, New York, Free Press.

Ansolabehere, S., and Iyengar, S. (1995b), "Winning through advertising: It's all in the context", in J. A. Thurber and C. J. Nelson (eds.), *Campaigns and Elections American Style*, Boulder, Westview, pp. 101–111.

Antonides, G. (1989), "An attempt at integration of economic and psychological theories of consumption", *Journal of Economic Psychology*, vol. 10, 77–99.

Arndt, J. (1978), "How broad should the marketing concept be?", *Journal of Marketing* vol. 42, 101–103.

Arndt, J. (1982), "The conceptual domain of marketing: Evaluation of Shelby Hunt's three dichotomies model", *European Journal of Marketing*, vol. 16, 27–35.

Arnold, S. D. (1995), "Political marketing in the European Parliamentary Elections: The Liberal Democrat campaign in Humberside. A case study", in S. C. Henneberg and N. O'Shaughnessy (eds.), *Political Marketing—Evolving Science or Maturing Art? Conference Proceedings*, Judge Institute of Management Studies, Cambridge University.

Assael, H. (1992), *Consumer Behavior and Marketing Action,* Boston, PWS-Kent.

Axford, B., and Huggins, R. (1995), "Political marketing and the aestheticization of political identities: Modernist politics and postmodern trends in the

UK, Italy and the USA", in S. C. Henneberg and N. O'Shaughnessy (eds.), *Political Marketing—Evolving Science or Maturing Art? Conference Proceedings*, Judge Institute of Management Studies, Cambridge University.

Baer, D. (1995), "Contemporary strategy and agenda setting", in J. A. Thurber and C. J. Nelson (eds.), *Campaigns and Elections American Style*, Boulder, Westview, pp. 47–61.

Bagozzi, R. P. (1974), "Marketing as an organized behavioral system of exchange", *Journal of Marketing*, vol. 38, 77–81.

Bagozzi, R. P. (1975), "Marketing as exchange", *Journal of Marketing*, vol. 39, 32–39.

Bagozzi, R. P. (1978), "Marketing as exchange: A theory of transactions in the marketplace", *American Behavioral Scientist*, vol. 21, 535–556.

Bagozzi, R. P. (1994), "Book Review: *Marketing Exhange Transactions and Relationships* by F. S. Houston, J. B. Gassenheimer, J. M. Masukulka", *Journal of Marketing*, vol. 58 (January), 155–157.

Bagozzi, R. P. (1995), "Reflections on relationship marketing in consumer markets", *Journal of the Academy of Marketing Science*, vol. 23, 272–277.

Banker, S. (1992), "The ethics of political marketing practices: The rhetorical perspective", *Journal of Business Ethics*, vol. 11, 843–848.

Barry, B. (1978), *Sociologists, Economists and Democracy*, Chicago/London, University of Chicago Press.

Barry, B. (1991a), "Is democracy special?", in *Democracy and Power: Essays in Political Thought*, Oxford, Clarendon, pp. 24–60.

Barry, B. (1991b), *Democracy and Power: Essays in Political Thought*, Oxford, Clarendon.

Bartels, R. (1974), "The 'identity' crisis in marketing", *Journal of Marketing*, vol. 38, 73–76.

Bartle, J. (1995), *Market Analogies, the Marketing of Labour and the Origins of New Labour*, Paper presented at the PSA Elections, Public Opinion and Parties Conference, Guildhall University, London, 15–17 September.

Bass, F. M. (1993), "JMR 30th Anniversary Guest Editorial: The future of research in marketing: Marketing science", *Journal of Marketing Research*, vol. 30, 1–6.

Bauer, H. H. (1995), "Ist Marketing (zu etwas) gut?", in H. H. Bauer and H. Diller (eds.), *Wege zum Marketing*, Berlin, Dunker & Humblot, pp. 137–160.

Bauer, H. H., Huber, F., and Herrmann, A. (1995), "Politik-Marketing—Inhalt, Instrumente und Institutionen", *Der Markt*, vol. 34, 115–124.

Bauman, S., and Herbst, S. (1994), "Managing perceptions of public opinion: Candidates and journalists reactions to the 1992 polls", *Political Communication*, vol. 11, 133–144.

Beach, L. R. (1993), "Image theory: An alternative to normative decision theory", *Advances in Consumer Research*, vol. 20, 235–238.

Becker, C. S. (1976), *The Economic Approach to Human Behavior*, Chicago, University of Chicago Press.

Behrena, G. (1991), *Konsumentenverhalren*, Heidelberg, Physica-Verlag.

Belk, R. W., Wallendorf, M., and Sherry Jr., J. F. (1991), "The sacred and the profane in consumer behaviour: Theodicy on the Odyssey", in H. H.

Kassarjian and T. S. Robertson (eds.), *Perspectives in Consumer Behavior*, Englewood Cliffs, Prentice Hall, pp. 511–562. [First published in *Journal of Consumer Research*, 16 (1989), 1-38.]

Bennet, W. L. (1981) "Perception and cognition", in S. L. Long (ed.), *The Handbook of Political Behavior, Vol. 1*, New York/London, Plenum Press, pp. 69–193.

Berelson, B. R., Lazarsfeld, P. F., and Merhee, W. N. (1954), *Voting*, Chicago, University of Chicago Press.

Bettman, J. R., and Zims, M. A. (1991), "Constructive processes in consumer choice", in H. H. Kassarjian and T. S. Robertson (eds.), *Perspectives in Consumer Behavior*, Englewood Cliffs, Prentice-Hall, pp. 166–181. [First published in *Journal of Consumer Research*, vol. 4 (1977), 75–85.]

Bike, W. (1998), *Winning Political Campaigns*, Alaska, Denali [a guide offering an insight into the nature of modern American political campaigning].

Blundell, R. (1988), "Consumer behaviour: Theory and empirical evidence—a survey", *The Economic Journal*, vol. 98 (March), 16–65.

Boll, B., and Poguntke, T. (1992), "Germany: The 1990 all-German election campaign", in S. Bowler and D. M. Farrell (eds.), *Electoral Strategies and Political Marketing*, New York, St. Martin's Press, pp. 121–143.

Bowen, E. R., and Balch, G. I. (1981), "Epistemology, methodology, and method in the study of political behavior", in S. L. Long (ed.), *The Handbook of Political Behavior, Vol. 5*, New York/London, Plenum Press, pp. 1–37.

Bowler, S., Broughton, D., Donovan, T., and Snipp, J. (1992), "The informed electorate? Voter responsiveness to campaigns in Britain and Germany", in S. Bowler and D. M. Farrell (eds.), *Electoral Strategies and Political Marketing*, New York, St. Martin's Press, pp. 204–222.

Bowler, S., and Farrell, D. M. (1992a), "The study of election campaigning", in S. Bowler and D. M. Farrell (eds.), *Electoral Strategies and Political Marketing*, New York, St. Martin's Press, pp. 1–23.

Bowler, S., and Farrell, D. M. (1992b), "Conclusion: The contemporary election campaign", in S. Bowler and D. M. Farrell (eds.), *Electoral Strategies and Political Marketing*, New York, St. Martin's Press, pp. 223–235.

Bowler, S., and Farrell, D. M. (eds.) (1992c), *Electoral Strategies and Political Marketing*, New York, St. Martin's Press.

Bradshaw, J. (1995), "Who will vote for you and why: Designing strategy and theme", in J. A. Thurber and C. J. Nelson (eds.), *Campaigns and Elections American Style*, Boulder, Westview, pp. 30–46.

Brady, H. E., and Sniderman, P. M. (1993), "The likability heuristic", in P. M. Sniderman, R. A. Brody and P. E. Tetlock, *Reasoning and Choice. Explorations in Political Psychology*, Cambridge, Cambridge University Press, pp. 92–119.

Brennan, C., and Lomasky, L. (1993), *Democracy and Decision: The Pure Theory of Electoral Preference*, Cambridge, Cambridge University Press.

Brown, S. (1996), "Art or science? Fifty years of marketing debate", *Journal of Marketing Management*, vol. 12, no. 4, 243–267.

Bryant, J. (1995), "Paid media advertising", in J. A. Thurber and C. J. Nelson (eds.), *Campaigns and Elections American Style*, Boulder, Westview, pp. 84–100.

Budge, I. (1994), "A new spatial theory of party competition: Uncertainty, ideology and policy equilibria viewed comparatively and temporally", *British Journal of Political Science*, vol. 24, 443–467.

Bunn, M. D. (1993), "Taxonomy of buying decision approaches", *Journal of Marketing*, vol. 57, 38–56.

Campbell, A., Converse, P. E., Miller, W. E., and Stokes, D. E. (1960), *The American Voter*, New York, Wiley.

Campbell, A., Gurin, C., and Miller, W. E. (1954), *The Voter Decides*, Evanston, Row, Peterson & Company.

Carman, J. M. (1972), "On the universality of marketing", *Journal of Contemporary Business*, vol. 2 (Autumn), 1–16.

Chubb, J. E., Hagen, M. C., and Sniderman, P. M. (1993), "Ideological reasoning", in P. M. Sniderman, R. A. Brody and P. F. Tetlock, *Reasoning and Choice: Explorations in Political Psychology*, Cambridge, Cambridge University Press, pp. 140–163.

Clifford, P., and Heath, A. (1994), "The election campaign", in A. Heath, R. Jowell and J. Curtice (with B. Taylor), *Labour's Last Chance?*, Aldershot, Dartmouth, pp. 7–23.

Collins, N., and Butler, P. (1995), "Considerations on market analysis for political parties", in S. C. Henneberg and N. O'Shaughnessy (eds.), *Political Marketing—Evolving Science or Maturing Art? Conference Proceedings*, Judge Institute of Management Studies, Cambridge University.

Cooper, M. (1991), "Ethical dimensions of political advocacy from a postmodern perspective", in R. B. Denton, Jr. (ed.), *Ethical Dimensions of Political Communication*, New York, Praeger, pp. 23–47.

Cox, C. W. (1990), "Multicandidate spatial competition", in J. M. Enelow and M. J. Hinich (eds.), *Advances in the Spatial Theory of Voting*, Cambridge, Cambridge University Press, pp. 179-198.

Crewe, I. (1993), "Voting and the electorate", in P. Dunleavy, A. Gamble, I. Holliday and G. Peele (eds.), *Developments in British Politics 4*, Basingstoke, Macmillan, pp. 92–122.

Crewe, I., and King, A. (1994), "Did Major win? Did Kinnock lose?", in A. Heath, R. Jowell and J. Curtice (with B. Taylor), *Labour's Last Chance?*, Aldershot, Dartmouth, pp. 125–147.

Crewe, I., et al. (1998), *Political Communications: The British General Election Campaign of 1997*, Cambridge, Cambridge University Press.

Crockett, L. (1974), "Commentaries on Katona, 'Psychology and Consumer Economics'", *Journal of Consumer Research*, vol. 1, 9–11.

Curtice, J., and Semetko, H. (1994), "Does it matter what the papers say?", in A. Heath, R. Joweel, and J. Curtice (with B. Taylor), *Labour's Last Chance?*, Aldershot, Dartmouth, pp. 43–63.

Czada, R. (1991), "Sozialstruktur und Stimmabgabe", in H.-G. Wehling (ed.), *Wahlverhalten*, Stuttgart, Kohlhammer, pp. 103–130.

Deaton, A. (1992), *Understanding Consumption*, Oxford, Clarendon Press.

Delvin, L. P. (1995), "Political commercials in American presidential elections", in L. Kaid and C. Holtz-Bacha (eds.), *Political Advertising in Western Democracies*, Thousand Oaks, Sage, pp. 186–205.

Demsetz, H. (1990), "Amenity potential, indivisibilities, and political competition", in J. E. Alt and K. A. Shepsie (eds.), *Perspectives on Positive Political Economy*, Cambridge, Cambridge University Press, 144–160.

Denton, R. E., Jr. (1991a), "Political communication ethics: An oxymoron?", in R. E. Denton, Jr. (ed.), *Ethical Dimensions of Political Communication*, New York, Praeger, pp. 1–5.

Denton, R. E., Jr. (1991b), "Primetime politics: The ethics of teledemocracy", in R. E. Denton, Jr. (ed.), *Ethical Dimensions of Political Communication*, New York, Praeger, pp. 91–114.

Denton, R. E., Jr. (ed.) (1991c), *Ethical Dimensions of Political Communication*, New York, Praeger.

Deshpande, R. (1983), "Paradigms lost: On theory and method in research in marketing", *Journal of Marketing* vol. 47, 101–110.

Dibb, S., Simkin, L., Pride, W. M., and Ferrell, O. C. (1994), *Marketing, Concepts and Strategies*, Boston/London: Houghton Mifflin.

Dichtl, E. (1983), "Marketing auf Abwegen?", *Schmalenbachs Zeitschrift für betriebswirtschaftliche Forschung*, vol. 35, 1066–1077.

Downs, A. (1957), *An Economic Theory of Democracy*, New York, Harper Row.

Duncan, C. P., and Olshavsky, R. W. (1982), "External search: the role of consumer beliefs", *Journal of Marketing Research*, vol. 19, 32–43.

Dunleavy, P. (1986), "Topics in British politics", in P. Dunleavy, A. Gamble and G. Peele (eds.), *Developments in British Politics 2*, Basingstoke, Macmillan, pp. 329–372.

Dunleavy, P. (1990), "Mass political behaviour: Is there more to learn?", *Political Studies*, vol. 38, 453–469.

Dunleavy, P. (1991), *Democracy, Bureaucracy and Public Choice: Economic Explanations in Political Science*, New York, Harvester/Wheatsheaf.

Dunleavy, P., Gamble, A., Holliday, I., and Peele, G. (eds.) (1993), *Developments in British Politics 4*, Basingstoke, Macmillan.

Dunleavy, P., Gamble, A., and Peele, G. (eds.) (1986), *Developments in British Politics 2*, Basingstoke, Macmillan.

Dunleavy, P., Gamble, A., and Peele, G. (eds.) (1990), *Developments in British Politics 3*, Basingstoke, MacMillan.

Duverger, M. (1959), *Political Parties*, London, Methuen.

Elster, J. (1990), *Solomonic Judgments*, Cambridge, Cambridge University Press.

Elster, J. (1991), *Sour Grapes: Studies in the Subversion of Rationality*, Cambridge University Press, Cambridge.

Elster, J. (1993a), *Nuts and Bolts and the Social Sciences*, Cambridge, Cambridge University Press.

Elster, J. (1993b), *Political Psychology*, Cambridge, Cambridge University Press.

Elster, J. (1994), *The Cement of Society*, Cambridge, Cambridge University Press.

Enelow, J. M., and Hinich, M. J. (1984), *The Spatial Theory of Voting*, Cambridge, Cambridge University Press.

Enelow, J. M., and Hinich, M. J. (1990a), "Introduction", in J. M. Enelow and M. J. Hinich (eds.), *Advances in the Spatial Theory of Voting*, Cambridge, Cambridge University Press, pp. 1–11.

Enelow, J. M., and Hinich, M. J. (eds.) (1990b), *Advances in the Spatial Theory of Voting*, Cambridge, Cambridge University Press.

226   BIBLIOGRAPHY

Engel, J. F., Blaekwell, R. D., and Miniard, P. W. (1993), *Consumer Behavior*, Fort
    Worth, Dryden Press.
Englis, B. C., and Pennell, C. E. (1993), "Candidates as engendered products:
    Protoypes in political person perception", *Advances in Consumer Research*,
    vol. 20, 612–619.
Enis, B. M. (1973), "Deepening the concept of marketing", *Journal of Marketing*,
    vol. 37, 57–62.
Etgar, M. (1977), "Comment on Hunt (1976)", *Journal of Marketing*, vol. 41, 14–16.
Evans, G. (1994), "Tactical voting and Labour's prospects", in A. Heath, R. Jowell
    and J. Curtice (with B. Taylor), *Labour's Last Chance?*, Aldershot, Dart-
    mouth, pp. 65–84.
Ezra, M., and Nelson, C. J. (1995), "Do campaigns matter?", in J. A. Thurber and
    C. J. Nelson (eds.), *Campaigns and Elections American Style*, Boulder, West-
    view, pp. 224–231.
Farrar, C. (1993), "Ancient Greek political theory as a response to democracy", in
    J. Dunn (ed.), *Democracy*, Oxford, Oxford University Press.
Farrell, D. M. (1989), "Change in the European electoral process: A trend towards
    Americanization", *Manchester Paper in Politics*, no. 6.
Farrell, D. M., and Wortmann, M. (1987), "Party Strategies in the electoral mar-
    ket: Political marketing in West Germany, Britain and Ireland", *European
    Journal of Political Research*, vol. 15, 297–318.
Field, W. (1994), "On the Americanization of electioneering", *Electoral Studies*,
    vol. 13, 58–63.
Fiorina, M. P. (1981), *Retrospective Voting in American National Elections*, New
    Haven, Yale University Press.
Folkes, V. S. (1991), "Recent attribution research in consumer behavior: A review
    and new directions", in H. H. Kassarhian and T. S. Robertson (eds.),
    Perspectives in Consumer Behavior, Englewood Cliffs, Prentice-Hall, pp.
    358–382. [First published in *Journal of Consumer Research*, vol. 14 (1988),
    548–565.]
Fowler, L. L. (1995), "Campaign ethics and political trust", in J. A. Thurber and C.
    J. Nelson (eds.), *Campaigns and Elections American Style*, Boulder, West-
    view, pp. 200–212.
Fox, K. F. A., and Kotler, P. (1980), "The marketing of social causes: The first 10
    years", *Journal of Marketing*, vol. 44, 24–33.
Foxall, G. (1980), "Marketing models of buyer behaviour: A critical view", *Euro-
    pean Research*, vol. 8, no. 5, 195–206.
Foxall, G. (1983), *Consumer Choice*, Basingstoke, Macmillan.
Foxall, G. (1984), "Marketing's domain", *European Journal of Marketing*, vol. 18, no.
    1, 25–40.
Foxall, G. (1985a), "Marketing *is* service marketing", in G. Foxall (ed.), *Marketing
    in the Service Industries*, London/Ottawa, Frank Cass, pp. 1–6.
Foxall, G. (1985b) (ed.), *Marketing in the Service Industries*, London, Frank Cass.
Foxall, G. (1986), "Theoretical progress in consumer psychology: The contribu-
    tion of a behavioural analysis of choice", *Journal of Economic Psychology*,
    vol. 7, 393–414.
Foxall, G. (1990), *Consumer Psychology in Behavioural Perspective*, London/New
    York, Routledge.

Foxall, G. (1993a), *The Behavioural Perspective Model of Purchase and Consumption: Refinement, Extension and Evaluation*, Working Papers in Consumer Research, CRU/93-01, University of Birmingham.

Foxall, G. (1993b), *Consumer Decision Making*, Working Papers in Consumer Research, CR/93-07, University of Birmingham.

Foxall, G., and Goldsmith, R. E. (1994), *Consumer Pychology for Marketing*, London/New York, Routledge.

Franklin, B. (1994), *Packaging Politics: Political Communications in Britain's Media Democracy*, London, Edward Arnold.

Franklin, B. (1995), "Priming the parish pump: Political marketing and news management in local political communications networks", in S. C. Henneberg and N. O'Shaughnessy (eds.), *Political Marketing—Evolving Science or Maturing Art? Conference Proceedings*, Judge Institute of Management Studies, University of Cambridge.

Freedman, P. F., and Freedman, A. (1981), "Political learning", in S. L. Long (ed.), *The Handbook of Political Behaviour, Vol. 1*, New York/London, Plenum Press, pp. 255–303.

Frey, B. S. (1990), *Ökonomie ist Sozialwissenschaft. Die Anwendung der Ökonomie auf neue Gebiete*, Munich, Vahlen.

Fuat Firat, A., Dhlolakia, N., and Venkatesh, A. (1995), "Marketing in a postmodern world", *European Journal of Marketing*, vol. 29, 40–56.

Fulbrook, F. S. (1940), "The functional concept in marketing", *Journal of Marketing*, vol. 4, 229–237.

Gabbott, M., and Hogg, C. (1994), "Consumer behaviour and services: A review", *Journal of Marketing Management*, vol. 10, 311–324.

Gabor, L. (1995), "Tall tales, dark deeds and one worn green", *Times Higher Education Supplement*, 4 August, p. 26.

Gardner, M. P. (1991), "Mood states and consumer behaviour: a critical review", in H. H. Kassarjian and T. S. Robertson (eds.), *Perspectives in Consumer Behaviour*, Englewood Cliffs, Prentice-Hall, pp. 253–80. [First published in *Journal of Consumer Research*, vol. 12 (1985), 281–300.]

Gibowski, W. G. (1991), "Wie wirkt sich die wirtschaftliche Lage auf das Wahlverhalten aus?", in H.-G. Wehung (ed.), *Wahlverhalten*, Stuttgart, Kohlhammer, pp. 122–138.

Gluchowski, P. (1987), "Parteiidentifikation", in D. Nohlen (ed.), *Pipers Wörterbuch zur Politik vol.1*, Munich, Piper, pp. 677–681.

Goldstein, W. (1995), "The ethics of political campaigns", in J. A. Thurber and C. J. Nelson (eds.), *Campaigns and Elections American Style*, Boulder, Westview, pp. 192–199.

Green, D. P., and Shapiro, I. (1994), *Pathologies of Rational Choice Theory*, New Haven/London, Yale University Press.

Gronbeck, B. E. (1991), "Ethical pivots and moral vantages in American presidential campaign dramas", in R. E. Denton, Jr. (ed.), *Ethical Dimensions of Political Communication*, New York, Praeger, pp. 49–68.

Grönroos, C. (1995), "Relationship marketing: The strategy continuum", *Journal of the Academy of Marketing Science*, vol. 23, 252–254.

Gundlach, C. T., Achrol, R. S., and Mentzer, I. T. (1995), "The structure of commitment in exchange", *Journal of Marketing*, vol. 59, 78–92.

Hamann, P., and Erichson, B. (1990), *Markforschung*, Stuttgart, UTB/Gustav Fischer Verlag.

Hamilton, W. R. (1995), "Political polling: From the beginning to the center", in J. A. Thurber and C. J. Nelson (eds.), *Campaigns and Elections American Style*, Boulder, Westview, pp. 161–180.

Hinsen, F. (1976), "Psychological theories of consumer choice", *Journal of Consumer Research*, vol. 3, 117–142.

Hargraves Heap, S., Hollis, M., Lyons, B. I., Sugden, R., and Weale, A. (1992), *The Theory of Choice: A Critical Guide*, Oxford, Blackwell.

Harris, P. (1994), *Political Lobbying or Machiavellian Marketing in Britain*, Paper for the British Academy of Management Conference, University of Lancaster, September.

Harris, P., and Lock, A. (1996), "Political marketing—Vive la différence!", *European Journal of Marketing*, vol. 30, 10–11.

Harrop, M. (1986), "Voting and the electorate", in H. Drucker et al. (eds.), *Developments in British Politics 2*, Basingstoke, Macmillan.

Harrop, M. (1990), "Political Marketing", *Parliamentary Affairs*, vol. 43, 277–291.

Harrop, M., and Miller, W. L. (1987), *Elections and Voters: A Comparative Introduction*, London, Macmillan.

Hasitschka, W. (1978), "Marketing für Nonprofit-Organisationen—Ein Forschungsstrategischer Typologisierungsansatz", *Der Markt*, vol. 65, 170–176.

Hasitschka, W. (1995), "Politik-Marketing", in B. Tietz, R. Kohler and J. Zentes (eds.), *Handwörterbuch des Marketing*, Stuttgart, Schaffer-Poeschl, pp. 2030–2042.

Hauser, J. R. (1986), "Agendas and consumer choice", *"Journal of Marketing Research*, vol. 23, 199–212.

Hauser, J. R., Urban, C. L., and Weinberg, B. D. (1993), "How consumers allocate their time when searching for information", *Journal of Marketing Research*, vol. 30, 452–466.

Heath, A. (1976), *Rational Choice & Social Exchange*, Cambridge, Cambridge University Press.

Heath, A., and Jowell, R. (1994), "Labour's policy review", in A. Heath, R. Jowell and J. Curtice (with B. Taylor), *Labour's Last Chance?*, Aldershot, Dartmouth, pp. 191–211.

Heath, A., Jowell, R., and Curtice, J. (1985), *How Britain Votes*, Oxford, Pergamon.

Heath, A., Jowell, R., and Curtice, J. (1994a), "Introduction", in A. Heath, R. Jowell and J. Curtice (with B. Taylor), *Labour's Last Chance?*, Aldershot, Dartmouth, pp. 1–6.

Heath, A., Jowell, R., and Curtice, J. (1994b), "Can Labour win?", in A. Heath, R. Jowell and J. Curtice (with B. Taylor), *Labour's Last Chance?*, Aldershot, Dartmouth, pp. 275–299.

Heath, A., Jowell, R., Curtice, J., Evans, C., Field, J., and Witherspoon, S. (1991), *Understanding Political Change*, Oxford, Pergamon.

Heath, A., Jowell, R., and Curtice, J. (with B. Taylor) (1994), *Labour's Last Chance?*, Aldershot, Dartmouth.

Hempelmann, B. (1995), "Generic marketing", in B. Tietz, R. Kohler and J. Zentes (eds.), *Handwörterbuch des Marketing*, Stuttgart, Schaffer-Poeschl, pp. 744–748.

Henneberg, S. C. (1995a), "Introduction", in S. C. Henneberg and N. O'Shaughnessy (eds.), *Political Marketing—Evolving Science or Maturing Art? Conference Proceedings*, Judge Institute of Management Studies, University of Cambridge.

Henneberg, S. C. (1995b), "The political 'market'—An analogy as foundation of political marketing?", in S. C. Henneberg and N. O'Shaughnessy, *Political Marketing—Evolving Science or Maturing Art? Conference Proceedings*, Judge Institute of Management Studies, University of Cambridge.

Henneberg, S. C. (1995c), *A Theoretical Approach of Categorising Research in Political Marketing*, Paper presented at the PSA Elections, Public Opinion and Parties Conference, London, 15–17 September.

Henneberg, S. C. (1996a), "Book review: B. Franklin, 'Packaging Politics'", *Party Politics*, vol. 2, no. 2.

Henneberg, S. C. (1996b), "Political marketing—Evolving science or maturing art?", *Party Developments*, vol. 2, no. 1.

Henneberg, S. C., and O'Shaughnessy, N. (eds.) (1995), *Political Marketing—Evolving Science or Maturing Art? Conference Proceedings*, Judge Institute of Management Studies, University of Cambridge.

Herrmann, A., and Gutiche, J. (1994), "Ein Modell zur Erfassung der individuellen Markenwechselneignung", *(Schmalenbachs) Zeitschrift für betriebswirtschaftliche Forschung*, vol. 46, 63–80.

Herrnson, P. S. (1995), "Field work, political parties, and volunteerism", in J. A. Thurber and C. J. Nelson (eds.), *Campaigns and Elections American Style*, Boulder, Westview, pp. 152–160.

Himmelweit, H., Humphreys, P., and Jaeger, M. (1985), *How Voters Decide,* Milton Keynes, Open University Press.

Hirschman, E. C. (1986), "Humanistic inquiry in marketing research: Philosophy, method, and criteria", *Journal of Marketing Research*, vol. 23, 237–249.

Hirschman, E. C. (1987), "People as products: Analysis of a complex marketing exchange", *Journal of Marketing*, vol. 51, 98–108.

Hogarth, R. M., and Reder, M. W. (1986), "Editors' comments: Perspectives from economics and psychology", *Journal of Business*, vol. 59, no. 4, S185–S207.

Holbrook, T. M. (1994), "Campaigns, national conditions, and U.S. presidential elections", *American Journal of Political Science*, vol. 38, 973–998.

Holt, D. B. (1995), "How consumers consume: A typology of consumption practices", *Journal of Consumer Research*, vol. 22, 1–16.

Holtz-Bacha, C., Kaid, L. L., and Johnston, A. (1994), "Political television advertising in Western democracies: A comparison of campaign broadcasts in the United States, Germany, and France," *Political Communication*, vol. 11, 67–80.

Homans, G. C. (1961), *Social Behavior*, London, Routledge & Kegan Paul.

Houston, F. S. (1986), "The marketing concept: What it is and what is it not", *Journal of Marketing*, vol. 50, 81–87.

Howard, J. A., and Sheth, J. N. (1969), *The Theory of Buyer Behavior*, New York, Wiley.

Hunt, S. D. (1976), "The nature and scope of marketing", *Journal of Marketing*, vol. 40, 17–28.

Hunt, S. D. (1983), "General theories and the fundamental explananda of marketing", *Journal of Marketing*, vol. 47, 9–17.

Hunt, S. D. (1991), *Modern Marketing Theory: Critical Issues in the Philosophy of Marketing Science*, Cincinnati, South-Western Publishing.

Hunt, S. D. (1992), "For reason and realism in marketing", *Journal of Marketing*, vol. 56, 89–102.

Hunt, S. D. (1993), "Objectivity in marketing theory and research", *Journal of Marketing*, vol. 57, 76–91.

Hunt, S. D. (1994a), "On the rhetoric of qualitative methods", *Journal of Management Inquiry*, vol. 3, 221–234.

Hunt, S. D. (1994b), "A realist theory of empirical testing: Resolving the theory-ladenness/objectivity debate", *Philosophy of the Social Sciences*, vol. 24, 133–158.

Hunt, S. D., and Morgan, R. M. (1995), "The comparative advantage theory of competition", *Journal of Marketing*, vol. 59, 1–15.

Hutt, M. D., Mowka, M. P., and Shapiro, S. J. (1986), "The politics of marketing: Analyzing the parallel political marketplace", *Journal of Marketing*, vol. 50, 40–51.

Jamieson, K. H. (1992a), *Dirty Politics*, New York/Oxford, Oxford University Press.

Jamieson, K. H. (1992b), *Packaging the Presidency*, 2nd edition, New York, Oxford University Press.

Jaworski, B. J., and Kohli, A. K. (1993), "Market orientation: Antecedents and consequences", *Journal of Marketing*, vol. 57, 53–70.

Johanneson, R. L. (1991), "Virtue ethics, character, and political communication", in R. E. Denton, Jr. (ed.), *Ethical Dimensions of Political Communication*, New York, Praeger, pp. 69–90.

Johnson, J., Meyer, R. J., and Chose, S. (1989), "When choice models fail: Compensatory models in negatively correlated environments", *Journal of Marketing Research*, vol. 26, 255–270.

Johnston, R. J. (1985), "Political advertising and the geography of voting in England at the 1983 General Election", *International Journal of Advertising*, vol. 4, 1–10.

Johnston, R. J., and Pattie, C. J. (1995), "The impact of spending on party constituency campaigns at recent British general elections", *Party Politics*, vol. 1, 261–273.

Johnston, R. J., Pattie, C. J., and Russell, A. T. (1993), "Dealignment, spatial polarisation and economic voting", *European Journal of Political Research*, vol. 23, 67–90.

Jones, N. (1995), *Soundbites and Spin Doctors: How Politicians Manipulate the Media and Vice Versa*, London, Cassell.

Jones, S. (1982), "Social marketing: Dimensions of power and politics", *European Journal of Marketing*, vol. 16, no. 6, 46–53.

Jung, M. (1991), "Der Wechselwähler—das unbekannte Wesen", in H.-G. Wehung (ed.), *Wahlverhalten*, Stuttgart, Kohlhammer, 208–223.

Kaid, L. L. (1991), "Ethical dimensions of political advertising", in R. E. Donton (ed.), *Ethical Dimensions of Political Communication*, New York, Praeger, pp. 145–169.

Karvonen, L. (1991), "The study of election campaigns: An introduction", *Scandinavian Political Studies*, vol. 14, no. 3, 195–203.

Kassarjian, H. H., and Robertson T. S. (eds.) (1991), *Perspectives in Consumer Behavior*, Englewood Cliffs, Prentice-Hall.

Kassarjian, H. H., and Sheffet, M. J. (1991), "Personality and consumer behaviour: An update", in H. H. Kassarjian and T. S. Robertson (eds.), *Perspectives in Consumer Behavior*, Englewood Cliffs, Prentice-Hall, pp. 281–303.

Katona, C. (1974), "Psychology and consumer economics", *Journal of Consumer Research*, vol. 1, 1–8.

Katz, R. S., and Kolodny, R. (1992), "The USA: The 1990 congressional campaign", S. Bowler and D. M. Farrell (eds.), *Electoral Strategies and Political Marketing*, New York, St. Martin's Press, pp 183–203.

Katz, R. S., and Mair, P. (1995), "Changing Models of Party Organization and Party Democracy: The Emergence of the Cartel Party", *Party Politics*, vol. 1, 5–28.

Kavanagh, D. (1995a), *Election Campaigning: The New Marketing of Politics*, Oxford, Blackwell.

Kavanagh, D. (1995b), "Speaking truth to power? Pollsters as campaign advisors", in S. C. Henneberg and N. O'Shaughnessy (eds.), *Political Marketing—Evolving Science or Maturing Art? Conference Proceedings*, Judge Institute of Management Studies, University of Cambridge.

Key, Jr., V. O. (1966), *The Responsible Electorate*, Cambridge, MA, Belknap Press of Harvard University Press.

Kinder, D. R., and Sears, D. O. (1985), "Public opinion and political action", in G. Lindzey and E. Aronson (eds.), *Handbook of Social Psychology, Vol. 2*, New York, Random House, pp. 659–741.

Kotler, P. (1972), "A generic concept of marketing", *Journal of Marketing*, vol. 36, pp. 46–54.

Kotler, P. (1979), "Strategies for introducing marketing into nonprofit organizations", *Journal of Marketing*, vol. 43, 37–44.

Kotler, P., and Andreason, A. R. (1991), *Strategic Marketing for Nonprofit Organizations*, Englewood Cliffs, Prentice-Hall.

Kotler, P., and Bliemel, F. (1992), *Marketing-Management*, Stuttgart, C. E. Poeschel Verlag.

Kotler, P., and Levy, S. J. (1969a), "Broadening the concept of marketing", *Journal of Marketing*, vol. 33, 10–15.

Kotler, P., and Levy, S. J. (1969b), "A new form of marketing myopia: Rejoinder to Professor Luck", *Journal of Marketing*, vol. 33, 55–57.

Kotler, P., and Zaltman, C. (1971), "Social marketing: An approach to planned social change", *Journal of Marketing*, vol. 35, 8–12.

Kroeber-Riel, W. (1979), "Empirische Entscheidungsforschung", *Marketing ZFP*, vol. 1, no. 4, 267–274.

Kroeber-Riel, W. (1991), "Activation research: psychobiological approaches in consumer research", in H. H. Kassarjian and T. S. Robertson (eds.),

Perspectives in Consumer Behavior, Englewood Cliffs, Prentice-Hall, pp. 225–239. [First published in *Journal of Consumer Research*, vol. 5 (1979), 240–250.]

Kroeber-Riel, W. (1992), *Konsumentenverhalten* [Consumer behaviour], Munich, Vahien.

Kuß, A. (1991) *Kauferverhalten*, UTB/Gustav Fischer, Stuttgart, 1991.

Laaksonen, P. (1994), *Consumer Involvement*, London/New York, Routledge.

Lacziniak, G. R., Lusch, R. F., and Murphy, P. E. (1979), "Social marketing: Its ethical dimensions", *Journal of Marketing*, vol. 43, 29–36.

Lane, R. (1993), *Voting and Buying: Political Economy on the Small Stage*, Paper presented at the Annual Meeting of the Society for the Advancement of Socioeconomics, New York School for Social Research, New York, March.

Lazarsfeld, P. F., Berelson, B., and Gaudet, H. (1968), *The People's Choice*, New York/London, Columbia University Press.

Lazer, W. (1969), "Marketings changing social relationships", *Journal of Marketing*, vol. 33, 3–9.

LeClaire, K. A. (1981), "Consumer processing of information: fact or fiction?", *European Research*, vol. 9, no. 4, 134–143.

Lehner, F. (1987) "Okonomische Theorien der Politik", in D. Nohien (ed.), *Pipers Wörterbuch zur Politik, Vol 1*, Marichen, Piper, pp. 630–635.

Levitt, T. (1960), "Marketing myopia", *Harvard Business Review*, vol. 38, 45–56.

Lidstone, J. (1985), "The marketing of professional services", in G. Foxall (ed.), *Marketing in the Service Industries*, London/Ottawa, Frank Cass, pp. 7–11.

Lindzey, G., and Aronson, E. (eds.) (1985), *Handbook of Social Psychology, Vol. 2*, New York, Random House.

Long, S. L. (ed.) (1981), *The Handbook of Political Behavior, vol. 1*, New York/London, Plenum Press.

Luck, D. J. (1969), "Broadening the concept of marketing—Too far", *Journal of Marketing*, vol. 33, 53–55.

Luck, D. J. (1974), "Social marketing: Confusion compounded", *Journal of Marketing*, vol. 38, 70–72.

Lutz, R. J. (1991), "The role of attitude theory in marketing", in H. H. Kassarjian and T. S. Robertson (eds.), *Perspectives in Consumer Behavior*, Englewood Cliffs, Prentice-Hall, pp. 317–339.

Lynch Jr., J. C., and Srull, T. K. (1991), "Memory and attentional factors in consumer choice: concepts and research methods", in H. H. Kassarjian and T. S. Robertson (eds.), *Perspectives in Consumer Behaviour*, Prentice Hall, Englewood-Cliffs, pp.101–129. [First published in *Journal of Consumer Research* (1982), 18–37.]

Majaro, S. (1985), "Marketing insurance services: The main challenges", in G. Foxall (ed.), *Marketing in the Service Industries*, London/Ottawa, Frank Cass, pp. 76–90.

Malafarina, K., and Loken, B. (1993), "Progress and limitations of social marketing: A review of empirical literature on the consumption of social ideas", *Advances in Consumer Research*, vol. 20, 397–404.

Manger, C. A. (1982), *Political Marketing*, New York, Praeger.

Marsh, D. (1986), "The media and politics", in P. Dunleavy, A. Gamble and G.

Peele (eds.), *Developments in British Politics 2*, Basingstoke, Macmillan, pp. 332–349.

Matthews, J. (1991/1992), *The Marketing of the Conservative Party in the 1992 General Election*, M.Phil. dissertation, Judge Institute of Management Studies, University of Cambridge.

Mauser, G. A. (1980), "Positioning political candidates—An application of concept evaluation techniques", *Journal of the Market Research Society*, vol. 22, 181–191.

McGuire, W. J. (1976), "Some internal psychological factors influencing consumer choice", *Journal of Consumer Research*, vol. 2, 302–319.

McKelvey, R. D., and Ordeshook, P. C. (1990), "A decade of experimental research in spatial models of elections and committees", in J. M. Endow and M. J. Hinich (eds.), *Advances in the Spatial Theory of Voting*, Cambridge, Cambridge University Press, pp. 99–144.

McNair, B. (1995), *Introduction to Political Communication*, London: Routledge.

Mercer, D. (1992), *Marketing*, Oxford, Blackwell.

Michalos, A. C. (1991), "Ethical considerations regarding public opinion polling during election campaigns" *Journal of Business Ethics*, vol. 10, 403–422.

Miller, W. L. (1990), "Voting and the electorate", in P. Dunleavy, A. Gamble and G. Peele (eds.), *Developments in British Politics 3*, Basingstoke, Macmillan, pp. 42–68.

Miller, W. L., Clarke, H. D., Harrop, M., Leduc, L., and Whiteley, P. F. (1990), *How Voters Change*, Oxford, Clarendon Press.

Mittal, B. (1990), "The relative roles of brand beliefs and attitude toward the ad as mediators of brand attitude: a second look", *Journal of Marketing Research*, vol. 27, 209–219.

Moorthy, K. S. (1993), "Theoretical modeling in marketing", *Journal of Marketing*, vol. 57, 92–106.

Morgan, R. M., and Hunt, S. D. (1994), "The commitment–trust theory of relationship marketing", *Journal of Marketing*, vol. 58, 20–38.

Muller-Hagedorn, L. (1986), *Das Konsumentenverhalten*, Wiesbaden, Gabler, 1986.

Muller-Rommel, R., and Poguntke, T. (1990), "Lebensstile und Wahlverhalten [Life-styles and voting behaviour]", *Der Burger im Staat*, vol. 40, no. 3.

Muller-Rommel, R., and Poguntke, T. (1991), "Lebensstile und Wahlverhalten [Life-styles and voting behaviour]", in H. G. Wehung (ed.), *Wahlverhalten*, Kohlhammer, Stuttgart, pp. 179–193.

Muncy, J. A., and Fisk, R. P. (1987), "Cognitive relativism and the practice of marketing science", *Journal of Marketing*, vol. 51, 20–33.

Newman, B. I. (1993), "The role of marketing in the 1992 US presidential election: How Bill Clinton was transformed from 'Slick Willie' to 'Mr President'", *Werbeforschung & Praxis*, vol. 38, 195–201.

Newman, B. I. (1994a), "The forces behind the merging of marketing and politics", *Werbeforschung & Praxis*, vol. 39, 41–46.

Newman, B. I. (1994b). *The Marketing of the President: Political Marketing as Campaign Strategy*, Thousand Oaks, Sage.

Newman, B. I. (1995a), "Political marketing as a governing tool", in S. C. Henneberg and N. O'Shaughnessy (eds.), *Political Marketing—Evolving Science or Maturing Art? Conference Proceedings*, Judge Institute of Management Studies, University of Cambridge.

Newman, B. I. (1995b), "Political marketing as a governing tool", *Werbeforschung & Praxis*, vol. 5, 163–167.

Newman, B. I. (1996), *The Role of Marketing in American Politics*, Paper presented at the PSA Conference, Glasgow.

Newman, B. I. (ed.) (1999), *Handbook of Political Marketing*, Thousand Oaks, Sage.

Newman, B. I., and Sheth, J. N. (1987), *A Theory of Political Choice Behavior*, New York, Praeger.

Nicosia, R. M. (1966) *Consumer Decision Processes*, Englewood Cliffs, Prentice-Hall.

Nicosia, R. M., and Mayer, R. N. (1976), "Toward a sociology of consumption", *Journal of Consumer Research*, vol. 3, 65–75.

Nie, N. H., Verba, S., and Retrocik, J. R. (1976), *The Changing American Voter*, Cambridge, MA, Harvard University Press.

Nimmo, D. (1970), *The Political Persuaders: The Techniques of Modern Election Campaigns*, Englewood Cliffs, Prentice-Hall.

Nohien, D. (ed.) (1987), *Pipers Wörterbuch zur Politik, vol. 1*, Munich, Piper.

Nord, W. R., and Perter, J. P. (1991), "A behavior modification perspective on marketing", in H. H. Kassarhian and T. S. Robertson (eds.), *Perspectives in Consumer Behavior*, Englewood Cliffs, Prentice-Hall, pp.130–143. [First published in *Journal of Marketing*, vol. 44 (1980), 36–47.]

North, D. C. (1990), "Institutions and a transaction-cost theory of exchange", in J. E. Alt and K. A. Shepsie (eds.), *Perspectives on Positive Political Economy*, Cambridge, Cambridge University Press, pp. 182–194.

Olshavsky, R. W., and Granbois, D. H. (1991), "Consumer decision making—fact or fiction?", in H. H. Kassarj ian and T. S. Robertson (eds.), *Perspectives in Consumer Behavior*, Englewood Cliffs, Prentice-Hall, pp.89–100 [First published in *Journal of Consumer Research*, vol. 6 (1979), 93–100.]

Olson, M. (1990) "Toward a unified view of economics and the other social sciences", in J. E. Alt and K. A. Shepsie (eds.), *Perspectives on Positive Political Economy*, Cambridge, Cambridge University Press, pp. 212–231.

Omura, C. S. (1979), "Role of attribute generality in cognition of political candidates", *Advances in Consumer Research*, vol. 6, 635–640.

Ordershook, P.C. (1990), "The emerging discipline of political economy", in J. E. Alt and K. A. Shepsie (eds.), *Perspectives on Positive Political Economy*, Cambridge, Cambridge University Press, pp.9–30.

O'Shaughnessy, J. (1987), *Why People Buy*, Oxford/New York, Oxford University Press.

O'Shaughnessy, J. (1988), *Voter Decisions Processes*. Unpublished paper.

O'Shaughnessy, J. (1992), *Explaining Buyer Behaviour, Central Concepts and Philosophy of Science Issues*, New York/Oxford, Oxford University Press.

O'Shaughnessy, J. (1995a), *Competitive Marketing: A Strategic Approach*, London, Routledge.

O'Shaughnessy, J. (1995b), *The Concept of Rationality and Flawed Rationality*, Paper presented at seminar, Judge Institute of Management Studies, University of Cambridge, February.

O'Shaughnessy, J., and Holbrook, M. B. (1988), "Understanding consumer behaviour: The linguistic turn in marketing research", *Journal of the Market Research Society*, vol. 30, 197–223.

O'Shaughnessy, N. (1987), "America's political market", *European Journal of Marketing*, vol. 21, 60–66.

O'Shaughnessy, N. (1988), "The peevish penmen: Direct mail and US elections", *European Journal of Marketing*, vol. 22, no. 6, 36–44.

O'Shaughnessy, N. (1989/90), "Political marketing: An ethical conundrum?", *Irish Marketing Review*, vol. 4, no. 3, 39–48.

O'Shaughnessy, N. (1990a), "High priesthood, low priestcraft: The role of political consultants", *European Journal of Marketing* vol. 24, no. 2, 7–23.

O'Shaughnessy, N. (1990b), *The Phenomenon of Political Marketing*, Basingstoke, Macmillan.

O'Shaughnessy, N. (1996), "Social propaganda and social marketing: A critical difference", in S. C. Henneberg, N. O'Shaughnessy and S. Eghbalian (eds.), *Political Marketing. Conference Proceedings*, Judge Institute of Management Studies, Cambridge University.

O'Shaughnessy, N., and Holbrook, M. D. (1988), "What U.S. businesses can learn from political marketing", *Journal of Applied Business Research*, vol. 4, no. 3, 98–109.

O'Shaughnessy, N., and Peele, C. (1985), "Money, mail and markets: Reflections on direct mail in American politics", *Electoral Studies*, vol. 4, 115–124.

O'Shaughnessy, N., and Wring, D. (1994), "Political marketing in Britain", in H. Tam (ed.), *Marketing Competition and the Public Sector*, Harlow, Longman, pp. 246–270.

Ostrom, A., and Iacobucci, D. (1995), "Consumer trade-offs and the evaluation of services", *Journal of Marketing*, vol. 59, 17–28.

Panebianco, A. (1988), *Political Parties' Organisation and Power*, Cambridge, Cambridge University Press.

Paulson, B. (1994), "The economy and the 1992 election: Was 1992 Labour's golden chance?", in A. Heath, R. Jowell and J. Curtice (with B. Taylor), *Labour's Last Chance?*, Aldershot, Dartmouth, pp. 84–106.

Peele, G. (1982), "Campaign consultants", *Electoral Studies*, vol. 1, 355–362.

Perloff, R. M., and Kinsey, D. (1992), "Political advertising as seen by consultants and journalists", *Journal of Advertising Research*, vol. 32 (May/June), 53–60.

Peter, J. P. (1992), "Realism or relativism for marketing theory and research: A comment on Hunt's scientific realism", *Journal of Marketing*, vol. 56, 72–79.

Peterson, R. A. (1995), "Relationship marketing and the consumer", *Journal of the Academy Marketing Science*, vol. 23, 178–281.

Petrocik, J. R. (1995), "Reporting campaigns: Reforming the press", in J. A. Thurber and C. J. Nelson (eds.), *Campaigns and Elections American Style*, Boulder, Westview, pp. 126–137.

Petty, R. E., Cacioppo, J. T., and Schumann, D. (1991), "Central and peripheral routes to advertising effectiveness: The moderating role of involvement", in H. H. Kassarjian and T. S. Robertson (eds.), *Perspectives in*

Consumer Behavior, Englewood Cliffs, Prentice-Hall, pp. 340-357. [First published in *Journal of Consumer Research*, vol. 10 (1983), 135–146.]

Philo, C. (1995), "Political advertising and political economy", in S. C. Henneberg and N. O'Shaughnessy (eds.), *Political Marketing—Evolving Science or Maturing Art? Conference Proceedings*, Judge Institute of Management Studies, University of Cambridge.

Popkin, S. L. (1994), *The Reasoning Voter*, Chicago/London, University of Chicago Press.

Popkin, S. L. (1995), "Strategic perspectives on the 1992 campaign", in J. A. Thurber and C. J. Nelson (eds.), *Campaigns and Elections American Style*, Boulder, Westview, pp. 213–223.

Raffee, H., and Specht, C. (1974), "Basisverurteile der Marketing-Wissenschaft", *Schmalenbachs Zeitschrift für betriebswirtschaftliche Forschung*, vol. 26, 373–396.

Raffee, H., and Wiedmann, K-P. (1995), "Nonprofit-marketing", in B. Tietz, R. Kohler and J. Zentes (eds.), *Handwörterbuch des Marketing*, Stuttgart, Schaffer-Poeschl, pp. 1930–1942.

Rauen, B. (1994), "Berlusconi: Wahlkampf mit den eigneen Medien", *Media Perspecktiven*, vol. 7, 349–361.

Reid, D. (1988), "Marketing the political product", *European Journal of Marketing*, vol. 22, 34–47.

Richardson, P.S., Dick, A. S., and Jam, A. K. (1994), "Extrinsic and intrinsic cue effects on perceptions of strong brand quality" *Journal of Marketing*, vol. 58, no. 4, 28–36.

Riggle, E. D., Ottati, V. C., Wyer, R. S., Kuldinsid, J., and Schwarz, N. (1992), "Bases of political judgments: The role of stereotypic and nonstereotypic information", *Political Behavior*, vol. 14, 67–87.

Riker, W. H. (1990), "Political science and rational choice", in J. A. Alt and K. A. Shepsie, *Perspectives on Positive Political Economy*, Cambridge, Cambridge University Press, pp. 163–181.

Riley, M. (1988), *Power Politics and Voting Behaviour*, New York, Harvester.

Roberts, M., and McCombs, M. (1994), "Agenda setting and political advertising: Origins of the news agenda", *Political Communication*, vol. 11, 249–262.

Robin, D. P. (1977), "Comment on Hunt (1976)", *Journal of Marketing*, vol. 41, 136–138.

Robin, D. P. (1978), "Comment on Hunt (1976), and Hunt (1978)", *Journal of Marketing*, vol. 42, 6, 42.

Robinson, W. (1995), "Organizing the field", in J. A. Thurber and C. J. Nelson (eds.), *Campaigns and Elections American Style*, Boulder, Westview, pp. 138–151.

Ross, W. H. (1977), "Comment on Hunt (1976)", *Journal of Marketing*, vol. 41, 10, 146.

Rothschild, M. L. (1978), "Political Advertising: A Neglected Policy Issue in Marketing", *Journal of Marketing Research*, vol. 15, 58–71.

Ryan, M. J., and Bofield, E. H. (1980), "Fischbein's intentions model: a test of external and pragmatic validity", *Journal of Marketing*, vol. 44 (Spring), 82–95.

Sackman, A. (1992), *The Marketing Organisation Model: Making Sense of Modern*

Campaigning in Britain, Paper presented at the UK Political Studies Association Annual Conference, Belfast, April.

Sanders, D. (1994), *The Economy, Political Forecasting and the Marketing of UK Political Parties*, Paper presented to the Conference on Political Marketing, Judge Institute of Management, Cambridge University, March.

Scammell, M. (1991), *The Impact of Marketing and Public Relations on Modern British Politics: The Conservative Party and Government under Mrs. Thatcher*, Ph.D Thesis, London School of Economics and Political Science, University of London.

Scammell, M. (1994), "The phenomenon of political marketing: The Thatcher contribution", *Contemporary Record*, vol. 8, no. 1, 23–43.

Scammell, M. (1995), *Designer Politics*. Basingstoke, Macmillan.

Scammell, M. (1998), "The wisdom of the war room: US campaigning and Americanization", *Media Culture and Society*, vol. 20, no. 2, 251–275.

Schanz, G. (1975), *Einführung in die Methodologie der BWL*, Cologne, Kiepenhauser & Witsch.

Schedler, A. (1994), "Die (eigensinnige), kommunkative Struktur demokratischer Wahlen", *Zeitschrift für Politik*, vol. 41, 22–43.

Schultre, R. O. (1983), "Wählerverhalten", in D. Nohlen (ed.), *Pipers Wörterbuch zur Politik, vol. 1*, Munich, Piper, pp. 497–507.

Schultre, R. O. (1987), "Wahlverhalten", in D. Nohlen (ed.), *Pipers Wörterbuch zur Politik, vol. 2*, Munich, Piper, pp. 1124–1129.

Schultre, R. O. (1991), "Wählerverhalten und Parteiensystem", in H.-U. Wehling (ed.), *Wahlverhalten*, Stuttgart, Kohlhammer, pp. 11–43.

Schulz, W. (1994), "Wird die Wahl im Fern sehen entschieden?", *Media Perspektiven*, vol. 7, 318–327.

Schumpeter, J. A. (1950), *Kapitalismus, Soczialismus und Demokratie*, Tübingen/Basel, UTB, Francke.

Sellien, R. and Sellien, H. (eds.) (1988), *Gabler Wirtschafts-Lexikon*, 6 vol., Wiesbaden, Gabler.

Selnow, C. W. (1991), "Polls and computer technologies: Ethical considerations", in R. E. Denton, Jr. (ed.), *Ethical Dimensions of Political Communication*, New York, Praeger, pp. 171–197.

Semetko, H., and Scammel, M. (1995), "Political Advertising in Television", in L. Kaid and Holtz-Bacha, C. (eds.), *Political Advertising in Western Democracies*, Thousand Oaks, Sage.

Semetko, H., Scammel, M., and Nossiter, T. (1994), "The medias coverage of the campaign", in A. Heath, R. Jowell and J. Curtice (with B. Taylor), *Labour's Last Chance?*, Aldershot, Dartmouth, pp. 25–41.

Sen, A. (1992), *On Ethics & Economics*, Oxford, Blackwell.

Shapiro, B. P. (1975), "Marketing for nonprofit organizations", *Harvard Business Review*, vol. 51 (September/October), 123–132.

Shepsie, K. A., and Cohen, R. N. (1990), "Multiparty competition, entry, and entry deterrence in spatial models of elections", in J. M. Enelow and M. J. Hinich (eds.), *Advances in the Spatial Theorv of Voting*, Cambridge, Cambridge University Press, pp.12–45.

Sheth, J. N., Gardner, D. M., and Garrett, D. E. (1988), *Marketing Theory: Evolution and Evaluation*, New York, Wiley.

Sheth, J. N., and Parvatiyar, A. (1995), "Relationship marketing in consumer markets: antecedents and consequences", *Journal of the Academy of Marketing Science* vol. 23, 255-271.

Simmons, C. J., Bickart, B. A., and Lynch Jr., J. G. (1993), "Capturing and creating public opinion in survey research", *Journal of Consumer Research,* vol. 20, 316-329.

Simon, H. A. (1985), "The dialogue of psychology with political science", *American Political Science Review,* vol. 79, no. 2, 293-304.

Simon, H. A. (1955), "A behavioral model of rational choice", *Quarterly Journal of Economics,* vol. 69, 99-118.

Smith, G., and Saunders, J. (1990), "The application of marketing to British politics", *Journal of Marketing Management,* vol. 5, 295-306.

Sniderman, P. M., Brody, R. A., and Tetlock, P. E. (1993a), "Introduction: Major themes", in P. M. Sniderman, R. A. Brody and P. E. Tetlock, *Reasoning and Choice: Explorations in Political Psychology,* Cambridge, Cambridge University Press, pp. 1-13.

Sniderman, P. M., Brody, R. A., and Tetlock, P. E. (1993b), *Reasoning and Choice: Explorations in Political Psychology,* Cambridge, Cambridge University Press.

Sniderman, P. M., Brody, R. A., and Tetlock, P. E. (1993c), "The role of heuristics in political reasoning: A theory sketch", in P. M. Sniderman, R. A. Brody and P. E. Tetlock, *Reasoning and Choice. Explorations in Political Psychology,* Cambridge, Cambridge University Press, pp. 14-30.

Sniderman, P. M., Brody, R. A., Tetlock, P. E., and Spranca, M. D. (1993), "Retrospect and prospect", in P. M. Sniderman, R. A. Brody and P. E. Tetlock, *Reasoning and Choice. Explorations in Political Psychology,* Cambridge, Cambridge University Press, pp. 261-272.

Sniderman, P. M., Glaser, J. M., and Griffin, R. (1993), "Information and electoral choice", in P. M. Sniderman, R. A. Brody and P. E. Tetlock, *Reasoning and Choice: Explorations in Political Psychology,* Cambridge, Cambridge University Press, pp. 164-178.

Sniderman, P. M., Hagen, M. B., Tetlock, P. E., and Brady, H. E. (1986), "Reasoning chains: Causal models of policy reasoning in mass publics", *British Journal of Political Science,* vol. 16, 405-430.

Sniderman, P. M., Hagen, M. B., Tetlock, P. E., and Brady, H. E. (1993), "Reasoning chains", in P. M. Sniderman, R. A. Brody and P. E. Tetlock, *Reasoning and Choice: Explorations in Political Psychology,* Cambridge, Cambridge University Press, pp. 71-92.

Sniderman, P. M., Tetlock, P. E., Glaser, J. M., Green, O. P., and Hout, M. (1993), "Democratic values and mass publics", in P. M. Sniderman, R. A. Brody and P. B. Tetlock, *Reasoning and Choice: Explorations in Political Psychology,* Cambridge, Cambridge University Press, pp. 120-139.

Sparrow, N., and Turner, J. (1995), "Massages from the spiral of silence: Developing more accurate market information in a more uncertain political climate", in S. C. Henneberg and N. O'Shaughnessy (eds.), *Political Marketing—Evolving Science or Maturing Art? Conference Proceedings,* Judge Institute of Management Studies, University of Cambridge.

Stoiber, E. (1983), "Marketing und Politik", *Marketing ZFP,* vol. 5, no. 2, 98-102.

Street, J. (1998), *Popular Culture and Politics*, Cambridge, Polity.

Sweeney, W. R. (1995), "The principles of planning", in J. A. Thurber and C. J. Nelson (eds.), *Campaigns and Elections American Style*, Boulder, Westview, pp. 14–29.

Tam, H. (ed.) (1994), *Marketing Competition and the Public Sector*, Harlow, Longman.

Thomassen, J. (1994), "Introduction: The intellectual history of election studies", *European Journal of Political Research*, vol. 25, pp. 239–245.

Thurber, J. A. (1995), "The transformation of American campaigns", in J. A. Thurber and C. J. Nelson (eds.), *Campaigns and Elections American Style*, Boulder, Westview, pp. 1–13.

Thurber, J. A., and Nelson, C. J. (eds.) (1995), *Campaigns and Elections American Style*, Boulder, Westview.

Tietz, B. (1993a), "Die bisherige und künftige Paradigmatik des Marketing in Theorie und Praxis, Teil 1", *Marketing ZFP*, 149–163.

Tietz, B. (1993b), "Die bisherige und künftige Paradigmatik des Marketing in Theorie und Praxis, Teil 2", *Marketing ZFP*, 221–236.

Tietz, B., Koehler, R., and Zentes, J. (eds.) (1995), *Handwörterbuch des Marketing*, Stuttgart, Schaffer-Peoschl.

Topf, R. (1994), "Party manifestos", in A. Heath, R. Jowell and J. Curtice (with B. Taylor), *Labour's Last Chance?*, Aldershot, Dartmouth, pp. 149–171.

Trommsdorff, V. (1993a), "Kauferverhalten", in W. Wittmann et. al. (eds.), *Handwörterbuch der Betriebswirtschaft*, Stuttgart, Schaffer-Poeschel, pp. 2139–2160.

Trommsdorff, V. (1993b), *Konsumentenverhalten*, Stuttgart, Kohihammer Verlag.

Tscheulin, D. K. (1994), "'Variety-seeking-behavior' bei nicht-habitualisierten Konsumentenentscheidungen", *(Schmalenbachs) Zeitschrift für betriebswirtschaftliche Forschung*, vol. 46, 54–62.

Tversky, A., and Kahneman, D. (1991), "The framing of decisions and the psychology of choice", in H. H. Kassarjian and T. S. Robertson, *Perspectives in Consumer Behavior*, Englewood Cliffs, Prentice-Hall, pp.154–165. [First published in *Science*, vol. 211 (30 January 1981), 453–458.]

Vallely, P. (1995), "Politicians rely on them, tycoons swear by them, even the Queen has one: The unstoppable use of the spin doctors", *The Independent*, section 2, Friday, 15 September, pp. 2–3.

Van den Doel, H., and van Velthoven, B. (1993), *Democracy and Welfare Economics*, Cambridge, Cambridge University Press.

Van Raaij, W. F. (1991), "Economic psychology", in H. H. Kassarjian and T. S. Robertson (eds.), *Perspectives in Consumer Behavior*, Englewood Cliffs, Prentice-Hall, pp. 383–395. [First published in *Journal of Economic Psychology*, vol. 1 (1981), 1-24.]

Van Waterschoot, W., and van den Bulte, C. (1992), "The 4P classification of the marketing mix revisited", *Journal of Marketing*, vol. 56, 83–93.

Voggenreiter, D. (1988), "Politische Ökonomie", in R. Sellien and H. Sellien (eds.), *Gabler Wirtschafts-Lexikon*, 6 vol., Wiesbaden, Gabler, pp. 914–917.

Wagner, U., and Taudes, A. (1987), "Stochastic models of consumer behaviour", *European Journal of Operational Research*, vol. 29, 1–23.

Wangen, E. (1983), *Polit-Marketing: Das Marketing-Management der Politschen Parteien*, Opladen, Westdeutscher Verlag.

Ware, A. (1984), "Review article on C. A. Mauser 'Political Marketing: An Approach to Campaign Strategy", *Political Studies*, vol. 32, no. 2, 325–326.

Wattenberg, M. P. (1995), "Why Clinton won and Dukakis lost: An analysis of the candidate-centered nature of American party politics", *Party Politics*, vol. 1, pp 245–260.

Webb, P. (1992), "Britain: The 1987 campaign", in S. Bowler and D. M. Farrell (eds.), *Electoral Strategies and Political Marketing*, New York, St. Martin's Press, pp. 43–62.

Weaver, D. (1994), "Media agenda setting and elections: Voter involvement or alienation?", *Political Communication*, vol. 11, 347–356.

Wehung, H. G. (ed.) (1991), *Wahlverhalten*, Stuttgart, Kohlhammer.

Weinberg, P. (1980), "Vereinfachung von Kaufentscheidungen bei Konsumguten", *Marketing ZFP*, vol. 2, no. 2, 87–93.

Wensley, R. (1990), "The voice of the consumer? Speculations on the limits to the marketing analogy", *European Journal of Marketing*, vol. 24, no. 7, 49–60.

Westbrook, R. A., and Fornell, C. (1979), "Patterns of information source usage among durable goods buyers", *Journal of Marketing Research*, vol. 16, 303–312.

White, J. (1986), "The domain of marketing—Marketing and non-marketing exchanges", in *Quarterly Review of Marketing*, vol. 11, no. 2, 1–6.

Whiteley, P. F., and Seyd, P. (1994), "Local party campaigning and electoral mobilization in Britain", *Journal of Politics*, vol. 56, 242–252.

Williams, K. C. (1985), *Behavioural Aspects of Marketing*, London, Heinemann.

Wilson, R. M. S., Gilligan, C., and Pearson, D. J. (1992), *Strategic Marketing Management*, Oxford, Butterworth/Heinemann.

Wiswede, G. (1985), "Eine Lerntheorie des Konsumverhaltens". *Die Betriebswirtschaft*, vol. 45, 544-557.

Wiswede, G. (1991), *Einführung in die Wirtschaftspsychologie*, Munich, Ernst Reinhardt Verlag/UTB.

Wittman, D. (1990), "Spatial strategies when candidates have policy preferences", in J. M. Enelow and M. J. Hinich (eds.), *Advances in the Spatial Theory of Voting*, Cambridge, Cambridge University Press, 66–98.

Wittmann, W., et al. (eds.) (1993), *Handwörterbuch der Betriebswirtschaft*, Stuttgart, Schaffer-Poeschel.

Wohe, G. (1986), *Einführung in die Allgemeine Betriebswirtschaftslehre*, Munich, Franz Vahien.

Wolfinger, R. E. (1995), "The promising adolescence of campaign surveys", in J. A. Thurber and C. J. Nelson (eds.), *Campaigns and Elections American Style*, Boulder, Westview, pp. 181–191.

Woodward, G. C. (1991), "Political news: Narrative form and the ethics of denial", in R. F. Denton, Jr. (ed.), *Ethical Dimensions of Political Communication*, New York, Praeger, pp. 199–223.

Wortmann, M. (1989), *Political Marketing—A Modern Party Strategy*, Ph.D. thesis, European University Institute, Florence.

Wring, D. (1995a), "Political marketing and intra-party power: Perspectives on Labour, 'Old' and 'New'", in S. C. Henneberg and N. O'Shaughnessy (eds.), *Political Marketing—Evolving Science or Maturing Art? Conference Proceedings*, Judge Institute of Management Studies, University of Cambridge.

Wring, D. (1995b), *Political Marketing and Organisational Development: The Case of the Labour Party in Britain*, Research Papers in Management Studies, University of Cambridge.

Wring, D. (1996), "Political marketing and party development in Britain: A 'Secret' History", *European Journal of Marketing*, vol. 30, no. 10/11, pp. 100–111.

Wring, D. (1997), "Reconciling marketing with political science: Theories of political marketing", *Journal of Marketing Management*, vol. 5, 295–306.

Zajonc, R. B., and Markus, H. (1991), "Affective and cognitive factors in references", in H. H. Kassarjian and T. S. Robertson (eds.), *Perspectives in Consumer Behavior*, Englewood Cliffs, Prentice-Hall, pp. 240–252 [First published in *Journal of Consumer Research*, vol. 9 (1982), 123–131.]

Zeithaml, V. A. (1991) "Consumer perceptions of price, quality, and value: A means–end model and synthesis of evidence", in H. H. Kassarjian and T. S. Robertson (eds.), *Perspectives in Consumer Behavior*, Englewood Cliffs, Prentice-Hall, pp. 27–53. [First published in *Journal of Marketing*, vol. 52 (1988), 2–22.]

Zinkhan, G. M., Roth, M. S., and Saxton, M. J. (1992), "Knowledge development and scientific status in consumer-behavior research: A social exchange perspective", *Journal of Consumer Research*, vol. 19, 282–291.

Index

About the Editors and Contributors

BARRIE AXFORD is Professor of Politics at Oxford Brookes University. Previously he has held posts at Stanford University (California) and the University of Southampton. He has been Visiting Professor at Stanford University, the University of Genoa, and the University of Tampere. Recent publications include *The Global System: Economics, Politics and Culture* (1996), *Modernity–Postmodernity: From the Personal to the Global* (1996), *Politics: An Introduction* (co-author, 1997), *Unity and Diversity in the New Europe* (co-editor, 2000), and *The New Media and Politics* (co-editor, 2000). He is working currently on a major study of *Networks and Border-lines in the Global System* and on a book about democracy and democratisation.

JOHN BARTLE is a British Academy Post-Doctoral Fellow and Lecturer in the Department of Government at the University of Essex, specialising in voting behaviour and British politics. He has publications in *The British Journal of Political Science, Political Studies and the British Elections and Parties Review* and also co-edited *Political Communications: Why Labour Won the General Election of 1997* (1998).

PATRICK BUTLER is a Lecturer in Business Studies at Trinity College, Dublin, where he teaches marketing subjects on a range of undergraduate, postgraduate and executive education programmes. His research interests include marketing strategy, political marketing and public-sector marketing.

NEIL COLLINS is Professor of Government at National University of Ireland (Cork). He has written extensively on Irish politics, and his co-authored *Irish Politics Today* (4th edition 2002) has become a standard text in the field.

STEFAN EGHBALIAN is completing a PhD at Cambridge University and is a former Junior Research Fellow of Hughes Hall. He is a former marketing director of Name Planet, an Internet company, and he now works for the marketing consultants Ventura Practice.

DYLAN GRIFFITHS is a lecturer in Politics in the Department of Politics at the University of Newcastle upon Tyne. He specialises in British territorial politics (particularly Wales), referendums and devolution. He has published in Public Administration. He has also published *Thatcherism and Territorial Politics: A Welsh Case Study* (1996).

STEPHAN C. M. HENNEBERG completed a PhD in political marketing at the Judge Institute of Management, Cambridge University. He was a Junior Research Fellow and is currently a Senior Associate of Hughes Hall, Cambridge. He organised several annual conferences at Cambridge on the topic and published widely in the area of strategic marketing. He is now a senior consultant with McKinsey & Co.

RICHARD HUGGINGS is Deputy Head of School, Social Sciences and Law at Oxford Brookes University. In recent years he has been involved in a number of research projects related to issues of public policy, social order and crime. He has undertaken commissioned research work for the Thames Valley Police, Oxfordshire DAAT, Oxfordshire County Council, Oxford City Council and Oxfordshire Health promotion. He has extensive experience of research in a number of related areas of social science inquiry and has published a number of books and articles in recent years, including *Politics: An Introduction* (co-author, 1997) and *New Media—New Politics* (2000).

NICHOLAS J. O'SHAUGHNESSY is Professor of Marketing at the University of Keele. Previously he was a University Lecturer at Cambridge University and a Fellow of Hughes Hall. His publications include *The Phenomenon of Political Marketing* (1990) and *The Marketing Power of Emotion* (2002). He is completing a book about propaganda.

DOMINIC WRING is Lecturer in Communication and Media Studies in the Department of Social Sciences, Loughborough University. His work on political communication and marketing has been published widely. Currently he is co-convener of the UK Political Studies Association Media and Politics Group.